Globalization

Blessing or Curse?

HAN S. PARK

Sentia Publishing

2022

Printed in the United States of America.
ISBN 979-8-9864465-8-5

Table of Contents

A Note from the Author for the 2nd Edition:

In the five years since the original publication of this book, there has been ample evidence that the once dominant ideologies underlying our world order have been showing signs of weakening, if not failing. Toward addressing this, a new chapter (Chapter 16) has been included in an attempt to outline a broad roadmap for modeling a new world order. Here, in the spirit of optimism, I advance the idea that an ideology based on the tenets of Human Rights can be a guiding principle in the pursuit of global peace and harmony.

Preface

The impetus for writing this book may be traced back to several landmark experiences in my personal life. First and foremost among these experiences was as a child surviving war-torn Northeast China during the Chinese civil war that eventually led to the birth of Mao's China, and later living under horrific conditions during the Korea War. The lingering question from these early life experiences: Why can we not live together without killing each other?

The inevitable question, then, is: Will humanity survive the 21st Century and beyond? It may not! That is, if the course of social change fails to avert its present heading, the human race may indeed be doomed, and humanity will not likely be around to celebrate the arrival of the 22nd century.

We, the inhabitants of this planet, are faced with a number of fatal problems threatening the very survival of mankind. Any one or combination of our "global ills" could lead to the end of history as we know it: environmental decay and disequilibrium, the accumulation and proliferation of weapons of mass destruction, the continued degeneration of social and political institutions that have become dysfunctional, moral and cultural decay forcing members of society to become mutually irrelevant, and distributive injustice at all levels of the political system, to name a few. The human race is faced with the ultimate choice between extinction and survival. If we opt to take our chances with our current course, the consequence is simple: we will simply drift away with the tide of historical evolution as we currently experience it. But if wish to do something about the fatal destination of mankind, we must do a number of things with an utmost sense of urgency. This book is in response to this desperate call!

Yet, this book is not about telling a doomsday story, nor is it merely about issuing normative value prescriptions. Rather, this book is a rigorous attempt to scientifically and empirically **identify, explain, and predict** the nature of human, social, and political problems associated with the process of globalization. Such analyses will naturally lead to a series of normative **prescriptions** that are designed to address the root causes of specific global human problems.

In truth, this book is not just another product of my intellectual articulations; it is in fact the direct reflection of my life journey and intellectual soul search. I was born in China to immigrant parents

1

who had escaped from Japanese oppression during its colonial rule of Korea (1905-1945). While there, I experienced first hand the horrific policies of Japanese colonial exploitation; I also witnessed the cruel and brutal scenes of dead bodies and executions carried out with rudimentary weapons such as bamboo sticks, axes, and sickles during` the Chinese civil war. Those images left me with a penetrating sense of human helplessness and man-made misery. The senseless destruction and killing witnessed during the three long years of the Korean War (1950-1953), which has never truly been concluded, left me with a greater sense of frustration over the impotence of the individual against the capricious power of vicious political forces and brutal regimes. Those years of my early life instilled in me an incredible fear of military conflict leading to mass killings of innocent human beings and the destruction of life environments beyond repair.

I came to the United States from Korea as a foreign student in 1965 with little money in my possession and no financial support system. The ensuing years of economic and social hardship, during which I married a fellow Korean whom I dated before coming to the Land of Opportunity, opened me up to a much deeper and broader perspective of life itself. In 1967, I moved to the Twin Cities to pursue my doctoral degree at the University of Minnesota. There, my dreams as an aspiring young student came true as I was exposed to an incredibly rich intellectual environment. I was quickly overwhelmed by such intellectual giants as Don Martindale, Arnold Rose, and Gregory Stone in Sociology; Herbert Feigl and May Broadbeck of Philosophy, and Mulford Sibly, Robert Holt, and Edwin Fogelman of Political Science. To this day, nothing has inspired me more than being part of the great seminars they offered in a number of areas. They helped me to think logically, to reach out for answers wherever my intellectual curiosity led me, and to broaden my academic orientation beyond any one disciplinary confinement. During my three years at Minnesota (1967-1970), I became particularly fascinated by the works of Max Weber, Reinhold Niebuhr, and Abraham Maslow. As a scholar in the Deep South since 1970, I have been profoundly inspired by the exemplar writings and lives of Daisaku Ikeda, Johan Galtung, and Glenn Paige. How can I leave out Martin Luther King, Jr. as a source of inspiration! I grew up admiring Mahatma Gandhi when I as a young student practiced non-violence and conscientious objector to wars. In King, I was able to touch the sphere of God! All the profound discoveries of wisdom he articulated and expressed so eloquently in his life span of 39 years would not have been possible if he had been just a smart person. As a man od wisdom and intellectual inspiration, I must acknowledge Johan Galtung who has been a source of inspiration in my search for the realm of Positive Peace as he captivated me with the profound idea that the concept of peace must be given a positive meaning, not just the negative concept of the absence of war or conflict.

Then, there are countless students of my own I have encountered over the last 45 years in the United States. When I joined the faculty of the University of Georgia in 1970, I quickly realized that Georgia, like many states in the Deep South, was a place where racial prejudice, if not outright discrimination, was still rampant. But my students embraced me with open hearts, and accepted me as their teacher. I am enormously indebted to them and to the countless other people who inspired me and guided my scholarly life toward meaningfulness and relevance.

I would love to acknowledge the most significant of all of my "significant others": my own family! I should begin with my parents: My father was a farmer and student of Confucian classics who taught me never to undermine the value of education. My mother had only modest education, but she was a devout Buddhist with a temple in the remote mountains where I had the opportunity to spend ample time with monks of all ages. There, I learned how precious it is to "empty" myself. I was fortunate enough to develop a loving relationship with a young lady who had been brought up in a Christian family and had subliminal wisdom about life and love. Among a Confucian father, a Buddhist mother, and a Christian fiancé, I could easily have been subjected to cross-current of religious persuasions that might have been detrimental to the healthy development of a youthful mind. On the contrary, however, such experiences enabled me to see where the great worldviews converged at the pinnacle of their respective maturities.

Then, there is Sungwon, the once girlfriend, then fiancé, whom I married in Washington, D.C. in 1965, a few months after we landed in America, who remains my wife of over 50 years. She taught me what a loving relationship should be, beginning with the ring she presented me at our engagement bearing the inscription: 1 + 1 = 1. This inscription defied science, mathematical knowledge, and worldly logic, yet it spoke an immutable truth. Since that day, she has inspired me with the truth that love overcomes any difficulties and adversities.

How can I miss mentioning my own children, all three of them! They have taught and showed me how human needs and wants are expressed and pursued, which became the benchmark of my own theory of development, as detailed in the ensuing chapters of this book.

Finally, there is the great pool of students whose lives have crossed with mine at various points throughout the last half-a-century. As their teacher, I have always tried to ground my instruction in the centuries-old Chinese dictum, *"Give a man a fish, he will eat for a day; teach a man to fish, he will eat for a life time!*

Yes, for all the ideas, conceptions, theoretical premises that made this book possible, I am thoroughly indebted to countless inspirers and significant others, but none of them will be responsible for any shortcomings and flaws imbedded in this book. They are mine, and mine only!

Written in Athens, Georgia, U.S.A.

October 2016

ORGANIZATION OF THE BOOK

*A brief description of each of the three parts is made below, where all the fifteen chapters are given a grand perspective.

PART ONE

To Begin With
Cognitive Preparation:
About "Knowing and Knowledge

We wish to know development in terms of what it is, what causes or explains it, and what are its consequences. Before we try to know development or, for that matter, to know anything else, we must know what the meaning of knowing is, to begin with.

To "know" is to cognizant which happens when linkages are made among concepts. Then, what is a concept? A concept is a meaningful term. What, then, is meaning? Meaning is a purposeful act is an action, and an action is always goal oriented. Then, what is and where does a goal originate?

At the human or individual level, the common goal for every human being and at all times might be satisfying needs and wants. In this regard, without necessarily being reduced to psychological reductionism, one might accept the premise of methodological individualism which suggests that the unit of perceptions and actions has to be human being! Humans are necessarily relative and subjective. Therefore, knowledge is subjective; there is no objective knowledge. The definition of "definition" is "subjective meaning-giving." Therefore, by virtue of its being defined, a concept *becomes* subjective. The power of knowledge is determined not by whether it is objective or subjective but by the degree to which a piece of knowledge shares inter-subjective consensus. We begin the introductory chapter, **Chapter 1**, with the question of the purpose of knowledge and education. **Chapter 2** discusses the challenges in the craft of theory building from the perspective of philosophy of science. In this chapter, we will establish a series of criteria for defining and theorizing development. **Chapter 3** actually assesses the quality of development studies by applying the criteria herein. Most conceptual and theoretical configurations of socio-political development that are used today have been advanced during the Cold War era (1950s through 1980s) and under the condition of polarized world politics. Without necessarily adhering to epistemic empiricism, we can safely suggest that those theorists who advanced their theories were the product of their times, and those theories advanced by them are expected to represent "biases" for the life world of their choice. Therefore, almost all the theorists in the United States are responsible for Western-bias theories. They also showed their obsession with *scientific* inquiry. We shall examine, in **Chapter 3**, how those theories were projected and claimed to be universally applicable and scientific, when in fact they were not.

PART TWO

Development as It is (Sein)

Following examining those "biased" theories of development, we shall propose an alternative and more relevant path in which a more legitimate and value-free theorization of development might be pursued in **Chapter 4** where I advance the theme of "Bringing Human Being to the Main Stage." In **Chapter 5**, I intend to formulate a theoretical construct in which a human centered paradigm of development is advanced. **Chapters 6-9** elaborate the various stages of development as espoused in the paradigm.

Chapter 10 offers a meaningful definition of globalization.

PART THREE

In Search of a Holistic and Synoptic Solution

In the foregoing analysis of the process of development from the agrarian society through the industrial society, the post-industrial society and eventually to the current global community, we have concluded that the historical progression of development along this track has forced humanity to the brink of self-extinction. Serious problems have risen from the integrity of identity of human existence to the breakdown of human communities. In the end, in this deceptively blessed world with technological brilliance may bring an end to human history. Human awareness of the severity of the problems has been there, and numerous solutions have been proposed and tried. Yet, in the end, we have been becoming worse off with the passing of time. There are reasons for this gloomy projection. First of all, cause-effect analyses have seldom dealt with real root causes, as most remedial ideas have largely dwelled around the symptoms, rather than the causes. Second, most efforts have been piecemeal, as opposed to comprehensive, and they are far too short and weak to produce a discernible impact in alleviating the problem itself. To address the first problem of proper diagnosis, we have developed an empirical paradigm of development which is based on the notion that development is a process in which human needs and wants are pursued. In the ensuing chapters, I will offer what I consider to be a synoptic or holistic paradigm of development as development should be or it ought to be. This normative or value-laden conceptual articulations are made at three spheres of human existence: the individual, the interaction of individuals, and the society or community. **Chapter 11** deals with the Individual Level, **Chapter 12** at the Interaction Level, and **Chapters 13** and **14** at the Community Level. **Chapter 15** offers an alternative definition of development with communicative capability as the engineering force. **Chapter 16** is a new Chapter added to the second edition of this book designed to explore the nature of post-globalism. The final chapter, **Chapter 16,** ends the book with offering a series of actionable and concrete policy recommendations for social engineering.

Chapter 1

The Purpose of Knowledge and Knowledge with Purpose: Ontological Epistemology

What is knowledge? Knowledge is a system of knowing, and to "know" is to make "linkages" involving "concepts." Thus, concepts are building blocks meant to be inter- connected in logical ways. To illustrate this point, one might think of the mathematical notion that 2 plus 2 or multiplied by 2 equals 4. In this case, each of the "2"s and the "4" are mere facts that become the constituent parts of knowledge with the help of the logic of "plus" and "multiply". Since it is safe to say that every conceivable concept is potentially related to every other conceivable one, the field of possible links is virtually unlimited. This suggests that knowledge is inherently unlimited and unrestricted, and is only limited by its intended purpose. In other words, only the purpose of knowledge will define its character, boundaries, and functions. In this sense, knowledge is a tool designed to serve the knower (a human being) in seeking what he or she intends to achieve.

Another way of arriving at the same conclusion concerning the meaning of knowledge is to view the pursuit of knowledge as a form of human behavior. Since all human behavior is goal-oriented action, it is necessary to ask what the pursuer of knowledge purports to achieve. The answer could be one or more of the following: a prescription of values for a desirable life, justification for a certain system of social and political orders, moral legitimacy for certain sets of beliefs and norms, explanation and prediction, and problem solving. In fact, each of these potential goals has been instigated as the central goal of knowledge in the course of intellectual history. One can say that the nature and structure of knowledge will be determined by the nature and structure of the purpose for which knowledge is pursued. Then, what determines the nature and structure of the purpose of knowledge?

Sociology of Knowledge

The "sociology of knowledge" contends that the nature of knowledge is to be determined in a way that it can fulfill its purpose in a concrete historical milieu of the time. Therefore, the perceived need for knowledge as a tool for achieving a goal will in turn determine the nature and structure of knowledge itself. We have witnessed a series of different purposes of knowledge in the course of intellectual history that have emerged in response to varying historical conditions.

In ancient Greece, there were many city-states, and many of them were conquered by Spartan and Athens and integrated into them. When the city-states were in constant conflict, philosophers of the ranks of Plato and Aristotle actively prescribed ideas and norms that described the state of a desirable society. Plato's seminal book, *Republic*, was a depiction of an ideal society in terms of who should rule and how. By putting forth the notion of the "philosopher king," Plato reasoned that the ruler must be virtuous, and knowledge is the source of virtue. Therefore, the ruler should be one with knowledge, and the "philosopher" is the possessor of such knowledge. The ruled, on the other hand, lack knowledge and therefore cannot be virtuous. This lack of virtue naturally deprives them of the ruling position. Thus, those who are not knowledgeable should be ruled for their own well-being.

According Plato, there are three levels (planes) of the world: one that is referred to as "history," and represents the reality observed in historical records; one that is managed by the help of "laws" and represents a subnormal life situation; and one that is ideal, which is ruled by "philosophy" as depicted in his *Republic*. In this vertical construct of the living world, the role of knowledge (and scholarship) is to elevate quality of life by articulating prescriptions for ideal relationships in a given society. Aristotle, in his justification of slavery, used the same argument that the slave is best served by subjecting himself to the benevolent leadership of the virtuous masters. In advancing perhaps the first typology of political systems, Aristotle juxtaposed three sets of political systems, each with an ideal form and a pervert form: The first set includes one-man-rule that is virtuous (monarchy) and perverse (tyranny), virtuous rule by a few (aristocracy) and perverse rule by a few (oligarchy), plural rule for the benefit of the people (polity), and plural rule in a selfish and perverse manner (democracy). Here, Aristotle attempted to differentiate the virtuous systems from the perverse, and suggested that the role of knowledge should be to prescribe "good" forms of governance.

The normative and prescriptive orientation of scholarship was not limited to the Western tradition of intellectual history. In fact, it was around the same time (2-5 B.C.) that the ancient Chinese scholars Confucius, Mencius, and their associates prescribed their own set of norms and values for ideal relationships in a society. The "five cardinal rules" of Confucianism, for example, prescribe "proper relationships" guiding nearly all conceivable forms of social interaction: ruler-ruled relationships defined by "righteousness," spousal relationships by "separation of roles," parent-children relationships by "intimacy," relationships between friends governed by "trust," and relationships between old and young by "proper order."

These guidelines have long been regarded as the moral imperatives for proper conduct in Confucian society. One must note that the life situation for the ancient Chinese thinkers was similar to that for the Greek philosophers in that there were numerous small kingdoms existing in a constant state of bloody confrontation ("one hundred kingdoms swirled by war"). In this turbulent historical milieu, the task of scholarship was to offer prescriptions for a desirable society. It is remarkably intriguing to note that ancient societies in the West and the East, despite the obvious absence of interaction, were faced with a similarly disruptive reality, and responded the same way.

In medieval times, when the world was sharply divided between ecclesiastical (religious) and temporal (secular) authority, thinkers focused their intellectual attention to the question: Who of the two authorities should prevail? St. Augustine (354 – 430 A.D.) clearly delineated the two separate authorities in his treaties of the "Two Cities." The "city of God" possesses the moral authority and responsibility to supervise and manage the "city of Man," as a matter of proper order. From Augustine to Thomas Aquinas (1225-1274 A.D.), many thinkers prescribed that there be defined order between the two authorities. Therefore, in the medieval times, one might say that the role of knowledge was to articulate the moral justification for the world order of their choice. In this case, the alternatives for choice-making were limited to the two contending authorities. Structural limits on intellectual innovation and creativity between the 5th and 15th centuries earned the "Dark Ages" its name. For a variety of reasons, the world order at this time was resistant to reconfiguration.

This ancient role of scholarship came to an end with the advent of Machiavellian doctrine as depicted in *The Prince* (1515). *The Prince* marked the beginning of a more modern concept of governance, whereby authority would be sustained by manipulation or application of power. This early-modern era was brief, followed by drastic changes in civilization (at least in the West), and characterized by the advent of philosophical individualism (Renaissance), economic *laissez-faire* doctrine

(Adam Smith), and political *social contract* theory (John Locke). Each of these developments contributed to the emergence of egalitarian movements in all spheres of political life, terminating human inequality as the basis of justification for power. No "philosopher king" was acceptable to the new breed of thinkers, and the notion that someone was more qualified to interpret God's providence and therefore should rule was rejected. The Machiavellian edict that "Might is Just" lost its appeal within the scholarly community. No theory of legitimate power arose to fill the void, leaving philosophical confusion as to who should rule and why.

From this vacuum, the era of ideologies began. Ideologies are designed to rationalize and justify the legitimate relationship between the ruler and the ruled. The earliest ideology was classical liberalism as espoused by John Locke's *Two Treaties of Government* (1688). Political ideologies have since become the tool with which the ruling elite justify their power. Ideologies have also functioned as an instrument for political integration and power solidification. The classical liberalists, in opposition to (and defiance of) the capricious political orders of early modern times, advocated the notion that a "minimum government is the best government," whereby civil liberties were defined primarily in terms of the absence of government intervention. The concept that government is a necessary evil justifies the "minimum government" doctrine. Here, government's power is to be limited and constrained by the terms of agreement with the people, thus, the "social contract" theory. This doctrine was reinforced by the *laissez-faire* principle of economic free enterprise in which the well-being of the whole society is equal to the aggregate well-being of its constituent parts. Adam Smith, as the father of this school of thought, envisioned in his seminal work, *The Wealth of Nations (1776),* that there should be natural harmonization (by the "invisible hand") in which the parts will serve the whole.

The classical liberalists expected that all citizens would be better off when the government left them alone as much as possible. But it soon became evident that collective good did not always result from the promotion of individual interests. The "invisible hand" in which Adam Smith banked his optimistic perspective on liberalism turned out to be either nonexistent or malfunctioning. The moment that private ownership was allowed and free entrepreneurship became the ground rule for economic life, inequality in wealth and lifestyle ensued. This was due in part to differences inherent in human physical and mental capability, as well as differences in socioeconomic status and behavioral propensities toward savings versus consumption.

Here, economic inequality and class differentiation became unavoidable consequences, paving the way for the Marxist and non-Marxist socialist movements. This invigorated the age of ideologies, during which contending ideas proliferated rapidly, claiming to advance "just" modes of distribution and stable social and political orders. The basic underlying premises fell at vastly different places along the continuum of liberty (liberalists) and equality (socialists). The two mutually incompatible ideological systems made the 19th and early 20th Centuries an unregulated market place for political ideologies, ranging from diverse types of anarchism, varieties of liberalism, Marxist and non-Marxist socialisms, and extreme forms of nationalism and ethnocentrism. The scholarly community was busily engaged in officiating the brawl.

The result was a world order that was divided by two broad ideological camps, and those camps were responsible for the creation of the Cold War politics in the middle of the 20th Century. Cold War politics were characterized by one distinct feature: the advent of political ideologies that not only provided legitimacy for the hegemonic powers, but were also employed as the moral justification for their respective powers. The two hegemonic powers of the United States and the Soviet Union became the bipolar centers of world power politics.

The two contrasting ideologies of capitalist democracy and socialist communism were not only ideologically mutually incompatible but also helped form a polarized world divided by mutual distrust and suspicion. Each of the two super powers pursued power supremacy over the other in order to advance aspirations of becoming an unchallenged empire. They competed for expansion of influence over the rest of the world, often forcing smaller countries to serve them as surrogate states. The Soviet annexation of the former Eastern European countries to form a greater Soviet bloc was countered by the expansion of American influence into Western Europe and the Third World. The Soviet Union's aborted military campaign in Afghanistan in 1979-1989 marked the phasing out of the Soviet influence in that region, while the defeat in the Vietnam War suffered by the United States in the mid 1970s signaled a decline in American global influence. In the end, the Soviet Union vanished through domestic implosion, followed by the demise of the socialist systems in Europe and eventually the Second World itself when China opted to embrace economic capitalism. Thus, the Cold War era effectively ended by the waning years of the 20th Century.

What followed was an age forged by the United States as the sole superpower on the planet. America began her reign with the presumption that the implosion of the "Evil Empire" was by divine will, and the march of American global influence was destined to succeed. This dangerous dogma will be discussed later in this book.

Half a century of Cold War politics left a legacy of pervasive militarism and unprecedented military buildup. The culture of militarism promoted a simplistic worldview of ideological dichotomy and zero-sum relationships in global human interaction. The economy of militarism engineered an arms race that was responsible for the never-ending and competitive stockpiling of weapons, paving the way for the runaway military-industrial complex. In the end, the human race had become hopelessly arrested by the fear of destruction and death. The arms race was intended to boost military preparedness to annihilate the other camp, but it ultimately resulted in the fatalistic acceptance of mutually assured destruction.

In this period, the belief systems in both camps were dominated by the *fear* of annihilation as a result of preemptive attacks from the adversarial side. This political and perceptional atmosphere created great anxiety and uncertainty regarding policy decisions by the opposite camp. Because this anxiety-provoking uncertainty needed to be reduced, thus *uncertainty reduction* became the challenge for scholarship throughout the second half of the Cold War era. This was the genesis of what is referred to as the "behavioral revolution" in political and social sciences. The epistemological basis of "behavioralism" was science.

The Age of Science and Scientific Revolution in Social and Political Inquiry

In answering the call for *explanation* and *prediction* to alleviate the fear of human self-destruction, social and political scientists focused their efforts by emulating concepts, theories, and methods from the "hard science" forerunners– physical or natural (normal) science that had been successful in explaining many of the physical world's phenomena. Social-political scientists responded to the challenges of this age by bringing the "behavioral sciences" to bear. In the generations since the introduction of David Easton's seminal work, *Political System* (1951), behavioral scientists in the United States have demonstrated their craftsmanship in several

14

important areas: building conceptual frameworks such as systems theory and structural-functionalism, developing models such as variations of the rational actor model, as well as the works of the "barefoot" empiricist and number-crunchers. Their painstaking efforts drove the proliferation of scientific publications and research output, but they failed to further or enrich the realm of *common sense* or the general sphere of wisdom. On the contrary, the cult of science and the growth of behavioralist research output have succeeded in casting doubts on a host of relationships that are commonsensical, and, as a result, have diminished the sphere of common sense and conventional wisdom, a point that will be revisited in the following chapters of this book.

After a half of a century under the domination of the cult of science, social and political inquiry helplessly submitted itself to a set of beliefs and practices that paralyzed academia. In this era, the academia was compartmentalized for the purpose of developing specialization and expertise, often with little interaction between disciplines. Research activities were obsessed with producing "objective" knowledge without realizing that social behavioral sciences are inherently subjective. Putting research methodology over substance alienated academia from historical reality, leading to a period of diminished relevance.

While orchestrating this scientific revolution in political and social inquiries, however, social scientists failed to meet the challenge of explaining policies and predicting policy behaviors. Thus, they were unable to address real problems themselves. In the meantime, the world has been engulfed by serious problems in such a way that many conscientious people have become pessimistic about the continuation of progressive social change and development. In other words, uncertainty was no longer the prevailing sentiment of the time. Instead, it was certainty about the eminent threat from varied sources of global problems such as environmental deterioration, global warming, proliferation of weapons of mass destruction (many of which are unaccounted for in the wake of the Soviet Union's collapse), rampage of terrorist acts, food shortages, and population explosion in the regions and countries where resources are most scarce, epidemic diseases such as HIV, global sectarian warfare, and even genocide, to name only a few. The world is plagued by these problems that are no longer uncertain or hypothetical, but real.

Bringing the Academia back to Life and Relevancy: The Imperative of Problem Solving

This shift in our life environment has triggered a change in intellectual orientation from the reduction of uncertainty through explanation and prediction to the pressing challenge of **problem solving.** If we are unable to meet this challenge in a timely and effective manner, we might indeed see the coming of an end to history and humanity itself. It is this grave sense of urgency that should guide the course of intellectual predisposition today.

Contemporary problems may be said to have a set of shared characteristics:

- Universality: The contemporary problems are common to all mankind, not limited to a particular region; they are trans-boundary, and defy differences in culture, ideology or institutional characteristics, as clearly evidenced by global warming, ecological deterioration, massively destructive warfare, and epidemic communicative diseases.

- Urgency: They threaten the very existence of our species here and now. If the problems are not alleviated in the near term, there will be no tomorrow. Unlike all the previous challenges for scholarship, contemporary problem solving cannot be postponed indefinitely into the future. It is now or never.

- Survival of mankind hangs in the Balance: As prefaced in this book, unless we steer the course of history in a different direction, we may not live long enough even to embrace the arrival of the 22nd Century. Indeed, the human race itself shares a common fate, and that fate, at present, does not seem promising.

- The Imperative of a Holistic Approach: The problems we are experiencing today are trans-disciplinary and cannot be solved while maintaining disciplinary boundaries. Specialization has been the dominant trend since the industrial revolution and even before; now we must unravel this and see things more holistically if we are even to define our problems— let alone solve them. Academics have emulated "science" in approaching problem solving. The focus has been on piecemeal analysis, for this is what has proven the most successful approach in normal science. Now, we must focus on the whole and on the interconnectedness of its parts, rather than on the dissection

16

of the whole and the analysis of its parts. Science has served us well up to this point; indeed, it has made this analysis possible, for without it, we would not have the basis of knowledge to *consider* the whole. But it is now time to move on to the real world and the manner in which global problems and their causes are interconnected.

The Stages of Problem Solving:

Problem solving in the area of social interaction requires a series of steps that must be taken in sequence. These steps are equivalent to the steps taken by medical professionals in dealing with physical illness: (1) the identification of problem; (2) explanation and prediction of the problem (diagnosis and prognosis); (3) policy recommendation (prescription); (4) policy implementation (treatment); (5) policy evaluation (monitoring the effect of treatment); (6) reshaping the policy, if needed (modification of the prescription). Each of these steps will be discussed briefly.

- *Problem Identification*: In order to identify a problem in society, one must first know what a healthy society (a society devoid of problems) looks like. In other words, to identify problems or abnormalities, the first and foremost step is to know the state of "wellness" which will serve as the standard by which the reality is evaluated. This requires the articulation of a visionary perception of an ideal society. This is a normative challenge, and it may appear to be only subjective. But the reality of a society that is desired by a consensus of people need not be so subjective. In fact, I contend in this book that there is a set of human needs and wants that are exceedingly universal, and the definition of an ideal society should be made in terms of human happiness that results from satisfying those human need and wants (this point will be elaborated greatly later in ensuing chapters.) In short, one has to have perceptions of "good" society towards which the *status quo* must be engineered. The conceptualization of an "ideal" and problem-free society must precede any effort to induce a desirable course of social change. This will require "normative" perspectives that have been utterly alienated from scholarship in the name of science and value-neutral inquiry. As discussed above, in the name of the behavioral science revolution, social sciences in general, and political science in particular, have avoided "normative" scholarship by placing faith in "scientific" modes of inquiry. In this new era for problem solving, one must bring normative inquiry back to the mainstream of the study of social and political change. As will be discussed in later chapters of this book, the concept of development is inherently a normative concept, and as such one must define this concept normatively. Historically, each of the main political ideologies and subsets thereof have advanced a variety of concepts to portray ideal societies: liberal democracy, utopian anarchists, Marxist and non-Marxist socialisms, variations of communisms, pluralist democracy, and participatory democracy, to name only a few. In this book, I will argue that the development of society *is* all about the satisfaction of human needs and wants. Therefore, development must be viewed empirically as a process in which human needs and wants are effectively pursued and eventually satisfied. This may sound too philosophical and complicated but in reality the notion of a "good" society should not be subjected to metaphysical assertions. Rather, it should be dealt with as common sense.

- *Explanation and Prediction (Diagnosis and Prognosis)*: Once a problem is identified, one must attempt to ascertain the cause that is responsible for the creation of the problem. This process is explanation. The explanation is an act of discovering the conditions and forces that "produced" the problem. In other words, explanation is a cognitive process in which "problem makers" are identified as the problem's *causes*. The cause-effect analysis, or causal analysis, that the behavioral revolution was unable to produce in the Cold War era must now be revisited. A greater rigor is in order in espousing the nature of causal explanation and its requisite conditions. As commonly understood in the philosophy of the social sciences, an explanation entails the unearthing of the "causal" factors that are both necessary and sufficient to produce the effect as the two become logically linked. As seen in the diagram, the causal factors are expected to *produce* the effect through a logical process law. One key factor is the fact that the cause will precede the effect in time. However, the presence of a regular time interval between two phenomena does not necessarily indicate a causal relationship. The phenomenon that the day comes always after the night does not mean that the latter causes the former. Despite the obvious pattern, there is no deductive logic (theory) telling us that the night produces the day. A true causal explanation requires three

18

methodological conditions: empirical regularity, time-lag, and logical (deductive) plausibility. Prediction is to be understood on a continuum of explanation in that the effect has not been empirically materialized.

- *Policy Recommendation*: Once a problem is identified and explained, we will have the ability to attempt to engineer the course of social change pertaining to the problem by manipulating the causal factors. A policy recommendation should be judged by its relevance to the causes of the problem and also by the degree to which it can be implemented. Whether or not a policy addresses a root cause of the problem or merely a symptom is crucially important. For instance, in dealing with a patient who exhibits symptoms of high fever and pain, the condition cannot be treated by simply covering the symptoms with aspirin. Whatever causes those symptoms must be dealt with. By the same token, in order to control terrorism, which is a hot topic today, one must deal with its possible root causes, such as a sense of relative deprivation caused by distributive injustice in the world or discriminatory policies toward the would-be terrorists by stronger nations. Instead, economic sanctions or military assaults are often used to subdue the terrorists. This will only exacerbate the problem of terrorism. In this case, policies are geared to fight the symptom, not the cause. The other criterion for determining policy is the question of moral and ethical practicability. We cannot recommend a policy to curb terrorism based on research that links ethnic or religious association with terrorist inclinations, because recommending that a particular religious or ethnic affiliation be wiped out is both heinous and offensive. There are a host of moral and political issues that need to be considered when determining the likelihood that a particular policy can be successfully implemented.

- The chore of policy recommendation is never easy or safe, but this chore must be the function of researchers and intellectuals, especially college professors. In regards to the role of professors, one should pay attention to the fact that professors, at least in the United States, are given the privilege of being awarded tenure. A tenured professor is protected from being dismissed from the job because of his/her expressed political views. Policy recommendations or opinions on public issues by a professor can be disliked by the ruling elite who may wish to punish the scholar, but the tenure system is designed to protect them from such intimidation. This privilege is given to federal judges for precisely the same reason. It is should be noted that the tenure system in academia is not properly understood when it is used (rather, abused) to reward publications and other "professional" accomplishments. If professors are not doing the job of policy recommendation for fear of jeopardizing their job security, the sustainment of the tenure system is not justified.

In summary, I have ascertained that the purpose of knowledge is problem-solving, and the challenge of problem-solving entails a series of processes beginning with problem identification. The eventual goal of social and political inquiry must be to develop and recommend policies to the various agencies and individuals that are responsible for treating tangible and real problems.

The Synoptic Approach to Prevention and Solution

As an alternative or complementary approach, the synoptic approach has found its place in the craft of scholarship. This approach is a holistic and comprehensive approach in that the organism of a political system or society as a whole is rehabilitated. Just like a healthy body, a healthy political community is one in which all parts are integrated and coordinated in such a way that the body itself is well fit to deal with adversity and unexpected disturbances by external factors. For this, it is essential that the concept and nature of an ideal, healthy body of community be firmly established. Here, too, as is the case is with the incremental approach, one must have a prescribed notion of a healthy society. In this case, though, the notion is to be prescribed normatively. In part three of this book, I will offer a perspective on the architecture of such a normative conception of development.

Organization of the Book

In order to adequately address all the major issues raised in this chapter, this book will consists of three parts. Part one is designed to set the cognitive and intellectual stage for parts two and three. Following this opening chapter, Chapter 2 establishes the criteria by which the concept of development should be defined. In Chapter 3, I will make an analytical assessment of the state of scholarship in the field of development studies prevalent in the United States and the Western hemisphere. In Part Two, I will introduce (reintroduce) an empirical paradigm of development that is far more consistent with the criteria of development established in Chapter 2. This paradigm (theory) of development and globalization is intended to accurately and correctly portray the dynamics and processes of political and social development in the way they are known to us in the contemporary era. Chapter 4 sketches an overview of an empirical paradigm of development with a definition of development that satisfies all the criteria for defining development as established in Chapter 2. This paradigm consists of a set of four stages of development: Regime Formation and Security, Political Integration and Identity, Resource Expansion and Prosperity, and Conflict Management and Relative Gratification. Each of the four stages will be dealt with in a separate chapter. A separate chapter (Chapter 10) was devoted to globalization as an extension of development. Part Three of the book is designed to offer a normative or desirable paradigm of development, which consists of a set of four Chapters (11-14): Chapter 11 is about human development at the individual level; Chapter 12 deals with the issue of human dignity, through human rights, at the level of relationships among individuals; Chapter 13 is about the virtue of peace the community and global level; and Chapter 14 proposes the concept of communication as the key to development at all levels of social complexity. This final chapter ends with a series of concrete exemplar steps that might be taken to realign the direction of social and political progress towards a desirable development outcome.

Chapter 2

In Search of a "Mind's Eye" or the Study of Development

"It is the theory that tells us what to observe."

--Albert Einstein

In the words of wisdom by Einstein depicted above, what we wish to "observe" is "development," and we need a theory to observe and analyze its properties. Such a theory must satisfy as much as possible the criteria for a good theory: (1) universal applicability, (2) usefulness in addressing pressing and relevant human problems, and (3) explanatory-predictive power.

A theory is a symbolic lens through which the world, basically a complex system of symbols, is observed. In this way, a theory is an instrument that is used to identify, analyze, and address social and political problems in a way that the goal of problem solving may be served most effectively. Even when dealing with a physical phenomenon, as opposed to a symbolic one, a theory is required to begin proper analysis. A symbolic phenomenon involving the human mind itself is likely to be very complex, and is certain to require a dynamic and encompassing theory. A theory may be analogous to a physical eye. As we can clearly conceptualize the requirements and conditions for a healthy and functioning eye, we should also be able to discern such conditions for the mind's eye.

Criteria for a Good Mind's Eye (Theory)

The health of the human eye may be diagnosed by a few criteria. First, an eye is judged on whether it can clearly see objects placed far away *and* nearby. An eye that is either farsighted or nearsighted is regarded as inadequate. Second, the ability to see a wider spectrum (peripheral vision) is also regarded to be a feature of a good and more desirable eye. Third, an eye that can see a moving object more clearly is considered to be a better eye. When a baseball batter accurately judges the speed, velocity, and trajectory of the ball thrown by the pitcher, we say that the batter has a "good eye." Finally, an eye that can discern objects of greater importance and significance would be regarded as a well-functioning eye.

A theory, like an eye, is only as good as its utility. No theory is inherently more valuable than another because of its structural beauty, conceptual richness, or the fame of its author. The value of a theory is to be solely determined by its functional utility for solving problems. Then, given the nature of contemporary problems and the challenges of problem solving established in Chapter 1, we might ascertain a set of criteria by which a new theory can be articulated or an existing theory can be evaluated. We can establish an analogy between the above criteria for a good physical eye and those of the symbolic "mind's eye" (theory).

Criteria for Admissible Theory

1. Universal Applicability

A superior theory is both *universally applicable* and can help us view both *macro and micro* phenomena. A theory must be able to capture the problem in its entirety no matter where and when it occurs. In dealing with global problems such as global warming, terrorism, proliferation of weapons, and distributive injustice, we need universally acceptable definitions, diagnoses, and treatments. A theory today must be judged by the degree to which its application is universal. As global problems are by definition shared by different people in diverse life situations, a theory designed to discover causal laws underlying disturbing problems must be more generally applicable as opposed to being parochial.

2. Relevance and Utility

A theory must be *useful* in *identifying* problems that are *relevant* and significant enough to be addressed. For a theory to be useful, it must be *relevant* to addressing human conditions. Given the acute nature of the problems threatening the survival of mankind, a useful theory must be able to help us to cleanly identify the problem in need of solving. It is only through a theory that is relevant to the problem that we can make a focused and meaningful observation and analysis. This requires the theory to be rigorous, and to *directly* address the existential issues of the human condition. Going back to the metaphor of human eye, the functional importance of the eye lies in its utility. One should never forget that a theory loses its raison d'etre if it is not *relevant* to the ultimate goal of solving a particular problem.

In practical terms, considering the complexities that characterize contemporary global issues, one might safely conclude that a theory must be interdisciplinary in order to be fully relevant. The interdisciplinary perspective is analogous to peripheral vision. When a theory is confined and restricted within a compartmentalized intellectual disciplinary enclave, it loses the ability to address reality as a whole. Virtually no global problem is non-interdisciplinary. Terrorism, for instance, is simultaneously a concern of psychology, sociology, economy, ideology, theology, and political science. All other conceivable "real world" problems are likely interdisciplinary in the same way.

The academic disciplines that house scholarly activities today are outdated and obsolete. Anyone who confines himself or herself to a single conventional discipline of social science and humanities, such as political science, sociology, economics, psychology, history, and philosophy, is unable to fully describe the nature of a single contemporary global problem, let alone explain and prescribe remedial solutions to it. The existing disciplines are the offspring of the labor-division and role-specialization syndrome mandated by the forces of industrial development. As industrial products are intended for market rather than domestic consumption, they necessarily become subject to competition. This market competition forces industries to reduce the manufacturing costs through mass production that, in turn, requires mechanization and division of labor. As the life situation evolves around the nexus of industry and market, institutions of the industrial society become patterned after this development. The division of intellectual disciplines is also designed to facilitate role specialization and division of work, transforming the field of intellectual inquiry into an economic mechanism.

Now that the global society is beyond the age of industrialization, we are faced with challenges and problems with which continuous industrial expansion cannot cope. In fact, blind industrialization is more likely to be a cause of further problems rather than a solution. In the present global society, the awesome challenge of problem solving cannot be left to the forces and fruits of industrialization. For this reason, any paradigm or theory that is a product of a lone conventional discipline is not likely to be useful in coping with a problem of global relevance. We must strive to formulate paradigms and theories that transcend the conventional disciplinary boundaries and meet the above requirements._

3. Explanatory-Predictive Power:

A theory must also have explanatory power. Without explanation, the cause(s) of a problem cannot be ascertained, thereby rendering prescription and treatment impossible. This requires that a theory employ rigorous internal logic enabling causal inferences among those concepts. In this sense, a "causal" theory is the only form of a legitimate theory. The notion of a descriptive theory should not be even used.

As mentioned above, explanation is a causal statement in which the cause-effect linkage is specified. A statement in the form of "if A, then B" must be present in the theory itself. As a theory is commonly defined as a system of laws, the theories we employ should be a system of "causal" laws.

Using the metaphor of the mind's eye, we can say that the ability to discern a moving object is perfectly analogous to a theory's *explanatory and predictive function*. A good theory should guide the researcher to establish causality -- the movement of the object over time. In the case of the baseball analogy, explanation and prediction would require the identification of all the factors, such as the grip of ball in the pitcher's hand, the speed and spin of the ball, as well as exogenous factors such as temperature, humidity, and latitude of the ball park. When the movement of the ball as it passes the batter, which would be the "dependent" variable, is linked to the causal factors, the "independent" variables, then we have an explanation. Prediction is the same in its epistemological structure as explanation, except for the fact that the dependent variable is yet to be realized in time.

Explanation, as diagramed below, is the process by which the linkage between causal facts and the resultant outcome is made plausible by an already established theory, conventional wisdom, and/or commonsense:

Fact-1 fact-2 .... fact-n

Laws, theories, conventional wisdom, commonsense

Outcome

Thus, facts, no matter how numerous and exhaustive they may be, cannot be thought to "cause" the outcome. It is the theory, conventional wisdom, or accepted commonsense that establishes causality. No matter how numerous the "independent variables" (causes) and no matter how many statistical regularities are discovered, empirical generalizations are never sufficient to establish causality. Night comes after day, and day comes after night with great regularity, but no one can say that one causes the other. Here, a theory's utility is found in its guidance to the identification of problems that need to be resolved, and in assisting with explanation and prediction to establish the cause-effect relationship.

In short, what a theory can do for *identification, diagnosis, prognosis, prescription, and treatment* of the problem in point will determine its quality. In this sense, the quality of a theory cannot be taken as being constant. Rather, it will change with the intellectual challenges of the time. As the intellectual challenge today is *problem solving*, we must strive for a theory (or theories) that is useful for this very purpose of scholarship.

Theorizing About What?

In political science in particular and social sciences in general, there have been numerous units or foci of analysis ranging from psychological or reductionist micro units to an array of macro phenomena. The micro unit of human psychological attributes, such as personality types, human attitudinal dispositions, and behavioral traits, has been extensively employed for the study of politics. At the same time, social relationships and institutions can be the unit of analysis, as can macro phenomena such as revolution and social uprisings. In this book, I am proposing that the concept of "*development*" within a political system be the unit of analysis.

Why is development a superior unit of analysis in comparison with the myriad units of analysis that have been used in the study of politics and social change? First and foremost, development is a concept that is universally applicable. Every political system pursues "development" as a desirable goal. Although much is needed to conceptualize development in a universal way, the concept itself is common enough to allow the effective comparison of political and social dynamics in different life situations. The goal of development is unquestionably universal, but there could be diverse paths or approaches toward the goal. As we will see in the next chapter, there are indeed many strategic paths or approaches designed to achieve the goal of development.

Second, the concept of development is a normative concept in the sense that all human beings, societies, political systems, and international or supranational communities prescribe development to be normatively desirable. It is a concept that allows a wide range of diverse definitions that will merge into a commonality of human aspirations regardless of cultural and ideological differences.

Third, development inherently refers to a process in which a goal is pursued through diverse approaches. As such, a theory of development can naturally be expected to contain broadly applicable explanatory and predictive elements. Finally, development directly affects the conditions of human existence. Thus, this concept is extensively relevant for addressing and understanding global problems in the contemporary world.

Conceptual and Methodological Issues of Development:

While the term "political development" has become the focal point of an entire body of literature in comparative studies of political and social sciences, few terms remain as ambiguous in their usage as this one. Indeed, one might even say that development theory remains one of the least developed areas of contemporary political and social scientific fields. Debate continues to rage in academic circles over what specifically the term is supposed to refer, how broadly (or narrowly) it should be defined, and with what purpose in mind (i.e., for purely descriptive analysis of Third World versus industrialized Western nations or for explanatorypredictive theories of political change). Indeed, many have even come to question whether political scientists at this point in time should continue to use it as a central, organizing concept in their attempts to deal systematically with the diverse problems induced by political change. Perhaps, they argue, political development is simply too broad a term to be defined in any precise and meaningful way and, therefore, we should abandon it as the focal point of our theories and concentrate instead on more concrete and theoretically manageable issues facing developing nations.[1]

Before taking a stand on this debate, we will examine some of the reasons for its emergence, and perhaps gain some insight into a proper strategy for resolving it. We can begin by pointing out that the continuing presence of criticism on the one hand and the everincreasing use of the term political development on the other may be attributed to the paradoxical qualities implicit in the term itself. While the term appears to be universally applicable, its high level of generality allows almost unlimited variations in conceptualization.

"Political development," or the development of a political system as a universally observable phenomenon, is a particularly appropriate subject around which to construct a scientific theory. Science, as an enterprise aiming at the construction of explanatorypredictive theories, requires that the units of theory construction be conceptualizations of universally observable phenomena. Although there are contending views of the meaning of political development, few would deny that every society is in constant change, and that "development" is a form of social change.[2] The requirement of conceptual universality is increasingly recognized by political scientists. Now, most universities offering political development as a course tend to define it in terms of the processes and dynamics of social and political change rather than the problems of a particular Third World region. While the problems of Asia, Africa, and Latin America may provide necessary data for the comparative study of the process of political development, the common issues of social change such as integration, stability, and mobilization constitute the basis of comparability in such a study, and thereby impart to it a universal applicability and explanatory-predictive capacity.

However, the conceptual universality of political development suffers from what might be termed its "operational diversity." A term that is so broad in scope permits an almost limitless variety of definitions and conceptual schemes to be subsumed under the term of "political development." However, as a theoretical construct,

---

1 Karl von Vorys discusses the relevance of political development to political science (Von Vorys 1967).

2 Helio Jaguaribe makes a systematic assessment of the leading views of the meaning of political development. (Jaguaribe 1973, 195-206)

"political development" encompasses such a broad ranging process of social and political change that, for the purposes of theory testing, it can be indicated and measured only by an index of multiple concomitants. Since such an index itself can be variously constructed depending upon the nature of the society (or societies) observed and the particular definition of the process that is used, a series of methodological problems emerge in the construction of such a theory, particularly with respect to the comparability problem in executing cross-cultural comparative analysis.[3]

In the subsequent chapters, we shall examine the use of the term "political development" in order to more clearly specify these methodological problems. But prior to introducing a set of widely used conceptions and theories of development, I shall introduce a series of criteria by which development may be defined. These criteria should be such that, if the scientist observes them, his/her theoretical construct of the development process would be devoid of these particular methodological pitfalls.

Criteria for Defining Political Development:

A definition (of anything) is a subjective bestowment of meaning. Yet, a definition can be superior to others if it is guided by well-conceived criteria and principles that are both logical and persuasive. The following set of criteria is articulated by examining the concept from a scientific perspective and in terms of the semantics of "development" itself.

(1) Political Development as Ideal Type

Although a definition is commonly held to be a meaning subjectively assigned to a term, most scholars would agree that this idea of "subjective meaning giving" is not in itself a sufficient ground for a random or arbitrary definition.[4] As Kaplan (1964, p. 72) concisely states, a definition should also provide a set of terms synonymous with the term being defined so that the term and its defining "descriptives" are each replaceable with the other. In other words, a definition identifies the characteristics that are necessary and sufficient to distinguish that term from all others.

---

3 Some of the methodological problems. Particularly the problem of comparability are brilliantly discussed by Adam Przeworski and Henry Teune (1970, Chapter 3).

4 References on the meaning of definition are many but for illustrative purposes, the following may be cited: Abraham Kaplan (1964, 72-73); May Brodbeck (1968, 3-6); Allan Isaak (1969, 59-77).

For example, a bird may be defined by listing all of its features, such as twolegged, feathered, warm blooded, and so forth. But one cannot say that bird is defined by simply indicating some of what might be shared by other animals as well. The set of identifying characteristics should be sufficiently broad and informative to clearly define one and only one term.

This simple meaning of definition has seldom been carefully considered in defining political development, which needs to be defined in such a way as to delimit that process by which we are to construct an explanatorypredictive theory. Yet, as will be discussed further in Chapter 3, most definitional bases of contemporary developmental theories are merely partial descriptions of what is observed in the "Western" world. More specifically, they usually consist of descriptions of either "Western" man in terms of his personality traits and associated sentiments (Pye, 1963), such as empathy (Lerner, 1958), achievement orientation (McClelland, 1961), and secularism (Parsons in Mitchell, 1967), or the institutional characteristics of economically advanced societies such as bureaucracy (Eisenstadt, 1963), roledifferentiation (Riggs, 1964), and social mobilization (Deutsche, 1961).

Definitions such as these have been rightly criticized for being valueladen or Western-biased. Furthermore, in defining political development in terms of the characteristics of selected (i.e. Western) societies, some preconceived definition (or at least perception) of development is unconsciously applied as a criterion for selecting the model society (or societies). As noted above, most contemporary studies of political development tend to view it as a process of social and political change. And while the economic achievements of many "Western" societies may in some sense represent some of the goals of nations that have only recently embarked upon this process, it is doubtful that "Western" society as a whole represents the fundamental ideal toward which less-developed nations are exclusively focusing their developmental efforts. Holsti (1975, p. 829) notes that we have often confused the aspiration for better quality of life with the assumption that everyone wants to adopt all Western institutions through Western forms of economic and political activity.

If a definition is to be derived through the observation of selected societies, the fact that a society is comparatively advanced economically does not necessarily mean that its political system is an ideal laboratory in which to observe the concomitants of a politically developed society. In the absence of causal links between economic and political development, it is conceivable that the goal of economic abundance could be achieved in a

31

variety of political milieus. Therefore, one should avoid restricting observations to those economically advanced societies of the industrialized West.

In view of this problem with empirically derived definitions of political development, it should be affirmed that a definition of development must be articulated as an *ideal type*. The *ideal type* definition is not intended to be an accurate representation of reality, but instead highlights those aspects of reality that, for theoretical reasons, are deemed most important. In this sense, an ideal type definition is used as a basis for comparison with whatever aspect of reality is under consideration. The ideal type is used as a yardstick by which a real situation may be compared. A definition of development as an *ideal type* should never be construed as the true depiction or representation of the development process, but as a theoretical construct emphasizing those aspects of the process that are felt, a priori, to have some importance in constructing a theory of development. In this manner, perhaps we can avoid the aforementioned shortcomings that seem characteristic of descriptiveempirical definitions.[5]

(2) Political Development as Explanadum

Since definition may be viewed as subjective meaninggiving, any definition of a term is justifiable to the extent that it succeeds in identifying the term's unique *definiens* (concepts with which a definition is made). Therefore, there could be numerous definitions of political development without any particular one being inherently superior to the others, at least in terms of "subjective meaninggiving." Hence, we need some basis of selection, and toward this end, the criterion of utility might suggest that the intended use of a definition should be the chief consideration in determining its composition.

If we acknowledge that theory construction is the aim of social scientific inquiry, then it would follow that concepts should be defined in such a way as to be useful to the social scientist in carrying out this task. Theory construction, as alluded to earlier, may be viewed as an enterprise intended to produce statements that are universally applicable, on one hand, and explanatorypredictive, on the other. Although both of these ideas have been mentioned elsewhere in this chapter, a more thorough discussion of them

---

5 This suggestion occurs with David Apter's view (1973, 3-15) that a "normative structural" or a "normative behavioral" research needs to be conducted for the process of modernization and development.

seems warranted in order to more fully explicate their implications for defining political development.

The question of universal applicability is widely acknowledged as a crucial methodological issue in empirical theory construction. The argument against the "ideologically biased" conception developed by Western scholars such as Huntington (1965) is based upon the scientific requirement of universal generalization. Perhaps the proliferation of such Western-biased or culturally-biased definitions in the behavioral era is attributable to the very premises of behavioralism itself. Social empiricism of the behavioralist orientation claims to pursue factual knowledge through observation. Yet, as alluded to earlier, this brand of empiricism provides the justifications for defining political development in terms of economically-developed Western industrial societies. What is observed in these societies is generally considered "developed," and the sociocultural attributes observed in less affluent and more agricultural societies are usually termed "underdeveloped."[6] Such views violate the requirement of universal applicability. It is in this sense that a certain valueneutrality must be considered as a criterion for definition.

Along with the construction of universal laws, explanation and prediction are commonly regarded as the core tasks of scientific inquiry. An adequate explanation requires logical conditions as well as empirical conditions. As Hempel and Oppenheim suggest, an explanation consists of an *explanadum* (statements describing the phenomenon to be explained), *explanans* (statements which are adduced to account for the phenomenon), and a logical deduction linking the *explanandum* with its explanans.[7]

A definition of political development in this case becomes the explanandum that is to be linked to the antecedent conditions in such a way that the conditions are expected, by a deductive framework, to cause or produce the phenomenon called political development. Hence, a utilitarian definition of political development for scientific analysis is one that, in giving structure to the phenomenon of political development, illuminates those conditions (*explanans*) from which a causal process of political development may be deductively ascertained. The Marxist theory of historical materialism and Walter Rostow's theory

---

6 The real problem with Western biased definitions, however, does not lie in the apparent moral bias implied in defining the Western life style as developed. Any selected bias violates the rules of science

7 Hempel and Oppenheim present a useful diagram to show the procedure of explanation (Hempel and Oppenheim 1945, 132-175).

(1952) of economic growth are examples of theories constructed for explanation and prediction. In defining each stage of the developmental process, these authors suggest the necessary and sufficient (i. e., causal) conditions for the achievement of each stage.

(3) Development as an Organismic Concept

The term "development" is most commonly associated with the organization of a living structure and its life processes. As Dale B. Harris (1957) maintains, a definition of development should essentially involve the idea of a living system. Now, if development is such an animate concept, "political" as an adjective of development should likewise be defined in terms of a living system.

A living being is one with inherent goals and propensities rather than assigned goals and imposed attributes. Whereas a raft unit such as a political system or a social system may seem to have apparent goals and functional imperatives, these goals are assigned or imposed upon the unit by its constituent human beings. Talcott Parsons' "functional requisites" (Parsons, 1949) are typical examples of such assigned goals. Thus, as long as development is a concept associated with living units, and "politics" is seen as a certain segment of the web of human interaction, "political development" should not be defined in terms of institutional imperatives but in terms relevant to the actual state of human beings.

To say that the human being needs to be the unit of analysis is not necessarily to endorse psychological reductionism. Obviously, political development is a macrolevel process involving wide-ranging types of social change. However, this fact does not preclude defining political development in terms of human attributes and explaining it in terms of their changing dynamics. This suggestion is in fact the essence of the perspective known as *methodological individualism.*[8] The individual man in this case is taken as the unit of analysis, but explanation of society as a whole remains the goal of analysis. In other words, look at the individual to talk about society. No pretense is made to solve the classical problem inherent in relating parts to the whole. It is simply assumed that the whole can be explained by the parts in the sense that there are no emergent qualities of the whole that the

---

8 For a concise discussion on methodological individualism, J. Watson (1957) and May Brodbeck (1968, 280-303).

individual cannot alter. The whole is exhaustively accounted for by the sum of its parts. This obviously debatable perspective of methodological individualism might be required for any kind of inductive social study.

In spite of this, the current literature frequently defines political development by employing the institutional setups of the political system as the definiens.[9] Although institutionalization may be an essential characteristic of modern society, institutions themselves are not "living" units with inherent goals or motivations or life cycles. Much of the sympathy for the "no growth" or "decay" concepts of social change and the widespread skepticism concerning the idea of assumed progressive social change stems from the fact that the human factor is largely neglected when institutions are used as the unit of observation.[10] An institution such as a bureaucracy, for instance, is neither inherently developed or underdeveloped. Its development can only be judged as a function of how well it achieves its assigned goals -- goals which are assigned by human beings because they are important to human beings.

It should be emphasized that an institution cannot be evaluated in any other way, for it is a human invention designed to pursue decidedly human needs.[11] For example, one would not evaluate the institutional setup of a university as a way of determining the state of "development" of the educational system. It is what the institution does, not what it consists of, that accounts for its development or underdevelopment. The obvious question, then, is what should an institution be doing? Of course, it should be doing what the human being, its inventor, designed it to do. What do we expect from the institution of government? This is a question we should confront in our attempt to define "political" and "development" and the answer should focus upon the human goals that institutions are created to pursue, not upon the characteristics of the institution itself.

---

9 Jaguaribe (1973, 201-202) discusses some of the institutionally oriented definitions of political development in his assessment of Deutsch , Pye, and Huntington..

10 Mulford Sibley (1966), B. D. Goulet (1965), and M. Diamant (1966), and R. Heilbroner (1974) are among those who brought up the importance of human dimensions of political development.

11 For an example of such interpretation of social institutions, see J. O. Hertzler (1946, 4-5) in which the author states that "social institutions are purposive... formed... to satisfy individual wants and social needs bound up with the efficient operation of any plurality of persons." An application of such institutional theory to the American society is made by Don Martindale (1960).

Without a doubt, developmental movements are affected by social institutions. An institution, as a human invention, is molded and characterized by the unique sociocultural environment in which it occurs. Thus, it is not unreasonable to expect that different societies with different cultural and social attributes, while pursuing the same goal, are likely to formulate different forms of a given institution in order to maximize effectiveness in achieving this goal. A society's institutional arrangement is as much determined by the attributes of that society as it is dictated by the goals themselves. For instance, the extended family system in China might perform the function of socialization, much as the conjugal family does in the West. However, the extended family has also been known to perform various other functions such as economic production and distribution and educational advancement that, in the West, require a multiplicity of secular institutions. Therefore, comparing the two family systems cross-culturally to evaluate the respective levels of development is not only valuesladen but also meaningless. By the same token, although both industrialization and agricultural enterprise may perform the same economic function (i.e., that of production), we cannot compare the two institutions crossculturally because production may not be the only function performed by agriculture or industry in a given societal context. We must conclude, then, that as long as the same goal is pursued by different institutional means in different societies, institutions provide us with a poor unit of comparative analysis.

(4) Development as Movement Over Time

As Dale Harris (1957, p. 3) emphatically maintains, development occurs only over time. More precisely, development occurs as movement over time toward the desired state of the living structure. A development, then, may be described schematically as follows:

S-1S-2S-3S-n

M-1M-2M-3M-n

T-1T-2T-3T-n

(T-1 through T-n represents the time needed for the state change from S-1 to S-n which is accomplished incrementally through movements (M-1 through M-n)

This structure of development implies, among other things, that a developmental theory should be designed to explain, as well

36

as describe, the sequential movements that represent the change occurring between *So* and *Sn*. This means that it should account for the process of change in the same unit of analysis. Theories or definitions derived from and aimed at comparing various units of analysis at a given time would not be adequate for scientific inquiry into the development process.

As we survey the literature on political development, we find that, until recently, most theories intended to describe and explain the phenomenon of development have been formed by the comparison of different societies at a given point in time rather than by the comparison of different levels of development within the same society at different points in time. For example, economic growth, perhaps the most common yardstick of development, has primarily been compared crossculturally with the questionable measurements of GNP per capita, proportion of industrial production, and the like. It would seem much more meaningful in this case to measure the rate of economic growth within the same society.[12]

Then, it might be suggested, as a rule for development theory construction, that one consider the rate as well as magnitude of change in the same unit of analysis.

(5) Development as a Stage Concept

A movement in the process of development represents an incremental progression toward the achievement of a goal. One way to represent movement in this manner is through a stage theory of development. This seems warranted for a number of reasons, especially when it is "political" development that is the focus of the theory.

From a purely semantic perspective, since development movements are incremental, the idea of a stage is a useful for designating each of the increments in the sequential chain. Furthermore, we must keep in mind that political development is an ongoing process. While a society may achieve its designated political goals, this does not mean the developmental process has been completed. Goal completion only gives way to new goals, and the developmental process resumes. Here, a stage theory might be useful in that the stages could be used to designate each of the

---

12 Such concern about the use of historical data became increasingly widespread as the inadequacies of earlier abstract models of political development had become more apparent. Almond (1970) and Rustow (1970), for example, acknowledged that the need for blending earlier models and applying them to sequences of historical events.

sets of goals, the sequential achievement of which constitutes the process of political development.

Unfortunately, however, not many theories concerning political development deserve to be called stage theories. There are several theories that suggest categories of development including John Kautsky's developmental categories (Kautsky, 1962) and Edward Shils' typology of transitional societies (Shils, 1962). In the strict sense of stage theory, no contemporary work, with the possible exception of Rostow's Process of Economic Growth, can equal Marxism as being a true "stage" theory. Excluding Rostow's work on the basis of its exclusive economic concern, Organski's work (1968) may be the best example of a stage theory of political development. However, as we saw earlier, it also suffers from a number of substantive and methodological problems. A stage theory should not only maintain clearcut boundaries between stages, but each stage upon its completion should provide the necessary and sufficient conditions for moving into the next stage. Put differently, a stage, when fully realized, should be able to produce the subsequent stage. Neither a genetic breakdown of various time periods for classificatory purposes nor a typology of development constitutes a stage theory of development. While Marxist stage theory incorporates the notion of inevitable causality into its logic of development, Organski's stages are much more flexible as the author admits:

> There is nothing inevitable about the stages here set forth, but it is striking that in all the world's many nations development has been in the same direction: toward industrialization, higher productivity, higher living standards; toward political complexity, political efficacy, and increased dependence upon the state (Organski, 196, p. 23).

Although the stages set forth by Organski, i.e., (1) primitive unification, (2) industrialization, (3) welfare state, and (4) abundance, appear to describe the historical pattern of growth for some Western societies, they fail to form the stage theory that we need for scientific analysis. First of all, Organski bases his theory upon a Western-biased definition in which economic development is treated as being synonymous with political development. Second, he fails to account for the mechanism of transition from one stage to the next. Third, he chooses not to recognize the sequential characteristics of the process of change, thus failing to construct a true stage theory. And finally, like Marx and Rostow, he fails to account for what happens after a "developed society" reaches the point of affluence. Economic abundance may indeed be what every society desires, but the abundant lifestyle does not stop the society and culture from changing -- witness the rapid changes taking place in North America and other postindustrial societies.[13]

We have discussed some of the problems that confront the researcher in conceptualizing and defining political development. The crucial definitional criteria have been identified within the perspectives of the philosophy of science and semantics. They may be summarized as follows:

- To satisfy the requirements of a definition, a definition of political development should identify the unique features of the terms that are necessary and sufficient to distinguish it from all other terms. An adequate definition is one in which the definiens and definiendum are mutually replaceable.

- The type of society defined as developed or underdeveloped needs to be an ideal type in the Weberian sense, in which the nature of the society should be determined as a hypotheticaldeductive construct rather than an empirically derived description of the observed society.[14]

- A definition, as the initial stage of scientific theory construction, needs to facilitate the formulation of explanatorypredictive laws. In order for the explanation of development to be feasible, the developmental unit should be an entity that is inherently motivated toward the achievement of goals. Thus, a human, rather than an institution, might be preferred as a unit of analysis.

- Since scientific inquiry is a nomothetic enterprise, a definition should be universally applicable. It should define the developmental process as it occurs in all possible social settings.

- The term "development" originated as a description of structural changes in living organisms, and it has commonly been applied to living systems. This suggests, as does criterion 4, that human beings need to be the unit of

---

13 It is this apparent "dead-end" assumption built into many development theories that Huntington (1965, 396ff), Eisenstadt (1964), and Riggs (1968), among others, were critical about and resentful to.

14 For the concept of "ideal type," refer to Don Martindale (1963); For Max Weber's original conception of the term, see Weber (1949).

analysis in a developmental theory and that the definition of political development should be in human terms.

- The term "development" implies a type of change over time. Hence, an adequate theory of the developmental process should be capable of explaining the mechanism involved in this change. This necessitates the use of longitudinal analysis of the same unit over time, rather than crosscultural comparisons of different units at fixed points in time.

- A developmental change over time involves various movements incrementally proceeding toward certain goals. These increments can best be represented as stages in a process, rather than categories or types that are minimally linked in a causal sequence. Hence, a stage theory appears to be the most appropriate approach to account for political development, and the definition of development should be such as to permit this.

- A stage theory should not only spell out the boundaries of stages but it should clarify the conditions for transition from one stage to another. This is minimally required if development is to be depicted as a sequential process of change.

- In order to be nomothetic, a stage theory should account for the further development of what have been inappropriately termed "developed" societies. Here, some type of cyclical theory might be suggested as a more powerful one than a linear progressive theory under the assumption that development of human society is not to be terminated.

Admittedly, it is a difficult task for any definition of political development to meet all the criteria discussed above. But having a set of acceptable rules for an adequate conceptualization of the term will be helpful not only in developing such a concept, but also in refining and assessing the leading current definitions (Appendix).

APPENDIX: What is Political Development?

Almond, C. (with C. Powell, 1966, p. 105)

"the increased differentiation and specialization of political structures and the increased secularization of political culture."

Apter, D. (1968, p. 2)

"a process which affects choice.... The modernization focus helps to make sense of the choices likely to be at our disposal."

Deutsch, K. W. (1961, p. 102)

"Social Mobilization (equivalently used with development) is the process in which major clusters of old social, economic, and psychological concomitants are eroded or broken and people become available for new patterns of socialization and behavior."

Diamant, A. (1966, p. 92)

"a process by which a political system acquires an increased capability to sustain successfully and continuously new types of goals and demands and the creation of new types of organizations."

Dorsey, J. (1963, p. 320)

"the changes in power structure and processes that occur concomitantly with changes in energy conversion levels in the social system, whether such conversion levels change primarily in their political, social, and economic manifestations or in various combinations of the three."

Eisenstadt, S. N. (1968, p. 184)

"The capacity of modern society to adapt itself to continuously changing demands, to absorb them in terms of policy making, and to assure its OWII continuity in the face of continuous new demands and new forms of political organization."

Goulet, D. (1968, p. 299)

"a crucial means of obtaining good life."

Huntington, S. (1965, p. 387)

"the institutionalization of political organizations and procedures."

Lerner, D. (1958, p. 50)

"Modern society is participant in that it functions by consensus."

Levy, M. (1965, p. 65, in Masannat 1973)

Considers "any society more developed the greater the ratio of inanimate to animate sources of power and the greater the extent to which human efforts are multiplied by the use of tools."

Organski, A. F. K. (1968, p. 7)

"increasing governmental capability in utilizing the human and material resources of the nation for national goals."

Pye, L. (1966)

"the capacity to maintain a certain level of public order, to mobilize resources for a specific range of collective enterprises, and to make and efflciently uphold types of international commitment."

Riggs, F. (1965 in LaPalombara, 1965, p. 122)

"a gradual separation of institutionally distinct spheres, the differentiation of separate structures for the wide variety of functions that must be performed in any society."

Chapter 3

The State of Development Theories: A Misguided Track

Returning to the wisdom of *Sociology of Knowledge* introduced in Chapter 1, we can ascertain that the life environment of the Cold War era dictated the nature of scholarship in the area of development studies. That era was dominated by polarized politics grounded on mutually incompatible sets of values and belief systems imbedded in capitalist democracy and socialist communism. There was practically no interaction between the academic communities of the two camps. Each was guided by "ideo-centrism" where each bloc developed an extreme sense of self-righteousness while demonizing each other. Development studies were in the center of this schism. Yet, not every country was divided into either of the two camps. The non-aligned countries, such as India, formed what is referred to as the Third World, reserving the label of the First World for the capitalist democracies and the Second World for the socialist communist systems. These two worlds expanded their hegemonic competition into the Third World in an attempt to create "surrogate" states for their respective power domains. The instruments for competition between them became diverse, ranging from the arms race to ideological and institutional clashes. Symptomatic in this confrontation was a lack of communication and mutual interest in academic discourse. Studies on development evolved separately across the divide: Whereas the socialist bloc did not encourage any intellectually creative activities that might be inconsistent with the official ideological and theoretical blueprint, the First World's scholars showed a degree of variation in advancing theories on development. In this chapter, we will examine these theoretical and conceptual expositions as witnessed in comparative studies in general and development studies in particular.

During the heightened decades of the Cold War Era, 1950s-1960s, there was a vibrant flurry of conceptual and theoretical scholarly activities, most of which was centered in the United States. There were three clusters of such activities: (1) The traditional-modern dichotomy where the traditional is regarded as backward and underdeveloped and the modern is considered advanced and developed; (2) structural-functionalism that juxtaposes the modern versus the traditional based on certain functions; (3) stage theories of development stating that the more advanced the stage, the more developed the system.

The "Traditional-Modern" Dichotomy

The process of retooling and reorienting comparative politics during the Cold War era, especially for the purpose of analyzing systemic changes during that period, quite naturally began with efforts to distinguish Western from nonWestern societies. The idea was that, if the industrialized West is "modern" or "developed" and the Third World is not, then we should begin by distinguishing these two system types as poles on a continuum. "Modernization" then becomes the process by which a nation moves from one end of the continuum to the other.

Hence, this gave rise to the first taxonomic endeavors aimed at constructing a traditionalmodern dichotomy, or some similar variant (e.g., ruralurban, agrarianindustrial, Westernnonwestern). The theoretical underpinnings of these efforts were largely derived from Talcott Parsons' elaboration of the "pattern variables," which refers to mutually exclusive value orientations, and the assertion that a particular society's value system will tend toward one or the other end of several specific dimensions of pattern variables (Parsons, 1951, pp. 24112). Pattern variables have formed the basis of a number of efforts aimed at distinguishing modern society from its traditional counterpart. The basic elements, present in some form or another in most of these works, include the following: (l) ascriptive versus achievement-based status, (2) functionally diffuse versus functionally specific roles, (3) particularistic versus universalistic values, (4) collective orientation versus self-orientation, and (5) affectivity versus affective neutrality. In each dichotomy, the former member is taken as characteristic of traditional society and the latter is typical of modern society (see Bill and Hardgrave 1973, p. 52 for a brief description of each).

Authors who have utilized this dichotomous scheme are numerous. Sutton (1963) proposed an "agriculturalindustrial" dichotomy. The former is characterized by ascriptive status norms, low spatial and status mobility, a simple and stable occupational system (functionally diffuse), and a differential stratification system. By contrast, in the latter system type we find achievement norms, high mobility, and a highly differentiated and functionally specific occupational system, (an "egalitarian" achievement system based on stratification). Similarly, Riggs (1957) extended Sutton's models for the analysis of administrative systems, using the polar opposites of *agraria* and *industria*. It should be noted that Riggs later elaborates this model into a more dynamic system, involving the fused, diffracted, and prismatic stages of social development (elaboration to follow in this chapter). Ward and Rustow (1964 pp. 67) provide a checklist of characteristics of the modern polity that a traditional polity presumably lacks.

Typically, then, the modern polity, in contrast to the traditional polity, is characterized by rationalized authority, differentiated and integrated structures, mass participation and positive affect toward the system and, consequently, the capacity to process a high volume of inputs and accomplish a broad range of goals. Modernization, then, is a lengthy, complex process that occurs in phases but ultimately revolutionizes social life in the traditional society (Huntington, 1971, pp. 288289).

A number of problems have been pointed out with respect to the validity and utility of the traditionalmodern dichotomy. Rustow (1967, p. 12) notes that while modernity can be affirmatively defined in terms of the characteristics of industrial societies, "traditional society" remains largely a residual concept. That is to say, those characteristics ascribed to traditional societies are, in many cases, simply the logical antitheses of characteristics ascribed to modern societies. It is doubtful that all or any of the socalled traditional societies manifested all these traits. At the very least, history shows that there was great diversity among traditional societies.

A second crucial problem with the dichotomous definitions is that they fail to distinguish between what is modern and what is Western. Indeed, modernity is virtually synonymous with the characterization of twentieth century Western European and North American society. The current dichotomy represents an empirical distinction of Western societies from Third World nations. Those scholars who use the dichotomy to define the two poles on the universal spectrum of change imply that the nature of Western society is the goal toward which all emerging nations aspire. As Holsti (1975, p. 829) notes, the evidence gathered from studies of developing nations argues largely against this inference.

Furthermore, the implicit teleological character of the change process implies that once a society has modernized or Westernized, change ceases. Surely, the persistence of change in socalled "developed" societies argues against this idea. Indeed, such a teleological conception of development contains an element of circularity: Some prior conception of development is needed to

45

explicate the characteristics of the developed society. This clearly violates the criterion for defining development as an ideal type established in the previous chapter.

Structural Functionalism and the "Transitional Society"

With the growing realization that the traditionalmodern dichotomy was of limited utility and accuracy, scholarly efforts began to focus on the idea of "transitional" systems. This new focus emerged from the realization that all societies possessed attributes of both the modern and the traditional ideal types. However, the enchantment with Talcott Parson's pattern variables and functional models remained.

In *The Politics of Developing Areas* (1960), Almond states his assumptions in terms of "four characteristics that all political systems have in common" and which thereby constitute the basis for the comparison of political systems. He asserts that all political systems have structures, which he defines as the legitimate patterns of interaction by means of which the order of society is maintained. Systems may be compared, then, in terms of the degree and form of structural specialization. These structures derive their *raison d'etre* from their performance of certain functions, and as a further basis of comparison, Almond postulates that there are certain functions that apparently are performed in all systems. Almond's eight "universal functions" are, on the input side, (1) political socialization, which involves the transmission of political culture from one generation to the next, (2) political recruitment whereby the new incumbents of political roles are selected and trained, (3) interest articulation by which demands are identified and transmitted from the society to the decisionmaking elite, (4) interest aggregation whereby these demands are consolidated into a manageable form for the elite to act upon, and (5) political communication, the process by which information is transmitted within the political system and between the political system and its environment. On the output side there are the functions of (6) rule making, (7) rule application, and (8) rule adjudication, which correspond to the legislative, executive and judicial functions in the democratic political system, as it is commonly conceived. Beyond this, Almond assumes that all structures, no matter how specialized, will be multifunctional in some sense and to some extent. And finally, all political systems are "mixed" systems in the cultural sense, in that no system is completely "modern," nor are there any "allprimitive" or traditional systems. In general, comparisons are made within this framework in terms of the probabilities of performance of the specified functions by the specified structures, and in terms of the differences in the style of their performance. Development is conceived of as the system's increase in the effectiveness of the performance of these functions (Almond and Coleman, 1960, p. 59).

The criticisms directed at Almond's initial formulation are numerous and multifaceted. They deal with, among other things, the lack of definitional clarity evident through this framework, weakness in the logical structure of the model, and questions concerning its capacity to meaningfully depict the process of change that must be central to any model of development.

First of all, we should note that in several ways the lack of definitional clarity in this construction severely limits its potential value as an explanatory device. Holt and Richardson (1970, pp. 3435) contend that Almond does not explicitly define several of the key structures in his framework, and those that he does define tend to be defined in terms of the functions that they perform. As long as this is so, there can be no probabilistic theory concerning the performance of a given function by a given structure, because that relationship is true by definition and therefore need not be tested empirically. Furthermore, Almond nowhere clarifies even what a function is, and his eight "universal" functions are defined at such a high level of generality that it is unclear what specific sets of empirical indicators could be used to measure the performance of these functions (Mayer 1972, p. 148). Since the increase in the effectiveness of their performance is what constitutes development, we must have some criteria by which to evaluate their performance if we are to explain development.

Besides these definitional problems, the explanatory power of Almond's model is also limited by Almond's use of the assumptions of universal functionalism. In particular, he never specifies why it is these eight functions, and not some others, whose effective performance results in political development (Bill and Hardgrave 1973, p. 213). In his first assumption, Almond states only that these functions are apparently sufficient for the effective performance of the system; he nowhere claims that their performance, and theirs alone, is necessary and sufficiently for the effective functioning of the system. While Mayer (1972, p. 143) notes that the differences between "universal" functionalism, such as the former case above, and requisite analysis, as would be the latter case above, appear semantic rather than logical, Almond can neither predict that the inadequate performance of these functions will result in system failure, nor infer their inadequate performance from systemic breakdowns unless he rules out the possibility of other unspecified functions contributing to the effectiveness of the system (Mayer 1972, p. 148).

There are questions as to whether Almond's framework really addresses an explanation of political change. It seems suitable for the comparison of different systems at different levels of development. But to compare the states of systems in such a static sense is not to explain the process of change over time in a given system. Thus, the model's conceptual scheme is illsuited for representing change over time in a given system. "Increasing effectiveness" of functional performance and "structural differentiation" are the only dimensions of change that are explicit in this formulation. Even ignoring the definitional problems with the variables discussed above, to define development as the quantitative increase along some single dimension of change is to neglect the qualitative changes that occur in the nature of the system as it develops. Development involves important identifiable changes beyond just the evolution of "more structures" performing the same functions more effectively.

Furthermore, having posited that there is a certain interdependence among the eight functions that is not necessarily harmonious, Almond fails to specify the nature of these interdependencies and therefore cannot predict that an increase in the performance of one function will not be deleterious to the performance of one of the other functions. In other words, unless it can be shown that the increased performance of one does not in fact detract from the effectiveness of the system by causing a decrease in the performance of another function, we cannot assert unequivocally that development results from increases in the performances of the eight functions. Hence, Almond's failure to specify the interrelationships among his eight functions limits his model's capacity to deal with the process of change in a meaningful way.

In *Comparative Politics: A Developmental Approach* (1966), Almond presents a much revised version of his functional model of development with the changes contained therein representing an attempt to correct some of the theoretical deficiencies attributed to his earlier formulation. Most importantly, perhaps, he expands his set of functional categories and attempts to establish some sort of relationships between them in an effort to infuse his model with the capacity to account for the dynamics of developmental change. In particular, Almond asserts that political systems must be evaluated in terms of three different "levels of functioning," which, ostensibly, are products of certain patterns of interrelationship among the various functional categories. On one level are the capability functions (regulative, extractive, distributive and responsive) that determine the performance of the political system in relation to its environment. On another level are the conversion functions (the inputoutput functions of the previous formulation) that are internal to the political system and involve the system's ability to meet demands (inputs) with authoritative decisions (outputs). The third level is that of the system maintenance and adaptation functions of political socialization and recruitment whereby the system ensures its own continuity (Almond and Powell 1966, pp. 2830).

Under this construction of the model, political development is driven when certain environmental conditions give rise to significant changes in the magnitude and content of political inputs. Such changes are deemed "significant" when it becomes apparent that the existing structural and cultural makeup of the political system is incapable processing the new demand load in a satisfactory manner. In such a situation, political development occurs when the political system undergoes structural differentiation and cultural secularization to such an extent that the needed increase in systemic capabilities occurs so that the new demands can be dealt with effectively (Almond and Powell 1966, p. 34).

Such challenges to the functional capacity of existing structural and cultural patterns occur in the form of what Almond designates as the "developmental challenges" of state building, nation building, participation, and distribution. Almond defines each of these in terms of their impact the three levels of political system functionality. Finally, he posits a sequence of their occurrence, although he claims no theoretical imperative for this particular order. It is simply that this is the order in which they have emerged in the political systems of Western Europe (Almond and Powell 1966, pp. 3637).

By means of these changes in the logic and conceptual content of his model, Almond has ostensibly answered the criticism of system states, yet he is still unable to explain the dynamics of the development process. The new model addresses the "what" and "how" of development: development is the acquisition of greater capabilities through the processes of structural differentiation and cultural secularization. The definitional clarity of his conceptual framework is sharpened somewhat by the greater number of concepts now explicit in the model. However, the model remains plagued by many of the same problems that elicited criticism of the earlier formulation. Despite the expansion of his set of functional categories, the concepts- even the new ones- are still defined at such a high level of abstraction that they cannot be operationalized without robbing them of some of the richness and complexity they retain in a strictly theoretical context. To operationalize these concepts without retaining most of their meaning in the empirical context would lead to unfair testing of the generated hypotheses (Flanigan and Fogelman 1967, p. 82).

Thus, while he uses the idea of the three "levels of functioning" to propose some very general relationships between the functions, these relationships are as yet untestable, since the critical concepts cannot be operationalized. And what relationships he has proposed between the adaptive functions of differentiation and secularization and the several capability functions represent only the bare beginnings of the interdependence patterns that would be necessary for a functionalist theory of political development. Almond, recognizing this weakness in his formulation, admits the theoretical necessity of such specification.

The theory of the political system will be designed to discover the relationships between various levels of functional capabilities, conversion functions, and system maintenance and adaptation functions (Almond and Powell 1966, pp. 29-30). Even the one relationship he proposed, that differentiation and secularization lead to enhanced capabilities, is of questionable validity, at least when the concepts are so vaguely defined. Bill and Hardgrave (1973, p. 73) pointed out that enhanced capabilities are by no means guaranteed by structural differentiation and cultural secularization. Differentiation without the concomitant integration of the new structural units may in fact reduce the system's capabilities, and cultural secularization may exacerbate rather than resolve system challenges by creating new demands (such as participation demands) at a time when the structure of the system is already overloaded with demands. To define development thus in terms of the instrumentalities of capabilities rather than capability itself is to cloud the distinction between political development and what Huntington (1965) has termed "political decay." Both are plausible outcomes of the differentiation and secularization processes. Almond ignores this, however, and therefore provides us with no additional criteria with which to predict what will occur in a given set of circumstances.

Thus, while Almond has at least attempted to inject the needed dynamism into his development scheme, the conceptual problems that plagued his first model remain critically unresolved here, as do the logical problems inherent in the universal functionalism paradigm. Perhaps the heuristic value of his model has been enhanced, but its desired explanatory power cannot be realized until these methodological dilemmas are resolved.

David Apter's works on modernization constitute a second instance of a functionalist approach to development theory. However, Apter's use of the idea of "structural requisites" and his more empirically based classification scheme for transitional societies distinguish his use of the functional mode from that of Almond. And, as would be expected, the theoretical propositions he generates within this framework differ from those of Almond with respect to both the aspects of the development process that are deemed to be of analytical importance and the way in which these phenomena are conceptualized. To begin with, Apter limited his analytical concern to the process of social development. He listed three preconditions for the inception of modernization: a social system (1) that can absorb innovation without disintegrating, (2) in which there are flexible, differentiated social structures, and (3) with the capacity to provide the skills and knowledge necessary for living in a technologically advanced world (Apter 1965, p. 67). It is this last condition that distinguishes modernization from development in general. Industrialization is the definitive economic and technological aspect of modernization. Hence, modernization is defined as the increasing complexity of social patterns resulting from the differentiation and integration of new functional roles, and, particularly, the spread and use of "industrial-type roles in nonindustrial settings" (Apter 1968, p. 334).

In order to analyze this process, Apter began by proposing a typology of transitional systems which, in their fulfillment of the above mentioned conditions, represent four analytically distinct alternative starting points for the modernization process. These "ideal type" constructs are distinguished according to whether they have a pyramidal or hierarchical authority structure, on the one hand, and whether their political actions are guided by consummatory (i.e., sacred or otherwise "ultimate") goals or instrumental (i. e., secular) goals (Apter 1965, pp. 19 24) on the other.

Secondly, he attempted to specify what activities must be performed in order for the system to maintain itself as a unit. He terms these "structural requisites," rather than "functional requisites," although it appears that what he meant to imply by use of this term is the institutionalization of the performance of what others would designate as functions. To illustrate this point, we note first that Apter's primary structural requisites are (1) authoritative decision-making, and (2) accountability. These two correspond roughly to what Apter calls the "functional requisites" of government, which are "coercion" and "information." Thus, in Apter's paradigm, "functional requisites" are the minimum tools a political system needs in order to perform the functions implied in the list of structural requisites (Mayer 1972, pp. 157).

Apter later increases his list of structural requisites to include (3) the structure of coercion and punishment, (4) the structure of resource determination and allocation, and (5) the structure of political recruitment and assignment (Apter 1968, p. 29). These appeared in his earlier formulation as "contingent structures" or "analytic substructures" of government (Apter 1965, pp. 245247).

Finally, within this conceptual framework, Apter attempts to derive theoretical propositions concerning the interrelationship between these structural requisites and the differences in these patterns of interrelationship. Since modernization involves the proliferation of "modern" roles throughout society, Apter examines the relative ability of each systemtype to foster such an expansion, and the major way of doing this is by affecting the society's stratification in such a way as to provide for the greater upward mobility of the "modern " roles and/or strata.

In assessing the explanatory utility of Apter's paradigm, Mayer (1972, p. 257) noted that because Apter's typology is based upon empirical rather than normative criteria, his scheme is capable of organizing and giving meaning to an otherwise amorphous and disparate group of political systems. To the extent that he can logically derive a precise set of developmental outcomes for each of the system types, his paradigm would represent a sound basis for the generation of testable propositions from which to construct a theory of development. In fact, Apter attempted to generate such scientific generalizations by linking characteristics of his "mobilization system" and "reconciliation system" with certain specified stages of the modernization process (Apter 1965, 1968).

However, the full explanatory potential of his paradigm is never fully realized due to many of the same reasons that limit Almond's model. Like Almond, Apter conceptualized the critical phenomena in his explanatory sequences at such a high level of generality that operationalization is all but impossible. Therefore, while he may be able to account logically for certain loosely defined relationships between system types and modernization phenomena, he cannot predict precisely defined outcomes from a given set of empirical preconditions unless the operational linkage is established between the preconditions and the concepts in his generalized explanatory sequences.

And like Almond, Apter does not pay sufficient attention to the specification of the relationships between his structural requisites. How does the functioning of one structure affect that of another, and vice versa? Unless such relationships are specified, we can never evaluate meaningfully the overall performance of the system. All that can be said is that the requisite structures, as a group, are functioning adequately if the system is still in existence. But such a conclusion is of no analytical value, and simply accentuates the tautological implications of Apter's use of requisite analysis.

As for this idea of "structural requisites," it also creates certain logical problems for Apter's paradigm, even though it should allow Apter to avoid those problems associated with "universal functionalism." There is no theoretical justification for the claim that Apter's set of requisites, and not some other, is the only possible set of structures by which a system can maintain itself. Since Apter's chief concern here is the explanation of modernization, it would be reasonable to assume the validity of his requisites and test the validity of this assumption later when the explanatory potential of the model has been established. However, Mayer (1972 p. 158) contended that, at the very least, the postulate of structural requisites should be defined with enough precision as to allow for the operationalization for such testing. In this respect, Apter's requisites offer little empirical utility.

Even given the assumption of structural requisites, it appears that the explanatory power of Apter's paradigm is enhanced little, if any, by its inclusion. All this assumption does is distinguish surviving systems from those that do not survive in terms of the former's performance (and the latter's nonperformance) of all of the implied requisite functions. Since political scientists are, in general, concerned only with systems that have maintained themselves, this distinction is meaningless from an analytical standpoint. The assumption of requisites contributes nothing toward the identification and explanation of the differences among systems that do survive, which is the central analytical concern of political science and comparative politics (Mayer 1972, p. 158).

Finally, there is a certain teleological aspect of Apter's model that limits its ability to explain the process of modernization. Apter, like Almond and Coleman before him, represents the process of modernization in terms of goals. That is, most of his attention is directed toward describing the starting points of the process (e.g. his typology) and its end state, the modernized society, while saying little about the dynamics of the process by which a system moves from the former state to the latter. To list the elements of the desired outcome of a process is not to explain the process itself

(Golembiewski et al. 1969, pp. 252253). And since it is the process of change that is by definition the focus of development analysis, Apter's model can contribute little toward the realization of this central explanatory goal.

The third instance of a functional approach to political development is contained in the work of the Social Science Research Council (SSRC). In essence, the SSRC simplified and relaxed some of the analytical restrictions of Almond and Powell's model in order to allow a maximum amount of investigative freedom for researchers while maintaining a general basis for the comparison and integration of the various findings.

In *Aspects of Political Development* (19xx), Lucien Pye summarized the approach employed by the Social Science Research Council (SSRC). Briefly, political development is seen as the interaction of the processes of structural differentiation, the imperatives of equality, and the integrative, adaptive and responsive capacities of the political system (Pye 1966, pp. 4547). Development in terms of these three categories of variables, which together make up the development syndrome, occurs in response to one or more of six crises that systems must face in the course of becoming modern nation states. These crises are: (1) the identity crisis (i.e., nation building), (2) the legitimacy crisis, (3) the penetration crisis (i.e., state building) (4) the integration crisis, (5) the participation crisis, and (6) the distributive crisis. The particular pattern of a country's development will depend upon the sequence in which these crises arise and the ways in which they are resolved (Pye 1966, pp. 6366).

Since this analytical scheme is simply intended as a guide to research and not a formal model, it is difficult to criticize it by the same criteria used above. However, the amount of guidance it can afford researchers is limited by the same conceptual problems that plagued Almond's model. It lacks clear operational criteria, meaning different researchers in different countries have no basis upon which to evaluate the equivalence of their operational definitions. Accordingly, the cross-cultural validity of any findings must be considered suspect. Relations between the elements of the syndrome are unspecified, and Pye's insistence on equating development with democratization (Pye 1966, p. 71) envelops the scheme in a cloud of ethnocentrism.

Dissatisfied with the largely descriptive and nonformal explanatory endeavors of the aforementioned studies, Fred Riggs attempted to construct a more coherent paradigm of political change (Riggs 1964). At a time when everyone was trying to devise some lawlike statement of comparisons among nations, he developed a more structured concept of the developing nation when he proposed that all transitional societies go through what he called the "prismatic society" stage. A prismatic society is one in which the social and political functions of institutions have been diffused but not yet integrated. Hence, a nation's degree of development may be described and compared in terms of the extent to which its institutional functions have become rationalized and specialized. Riggs defines political development as "a gradual separation of institutionally distinct spheres, and the differentiation of separate structures for the wide variety of functions that must be performed in any society" (Riggs in LaPalombara 1965, p. 122). He suggests that this is a rule of social change by which every society must be guided. As such, universal comparative theory, based on a clear conception of this common process, should be feasible. There are many who have chosen this "institutional specialization" concept as the unit of comparative inquiry, as we see from the works of Apter, Pye, Huntington, and Diamont.

Riggs' framework suffers, however, from failing to delineate the conditions that are both necessary and sufficient for changing from one state of affairs to another. Therefore, its value is restricted to its taxonomic utility since its explanatory and predictive capabilities have yet to be established.

Having discussed some examples of the functional approach to development, our task now should be to discern which criticisms are common to all three examples and what problems can be said to be intrinsic to the functional mode of analysis in general.

One criticism that was alluded to above is the apparent ethnocentric character of the functions defined by all the authors. Almond and Coleman admit that their functional categories are derived from political systems in which structural specialization and functional differentiation have occurred to the greatest extent (Almond and Coleman 1960, p. 16). Apter's structural requisites and Pye's development syndrome (and his crises) appear to be of similar derivation. In so doing, these authors in effect deny the possibility that alternative differentiation patterns might evolve in contexts different from that of the Anglo-American democracies (Golembiewski et al. 1969, p. 254). It is in this sense that their conceptual schemes are ethnocentric and, hence, of dubious theoretical utility.

A second point that should be made is that all of these authors deal with "modernization" rather than political development in general. While this is not a criticism of their work, it should be noted because this fact limits the applicability of their findings to a certain historical period and set of international preconditions. That is, they only account for the modernization of transitional societies in an international (comparative) context in which the societies are assumed to be moving toward the state of modern industrial nations. This assumption is no more plausible than assuming that India's tomorrow will be America's today. In short, their models are not universally applicable from a logical point of view, nor can they explain the development of all "developed" (i.e., modern) societies.

Stage Theories of Development

The grandest of all stage theories of development expressed belongs to Karl Marx. Consistent with his seminal work, *Das Kapital*, his *Communist Manifesto* (1848) advanced a set of clearly defined, qualitatively distinct stages of historical development portraying the evolution of history as a dialectical process both inevitable and virtuous. By progressing through feudalism, capitalism, and socialism, history will reach a perfected stage of classless society. Many believers in socialism adhered to versions of that ideology, notably, Lenin, Stalin, Mao Zedong, Fidel Castro, Ho Ji-Min, and more recent exponents of socialist economy in the Third World. The Soviet bloc during the Cold War era was subsumed under this ideological persuasion, resulting in a massive impact on world political and economic systems.

In response to the expansion of Marxist doctrine, some scholars in the United States offered their own versions of stage theory. Rostow in his well known, *The Stages of Economic Growth: Non-Communist Manifesto* (1960), proposed a five-stage process of development. He wanted to make sure that his theory countered Karl Marx's. Rowtow's five stages were:

1. "Traditional society": characterized by low levels of technology, a static, agrarian economy that is labor intensive.

2. "The preconditions of takeoff": here, scientific discoveries (or the intrusion of the West) are translated into technological advances.

3. "Takeoff": selfsustaining economic growth is achieved through increased investment, industrialization, and the commercialization of agriculture.

4. "The drive to maturity": outputs begin to exceed the increased demand generated by population growth.

5. "Mass consumption": the leading sectors of production shift to the production of durable consumer goods and service-oriented activities.

The weakness of this model is that it is solely a theory of economic development. Also, it is based largely upon one historical case (the U. S.) and is therefore time-bound and culture-bound.

Organski's (1965) stages of political development are similar to Rostow's and fall victim to the same criticisms. The stages of (1) primitive unification, (2) industrialization, (3) national welfare and (4) the politics of abundance are stages of economic growth again abstracted from the American case. The applicability of these two stage-oriented theories to the various systems in today's world is limited, as the value systems of these nations and the historical context of their developmental efforts are vastly different from those of the United States and the rest of the industrialized West.

Development and the Individual

Besides these grand theories that attempt to depict the development of entire political systems, there have been several works that focus upon the changes in individual attitudes, belief systems, and more general world views that seem to accompany the societal transition to modernity. The attraction of this approach for the behavioralist is that it is more clearly and directly linked to changes in behavioral patterns. Indeed, it focuses on the basic unit of behavior: the individual human actor. If developmental changes at the individual level can be accurately depicted in theory, then the broader systemic changes that occupied the structural functionalists become explainable in terms of these individual level changes. Systemic changes - and especially the different patterns of such changes that so baffled the structural functionalists - can be accounted for in terms of the differing institutional matrices within which ostensibly universal patterns of individual development have occurred.

One of the earliest attempts at comparing different societies through a similar individual-level conceptual framework is the work of Daniel Lerner (Lerner, 1958). Here, he used the concept of "empathy" or mobile personality as the yardstick with which to compare and explain the developmental dynamics of several

Middle Eastern countries. Development was defined as the movement of individuals toward this personality characteristic. Lerner and his associates conducted a comparative study in Turkey, Egypt, Lebanon, Syria, and Iran. They found that there were regularities in the life situations of individuals in these countries, making scientific theory construction possible at a crosscultural level of analysis. Although Lerner's general theory of modernization was not universally validated, his research suggested that the theory would be useful in affirming the universality of many specific positions and hypotheses. However, few of his hypotheses have been tested successfully in subsequent studies.

David McClelland, working from the assumption that economic development and modernization are ultimately explicable by the people's psychological motivations, particularly the need for achievement, attempted to assess various nations' development crossculturally by comparing the content of children's books. These books were taken as a measure of the degree to which the culture is grounded on achievementoriented values (McClelland, 1961). Here again, the author maintains that the direct relationship between achievement orientation and economic development may be suggested as an interesting hypothesis, but cannot as yet be enthroned as a proven theory.

A more ambitious comparative research project was conducted by Verba and Almond, culminating in the publication of *The Civic Culture* in 1963. The project, also known as the "five nations study," attempted to compare the U.S., the U.K., Germany, Italy, and Mexico in terms of people's political perceptions and attitudes as revealed by survey research methods. While this work represents a much more serious attempt at systematic comparative research, the introduction of this work provoked considerable discussion and debate as to the meaningfulness and validity of their crossnational and crosscultural comparisons.

These and other theorists who define political development in terms of individual predispositions appear to suggest that certain cultures are more "developed" than others, and individuals belonging to those cultures are assumed to be more developed than others in different cultural environments. As they specify cultural attributes such as achievement orientation (McClelland, 1963), mobile personality (Lerner, 1958), participant behavior (Verba, 1963), associational sentiment (Pye, 1962), and instrumentality (Apter, 1965) as being the characteristics of development, they are simply describing what is known to define Western Man.

Thus, these conceptions of development can hardly contribute to a science that is expected to be universal and value-neutral.

Modeling and Hypotheses Testing

The theories and conceptions of development discussed in this chapter are culturally and ideologically biased in favor of the Western political experience. Furthermore, they are grossly inadequate in view of the criteria for theory as established in the previous chapter. More importantly, they are not very useful for today's scholarly mission of problem solving.

The end of the Cold War brought about the beginning of the global era, guided by the dynamism of capitalist democracy and the pervasive market mechanism. The pace of social change has dramatically accelerated since that time. Since the dawn of the 21st Century, the world has indeed become inseparably interwoven by integrated networks of economy, politics, social institutions, communication, and virtually all spheres of human existence. In this period, global problems have intensified and yet, scholarship has been largely *atheoretical* with little interest in building theories of development. Indeed, intellectuals and their works have become largely irrelevant in the search for solutions to real-world problems. The typical nature of scholarly works and interests is geared to emulate and develop "scientific methods" practiced in the normal (physical) sciences. The notion of scientific "axiom" is mistakenly considered to be synonymous with "assumption" in that its validity is not subject to dispute. But an axiom in science is a universally verified and truthful attribute, whereas an assumption is always relative and subjective. A case in point: the assumption of rationality in human action is still an assumption. This assumption led to countless hypotheses for empirical testing, but little to show for it in terms of problem solving. The rationality thesis also paved a way to more refined conceptual frameworks such as *prospect theory*[15] and other variations of the rational actor model. Research via quantitative methods has become fashionable, and has fueled a cult of scholarship driven by the edict to "publish or perish." Yes, throughout this post-Cold War era, scholars have been quite prolific in publication, but how have these published works been useful in defining, explaining, and alleviating real problems?

---

15 In the sense that prospect theory builds it theoretical construct on the assumption of human choice making behavior is calculated and rational, this theory may be regarded as a variation of the rational actor model.

The scholarly community itself is least engaged with any aspect of problem solving. Instead, academia has been helplessly swirled into the culture and practice of commercialization, a topic that will be discussed further later in this book.

Chapter 4

Bringing Man Back to the Center Stage

The theories and conceptual frameworks we discussed in the previous chapter mostly emerged during the decades after the Cold War era. Most of these theories were developed in the Western bloc where the United States led the pack, and as a result, they were largely biased for ideological liberal democracy, Judeo-Christian ethics of individualism, free economic competition and the private incentive of capitalism, the norms and values of achievement, and scientism. The quality of development theories in general has been severely marred by ideological and cultural biases, on one hand, and science and quantification biases, on the other. Cold War-era theories from the Western world were constructed on the bias that what is Western is developed and modernized, and what is non-Western is underdeveloped and backward. The Cold War era was also the age in which the value of science reached ultimate supremacy. "The scientific way" became largely regarded as the methodological gold standard in scholarship.

Data Compilation and Empirical Generalizations

In spite of the persistent problems found in the various approaches introduced in the 1960s, researchers who had no choice but to comply with scientific expectations continued to demand more data rather than a more relevant conceptual schemes with which to structure the use of their data. As a result, comparative and development studies utilized whatever qualitative data was available, regardless of that data's relevance in practical terms. In order to comply with this demand, the researcher was forced to compile the numbers that were readily available. Countless data banks were established beginning with the compilation of aggregate data but spreading into attitude survey data, without a commensurate advancement of theoretical initiatives.

The growing use of massive volumes of data in comparative and development research has also necessitated the application of increasingly sophisticated statistical and methodological techniques, often giving research output the appearance of universal generality. However, due to conceptual and theoretical inadequacy, the contributions of such research are rarely valid or even convincing. For instance, several empirical studies on the conditions of democracy have fallen far short of agreeing as to what makes democratic institutions work.[16] The validity of these studies utilizing crossnational comparative data remains questionable, as generalizations resulting from these studies have seldom led to causal explanations. One must realize that statistical regularity or empirical generalization cannot produce causality. Rather, it is the theory that lends causality to an observed relationship between variables.

As an important factor in this validity problem, the problem of cross-national comparability of social and political indicators and measurements has received heightened attention from more alert researchers. For example, in their seminal work *The Logic of Comparative Social Inquiry* (1970), Teune and Przeworski introduced some possible means of conceptual renovation by raising the question of comparability. By establishing "equivalence" and "shifting levels of analysis," we might be able to enhance the comparability of social indicators in some cases. However, the fundamental issue of establishing comparable units of analysis and measurement remains basically unresolved, even in conceptual and theoretical terms. When it comes to the reliability and validity of measurements and data, the current state of comparative and international generalizations might well be described as one of persistent futility.

One proposed way of restoring cross-cultural comparability while still using comparative data is to utilize "longitudinal" analysis of historical data. This is essentially a "within-system comparison," and it thereby avoids many of the problems inherent in equating measures across systems. Despite the apparent promise of this technique, it introduces the issue of longitudinal comparability in addition to the unresolved problem of crosssectional comparability. If there is a comparability problem between nations with different cultures and varying levels of development, then there should also be the same problem in

---

16 Seymour M. Lipset, "Some Social Requisites of Democracy," in The American Political Science Review, Vol. 53, No. 1 (March 1958); Deane E. Neubauer, "Some Conditions of Democracy," in The American Political Science Review, Vol. 61, No. 4 (December 1967); Robert W. Jackman, "On the Relation of Economic Development to Democratic Performance," The American Journal of Political Science, Vol. 17, No. 3 (August 1973). These classical empirical studies on conditions of democracy may be subjected to this criticism.

crosstime comparisons within the same unit of analysis. For instance, in comparing levels of communication, one might use the volume of social networking as well as the number of television sets as measures. However, the predominant means of communication in the past might have been radios and newspapers, and the meaning of these facilities as communications media may well have changed over time. Thus, there is little basis for comparison. This situation would be analogous to comparing a developing country with an industrialized society in terms of their relative level of achievement in communications.

In the previous chapters, much has been said about quantification, measurement, and indices of comparable indicators in the field of comparative and development studies during the Cold War era. Indeed, comparison is commonly conceived of as a process leading to the sort of quantitative and uniform generalizations that enable us to talk about social and political objects in terms of *more* or *less*. Notice the casual way in which terms such as *more democratic, more developed, more industrialized*, and *more rational* are used. This places all nations and other units of analysis into a comparative (and hence competitive) perspective where they are reduced to a system of numerical values. These numerical values have motivated intense and continuous social and individual competition at all levels of social complexity. Individuals compete for higher appropriations of numbers (such as income) and nations compete for a superior position in various numerically-based hierarchies (such as GNP, military strength, and the like). As the world becomes more intimately interactive in both the physical and cultural sense, nations compete more intensely for commonly valued economic goods.

As the limits of world resources become more acutely felt, competition for the acquisition of such goods and values becomes more intense and social conflict more probable. Supremacy in social as well as international competition will be decided solely by "who has how much," and that will not be known or agreed upon until a common comparative yardstick is determined -- a prospect that, as discussed earlier, is not highly promising.

Moreover, I reject the notion of universal comparison by quantitative standards only. Such a comparison has done more harm than good in enhancing the quality of life conditions. The common desire to maximize and universalize the process of industrialization has indeed accelerated the irreversible processes of urbanization and mechanization, but at a high cost. Widespread social dislocations and popular disillusionment have emerged as the alltoofrequent concomitants of rapid modernization within traditional societies. Indeed, they have become rich enough to build apartment complexes and high-rise chimneys to symbolize their economic "achievement," but this has brought with it the notorious ills of industrialization. Many societies have become very similar to one other, and even more are approaching (or at least aspiring toward) uniformity. Old buildings - monuments to the uniqueness of traditional culture - are replaced with skyscrapers. Farmers are leaving their land and breaking the ties of extended kinship to migrate into cities. Crime rates in urban centers are increasing as rapidly as the population, both spurred by the influx of rural immigrants. More cars and factories are emitting poisonous exhaust. Onceluxurious and rare commodities are massproduced, and people everywhere stroll through the same Western-style shopping malls in search of the same bargains. More startlingly, remarkably similar curricula are being introduced in schools all over the world, all of this assuring us of an even more competitive and homogenized lifestyle in the near future. And much of this pattern may be attributable to the largely uncontested myth of "the bigger, the better."

In response to the human and moral consequences of the problematic ethos, an increasing number of social critics are proclaiming a new slogan of salvation: "Small is beautiful." This apparently humanistic movement attracts the largest number of sympathizers in the more advanced postindustrial societies.[17] It would be premature to make any conclusive judgment on this hopeful movement, but if the notion of "small" is perceived only as being diametrically opposed to the quantitative concept of "big," the movement will probably not provide much in the way of solutions. Perhaps it will only provide some psychic satisfaction for those who lament the passing of the "good old days," or it may excite some utopian thinkers who, like Saint Simon, Fourier, and Robert Owen long ago, insist that social selfmanagement is not only desirable but also feasible. Regardless, the commonality between the "bigger is better" and "small is beautiful" syndromes is their reliance on size as the criterion for appreciation. In this sense, they are not fundamentally different.

---

17 E.F. Schumacher's seminal work, *Small Is Beautiful* (1973) offered an insightful and provocative assessment of Western economics in response to the economic crisis in 1970s, and created the foundation of critical thinking about runaway capitalist economic growth.

"Apples and Oranges": Misguided Metaphor

In rationalizing the infeasibility of qualitative comparison, one uses the metaphor of "apples versus oranges" to suggest that objects that are different in form or kind cannot be compared. Following this metaphor, we have trained ourselves to reduce everything to a uniform dimension of quality that allows comparison in terms of quantity. We have fooled ourselves into believing that we can make all oranges into apples and, further, that while America is of a huge, delicious variety - the consummate apple, in fact -- underdeveloped tribal societies are, by comparison, pitifully shriveled, miserably rotten little offerings. Thus, we seldom hesitate to define development by such measures as GNP, industrial output, and urbanization. Some even define development in terms of certain attitudinal and behavioral traits that are common only in selected Western societies.

When we eat apples, we tend to take it for granted that everyone else is and should be eating apples, and that we are better off than others, depending on the size or amount of apples we possess. We ignore the fact that there are other fruits that can provide us what apples can. Pitiable is the undeniable fact that many people in the "nonapple eating" societies think that they need to change their dietary habits to achieve and maintain what the "appleeaters" have, even if their physical metabolism is not prepared for apple consumption. Still worse, they keep eating apples even when they see that the apple is not necessarily the best fruit, even for the original appleeaters themselves.

This appleeating analogy may not appear so unreasonable when we observe what is occurring in less-developed societies, as well as what has occurred in postindustrial societies. Third World countries have been rapidly industrializing, and many of them are entering the threshold stage of industrial society. Such successful Third World development may be attributed to three decisive factors: technology transfer, abundance of human and natural resources, and the increasing economic reliance of postindustrial societies upon Third World nations.

People in industrializing Third World countries have undergone profound changes in their value systems, steering their societies in the direction of economic rationality and pragmatism. Technical training has become a desired educational commodity in societies where, traditionally, technical education was either nonexistent (in any formal sense) or held in low esteem. As their economies have prospered, they have been able to send trainees abroad and hire foreign technicians and teachers to impart the advanced technology of the West. At the same time, they have utilized natural resources to apply the newly available technology, and exploited a relatively inexpensive labor force to produce commodities that compete favorably in international markets.

Finally, and perhaps most importantly, developed industrial societies have undergone an extensive change in their own economic structures as multinational corporate conglomerates have emerged as the capstone of the world economy. Multinational corporations have brought changes in the economic conditions of the world in general and Third World nations in particular. Third World nations not only carry the bulk of industrial production for the multinationals, they provide the most important sales markets as well. Thus, the development of a Third World economy is seen as a desirable factor for the sustained growth of developed societies, which forces all parties to maintain more cooperative economic relations with each other. In this regard, the main beneficiary is the Third World, and it is hastily but uneasily reaping the fruits of modern society.

However, developmental changes in Third World nations, particularly in the form of industrialization and technological transformation, are not occurring without the cost of cultural and social dislocations analogous to the physiological disorders that occur in a human following a sudden change in diet.

This critique of industrialization and modernization should not be interpreted as being onesided, for technological developments have resolved many individual and social problems and have contributed to the improvement of life conditions in numerous ways. Improvement of health care by advanced medical technology, resulting in prolonged life expectancy and the reduction of infant mortality, and increases in literacy rates may be cited as examples of the laudable accomplishments of modernization and technological innovation. What deserves criticism is the tendency toward encouraging cultural uniformity, homogenization, and quantitative aspirations, while uncritically rejecting or altering traditional value systems in favor of the cultural "yardstick." Also to be criticized is the manner in which modernization sends everyone in a scramble for "apples"—the fruit of Western society—resulting in ruthless economic competition and social struggle.

What is even more tragic is the servile mentality adopted by many intellectuals both in Western and developing societies. Many intellectuals, particularly the comparativists, have long concluded that "apples cannot be compared with oranges," and that the only way of sustaining a comparative science is to find what is common in both fruits. They believe that societies cannot be compared in the absence of a common index. As discussed earlier, the construction of such an index has a long way to go. The way is not only long but fraught with obstacles. It is blocked because no one concept can retain the same meaning in different social and cultural contexts. A sound and rich body of literature supports this rather pessimistic conclusion of "semantic empiricism" and even "epistemic empiricism." A term - be it democracy, income, education, human rights, or any other social idiom - needs to be given a "meaning" in order to become a useful concept, and "meaning" can only be given in reference to features in a specific context. Since this condition is endemic to social concepts, we must conclude that we simply don't have the kinds of well-defined concepts that the physical scientist uses in formulating physical laws.

As I alluded earlier, the proposal to transcend quantityconscious comparison was made not only because such a comparison is unlikely to yield workable comparisons. Rather, my argument rests on the belief that we can, in fact, compare oranges with apples, and that comparing apples and oranges will provide us with added dimensions and perspectives for comparative studies. Those who say that we cannot compare oranges with apples need only observe the shopper who rather routinely compares apples with oranges at the grocery store. Are we, who presumably are as intelligent and capable of abstract thinking as the shopper, conceding that we cannot develop an analogous logic of comparison while he/she goes on practicing such a logic so widely and so casually?

Today, we find ourselves practically conceding that a meaningful comparison of life situations cross-nationally and cross-culturally is infeasible. Nonetheless, we are prevented from drawing this pessimistic conclusion by our increased desire to make universal comparisons in order to deepen our sociological understanding of an intricately woven global community. Unfortunately, our desire alone is unlikely to increase the feasibility of such an endeavor. We must ask if the current concepts and theories of development truthfully portray what development is in real life situations. Are real life situations the true foci of analysis in the study of development? In the next few chapters, I will attempt to establish a depiction of development that is more valid than those previously employed.

From Comparison of Things to Comparison of People: Humanizing Comparison

Returning to the image of the grocery shopper, when he chooses to buy oranges instead of apples, there is likely some reason behind his decision. It could be that he has apples in his refrigerator or that the freshly harvested oranges appeal to him in that particular moment. In any event, he will compare the two fruits in terms of their relative meaning to him or his family, and the decision to buy oranges will indicate that he values oranges more than apples. Here, the comparison is in terms of the human conditions affected by the choices that are available. Thus, depending on the life situation of a particular choice-maker at a given point in time, the same apple may find different value.

Likewise, a dollar bill may provide a varying range of goods and services for the enhancement of human existence in different societies depending on the functional value of the money in each. A man could get a haircut, shampoo and styling, a shave, a back massage, and even a shoeshine for about a dollar in a country barbershop in rural China. For the same money, he could hardly get one side of his hair trimmed or one of his shoes shined in the United States. If the same service cost ten dollars in the U.S., the one dollar being used in China for that particular purpose should be considered functionally equivalent to ten dollars in the U.S.

This idea of establishing equivalence is not new in the literature of comparative logic. What is newly emphasized here is the principle of using equivalent human situations or value objects as a comparative yardstick, not the instrumental mechanism of money. This is to say that comparing an apple with another apple should be done in terms of its relative utility to the apple consumer in a particular situation. Any number of objects can serve the same human purpose. Furthermore, any one object can fulfill a number of human purposes. An artist may view an apple primarily as a subject for a drawing. Hence he values the color and appearance of the apple rather than its taste or size. And to this artist, a smaller apple could well be more precious than a larger one. There is no inherent meaning in the object of the apple itself, nor is any meaning of the apple held universally and constantly. This implies that any unit of a material resource can have a variety of meanings depending upon its use in a given cultural context. Its utility (even quantitative utility) cannot be carried over unaltered to a different social context. This would imply that a country with a greater GNP should not necessarily be regarded as a more developed nation. For this reason, comparative studies ranking nations by aggregate indices of social and economic characteristics are grossly misleading, as these indices may be only spuriously related to the quality of human life conditions.

We should never forget that all social institutions and material resources that we exploit are to serve human beings, and their very *raison d'etre* lies in their relationship with and utility to human beings. When people are alienated, their resources and institutions become meaningless for them because they are not serving to enhance the quality of life. There is no business more urgent than that of putting human beings in the driver's seat where they belong.

Beethoven and Picasso: From Objects to the Consumer

If someone were to ask you whether Beethoven or Picasso is the greater artist, you would probably reply that the question is a meaningless one because there is little basis for comparison, and you may be right. But that would not stop comparative analysts, preoccupied with the imperative of quantitative comparison, from busily comparing Beethoven and Picasso in terms of their weight, height, hair color, the size of their big toes, and so forth, omitting what is truly significant about them. In studying development, analysts have similarly produced comparative statements on income, industrialization, occupation, urbanization, and consumption of petroleum in a number of countries. They have developed correlations, regression coefficients, and a host of other impressive quantifiers. But what good are these achievements if they do not represent what is meaningful about different societies? It is deplorable to assume that America would become an India should the values of her indices be reduced to the level of India's indices. We cannot assume that all there is to an individual is his income, occupation, formal education, his place of residence, and so forth.

However, avoiding or denying comparisons between Beethoven and Picasso does not provide a solution to the issue of comparability, although it may support the humanist provocation. As long as social objects - particularly humans - manifest qualitative differences, analogous to the case of Beethoven versus Picasso, some sort of comparative method will be essential, and the root of that method will lie in perceived meanings. Thus, to a musician Beethoven, might be considered the greater, and to a painter, Picasso. But we must not forget that there is a significant difference between the case of "apples and oranges" and the case of Beethoven and Picasso. The two men were great achievers, exceeding by far the average person's accomplishments. We do not consider the fruits to be the achievers in themselves, but means by which human achievement is made possible.

Here, I would submit that, if comparison must be made, human beings should be compared in terms of their achievements. Human achievement in this case ought not to be determined solely by popularity or material possessions. Rather, it has to reflect the transformation of human attitudes and behavior as well as the more tangible achievements that result from attitudinal and behavioral makeup. It is beyond the scope of this chapter to dwell on the issue of measuring human achievement, for it is not an easy issue to resolve. We need only to point out that several major attempts have been made to trace the pattern of human growth and that much more study needs to be done in this area. Attempts by J. Piaget (1952) in his assessment of cognitive development, Kohlberg (1969) in his proposition of stages of moral development, Erickson (1950) in his psychosocial theory of human development, and Maslow's (1954) hierarchy of needs might be some examples of such relevant attempts. Indeed, Beethoven and Picasso probably would be seen as great achievers according to most of these theories, and a great number of other musicians and painters might be rated at much lower levels of achievement.

Human achievement can be evaluated by the fulfillment of human potential in relation to the resources available to realize such potential. Hence Beethoven's achievement could be considered greater since he was not adequately provided with material resources and was later handicapped by deafness. If so, the developmental level of a society may as well be rated by the degree to which potential has been actualized in relation to resource availability.

In accordance with the edicts of postbehavioralist thought, in which resolving relevant human problems is singled out as the most important task of political scientists, this chapter advances the proposition that comparing "development situations" ought to be done in terms of human situations themselves rather than material or institutional situations. This led to a critical review of some major trends in the field of comparative social inquiries. We concluded that establishing a common yardstick (index) with which all societies may be objectively compared is simply an unrealistic aspiration, partly because of the somewhat unique nature of social concepts and behavioral sciences. Furthermore, I proposed that quantitative studies attempting to generate universal laws are not only infeasible but, more importantly, morally inhumane.

Having concluded that we need to radically re-conceptualize the idea of "comparison," I attempted to show with specific examples that the concept may be expanded to include qualitative comparison as well. Such a new concept of comparison is conducive to dealing with human and social problems more intimately and is more feasible than the conventional quantitative mode of comparison.

Admittedly, much work needs to be done toward operationalizing the "qualitative comparison," and the present discussion did not go far in this direction. However, I am content if I have helped to put the practice of comparing life situations on the correct track toward a theory that will be more universally applicable, explanatory, and predictive with process-laws. How far the train will travel will depend on further efforts and studies, but a train on the right track and stationary seems better than a derailed train traveling in an unwanted direction.

Why Not Human Needs and Human Wants?

A word of clarification is needed at this point in the book. In ascertaining the status of development studies, I have labeled most existing studies (Chapter 3 and this chapter) as being wrong and incorrect in that they are normatively wrong and they are incorrect in portraying the empirical reality of development. In order that we advance a theory that might be both right and correct, we will offer a correct process of theorization, although that too may be wrong from a normative perspective. Then, a grant theory of development that might be claimed to be both right (development as it should be) and correct will be articulated in Part Three of this book. This chapter will conclude with the suggestion that a far more accurate definition of development as it has historically and actually been can be ascertained by analytically differentiating the two separate spheres of "goals" and "strategic means" whereby, in this case, the goal is human need/wants satisfaction and the strategic means is development. Development may refer to a series of defining concepts such as economic growth, institutional effectiveness, certain ideological values or cultures, or social structural sophistications, but all these concomitants may be viewed as the strategic means to aid in the satisfaction of human needs and wants. Needs/wants satisfaction has always been the very purpose of human actions at all levels of social complexity (that

71

is, the individual, group, and societal levels). Thus, a legitimate definition and explanation of development must evolve around the ultimate goal of human existence: the satisfaction of needs/wants, which is universally valid and is a direct source of human happiness as observed throughout the course of human history. By conceptualizing human needs/wants in a way that they are not only universal but also structured in a manner that can be explained and predicted, we might find a theory of development that is better in terms of the criteria for theory and for defining development as established in Chapter 2. Such a theory cannot only be universal, but can also wield greater explanatory/predictive potential than those theoretical frameworks discussed in Chapter 3. Furthermore, the elements of human needs/wants are qualitatively different from one another in that the process of needs/wants satisfaction represents a process of qualitative transformation, rather than a process that is quantitatively contiguous. Therefore, the process cannot be uni-linear and necessarily progressive, but rather it is a process that contains varying stages. The stages of the agrarian society, industrial and urban society, the post-industrial society, and the global village are all qualitatively unique. For this reason, those stage theories of "development" by Rostow and Organski may be superior to others except, as we discussed in the previous chapter, for the fact that they merely describe the processes of select societies. Although Marxist stage theory of historical evolution does have explanatory and predictive power, it fails to be universally applicable or universally valid. We must strive toward articulating a theory that is value-neutral and that satisfies the criteria of defining development as discussed earlier in this book.

In the next chapter, I shall labor toward the creation of a paradigm of development. It is important to clarify the fact that the human needs/wants based paradigm describes and explains the process of development the way it is, not the way it should be. The considerable task of formulating a paradigm for the way development *should* occur will be attempted in Part Three of this book.

Chapter 5

The Pursuit of Human Needs and Wants: The Real Course of Development

It was suggested in the previous chapter that the concept of human needs/wants might be explored to develop a more universal, explanatory-predictive theory of development. This chapter is designed to dissect this concept for advancing a theory of development that captures historical reality more accurately than the major theories of development examined in earlier chapters.

The Structure of Human Needs and Human Wants

For the incremental and conscientious pursuit of human needs, man is likely to order his needs hierarchically based on urgency and desirability. As alluded to earlier, such an orderly approach is implied in the definition of *goaloriented* action itself.[18] Some goals are more urgent than others, and we can expect these to be pursued prior to the pursuit of other, less urgent goals. The concept of preference ordering (Friedman, 1953) is a more formal version of this idea. At any rate, in view of our emphasis upon the qualitative dimension of the concept of development, some structure of human needs must be assumed in the interest of constructing an explanatorypredictive theory.

Conforming to most of the basic premises underlying Maslow's conception of the "hierarchy of human needs," as well as the psychological perspectives of cognitive development, I suggest here a fourfold hierarchical structure of human needs. They are (1) survival, (2) belongingness, (3) leisure, and (4) control.

These needs are hierarchical in that one level will not emerge as the primary behavioral motivator until the previous level as been satisfied. Thus, the organism is dominated and its behavior

---

18 Human behavior itself is defined as a goal-oriented action. Mere act may be random and aimless but "behavior" is not.

organized by the lowest rung in the hierarchy of needs that is, at present, inadequately satisfied.

Each of these four levels of human needs will now be explicated more fully, and in so doing, the incremental and progressive nature in which they are pursued will become more readily apparent.

(1) *Survival*: It may be accepted as an axiom that all living beings want to stay alive. This need constitutes more than just a conscious choice to survive. It appears to be inherent in the nature of all living things, and thus, can be considered instinctive. The emergence of all other human needs is contingent upon first meeting the conditions for survival. Because most people value survival so highly, as Lenski (1966, p. 37) maintains, anything that facilitates survival is also valued highly. Maslow's physiological and safety needs are considered essential, and when denied, they demand the individual's attention above all less immediate needs.

If mere physical survival were the only desire of humankind, we might be able to eliminate many social and political problems. But, in reality, humans want not only to survive but to survive "well." In this desire to survive "well," humans manifest additional needs.

(2) *Belongingness*: Once the chances of physical survival are believed to be good, a human being can be expected to seek others with whom to identify. Ever since Aristotle's description of man as a social animal, many studies have verified the heavy social orientation of human nature. This disposition may be termed the need for love and affection (Maslow, 1957) or "associational sentiment" (Pye, 1965), but in some form the desire for subjectively meaningful interpersonal relationships exists as a basic human need, meaning it begins to influence the behavior of most people at a very early age.

(3) *Leisure*: Since environmental resources are necessary to facilitate both primitive survival and the maintenance of basic levels of socialization, humans desire to maximize control over the environment for the extraction of these essential necessary material resources. Once humans acquire sufficient resources to ensure survival and socialization, however, their dispositions shift toward the desire for a leisurely mode of living. A leisurely lifestyle not only requires free time but also involves the consumption of material goods in amounts beyond what is necessary for mere physical survival. The desire to have a longer weekend, to ride in an automobile instead of on a

74

bicycle, to have an automatic dishwasher, a backyard swimming pool, and the desire to extend paid vacations are all appropriate examples of the human disposition for leisure. These types of consumption patterns are dictated by one's appetites, and not by the biophysical imperatives of survival or even the need for social esteem.[3]

(4) *Control*: Once man possesses the time and material resources necessary for a leisurely life, he will become preoccupied with the desire to maintain a "superior" life, superior relative to other individuals. At this point, man will become more selfconscious about his social status, or at least such considerations will become more salient among his motives. The subjective feelings of relative deprivation with respect to status might be only marginally important to a person whose primary motivations are to survive, but a status-conscious person's social behavior is easily dictated by his sense of relative achievement in his community. The desire to own material goods symbolic of high social status is evident in the actions of such a person.

This kind of material consumption, associated with the desire for social control or selfesteem, is what Veblen (1899) termed "conspicuous consumption." Consumers in economically advanced industrial societies often become conspicuous consumers, whereas the material needs of peasants in agrarian communities, although similarly stemming from a desire for material goods, would be characterized in terms of survival. We can distinguish between the two kinds of material goods more readily by recognizing that the goods, such as diamonds sought for the purpose of selfesteem or sense of superiority relative to others, attain their value mainly from their scarcity and from the social status that is attributed to their possessor, whereas the goods, such as food, needed for survival are always desired irrespective of their availability. The latter are valued in themselves rather than as the means to attaining social or interpersonal value.

This "social control" desire leads to fixedsum competitions. Social status is a relative value, thus winning by some necessitates losing by others. It is in this sense that we can say this desire may be morally undesirable but empirically undeniable. As Thomas Hobbes observed, man is a very rare animal with the instinct for killing. Even worse, man often kills not merely for survival but for glory. With enormous capacity to control the environment, contemporary man suffers even more complicated social and political problems than ever before, these having arisen precisely due to his desire to extend his control over other human beings. As Martindale (1962, p. 42) observes:

> More rarely the very abundance of nature places strain on society. Partners who have lived together during adversity find that success destroys what hard times does not.

The Incremental Progression of Human Needs/Wants

It is necessary, at this point, to clarify our central theme that these four common needs represent the incremental stages in structuring human needs. Further, they are distinct from one another not simply in quantitative terms, but also in terms of the qualitative nature of each need. That which is required for any one need's satisfaction is qualitatively different from that which is required for the satisfaction of any other need. No additional amount of food beyond what is required to survive will serve to satisfy the emergent belongingness needs of the individual.

The nature of this process is analogous to the progression of child from infancy to young adulthood. When a baby is newly born, the baby will cry, which indicates that the child must breath (by crying) to live. As an infant, a child instinctively seeks the nourishment that is necessary for its survival. Thus, this first stage represents survival, the most fundamental of human needs.

A newborn baby will usually sleep (a sign of physical satisfaction) when food and shelter are adequately provided, and the child will cry when such needs are not met.

Once the child grows further into infancy and toddlerhood, the child expresses the need to feel the presence of another human being, usually the mother. This is the stage in which the need for belonging first manifests, suggesting that the same child will not be fully content with food and comfortable physical surroundings alone. He will soon desire the presence of other persons such as his mother, and will demonstrate a desire to belong to groups (initially the family). At this stage of human growth, one seeks to develop an identity in relation to other human beings.

As the child feels physically comfortable and psychologically secure, he will demand and reach out for toys. Insofar as a child's desire for toys is concerned, there appears to be no cultural exception. There is absolutely no society where children's toys are irrelevant and absent! When a child is provided with a new toy, he or she will need some space of time to play with it, and thus the need for free time becomes apparent. Although a child may be initially satisfied with the toys he has, as he develops extrafamilial relationships with other children in the neighborhood, he starts to compare his toys with theirs and conclude that he needs more and better toys. This corresponds to the fourth level of human needs, in which competition arises over social and material values--the child wants to have the most and the best toys among his friends. At this stage, we can see the child's behavior may become competitive and even combative. I would submit that this pattern of development in children's attitudes and behaviors is absolutely universal.

Thus, to the extent that this observation of a child's developmental process is universally applicable, the structure of human needs might also be considered universal. As we maintain the analogy between childhood development and the universal human needs structure, one might question the relevance of children's needs to the motivations of adult members of the society. It is my belief that adults are not much more "mature" than children in terms of needs, since we differ only with respect to the instruments and means by which we pursue the same set of needs and wants. Instead of demanding the mother's presence to satisfy the need for belonging, the adult may seek lovers, peers, and memberships in unions, churches, country clubs, and political parties. In place of children's toys, the adult may desire golf clubs, sailboats, sports cars, and private jets. Indeed, the fact that an adult no longer attempts to possess more toys does not mean that he ceases to seek more money, more power, and more of just about everything than other people. The difference between a child and an adult in this regard is in instrumentalities and means. As a child outgrows the shell of the family, he becomes exposed to a much more complex and often hostile life environment. Therefore, instrumental means such as a family and toys can no longer sufficient to maintain a sense of psychological belongingness and a leisured life. In the same way, as the person's frame of reference expands, social competition becomes more intense, and winning in such a competition requires more resources and greater capabilities.

The assumptions and propositions underlying the literature of social stratification provide another means of demonstrating progressive nature of human needs. Although the stratification criteria vary-some by prestige, others by wealth, and still others by occupation-major stratification scales including the occupational prestige scale by the NORC (National Opinion Research Center) [19] in the United States is similar to the levels of human needs we have established in this chapter. The "unskilled workers," who are usually classified at the bottom of the social strata, are motivated primarily by survival. "Skilled" workers in Edward's category can be conceptualized as those pursuing economic opportunities in anticipation of social advancement. The whitecollar class may be viewed as those inclined to explore a variety of hobbies and leisure modes of life. Finally, the professional and managerial classes are those who pursue the highest need of our needshierarchy: selfesteem and social control. If, as Duncan and Blau (1966) assert, the social stratification scales that are prevalent today are not only mutually compatible but also historically consistent, the general correspondence of our needstages to the stratification scales could be an important aspect by which we might substantiate the progressive hierarchical nature of human needs. Additionally, if man is oriented toward status improvement, regardless of cultural and historical background, we can assert this as evidence of the universal applicability of the incremental needs/wants structure.

Based on the premises discussed above, one can measure the level of development by the proportion of members of the society who seek different kinds of human needs. Figure 1 shows the "ideal type" cases of the developed, developing, and underdeveloped societies. These three names for developmental stages–Underdeveloped, Developing, Developed–are strictly based on the state of human life condition in terms of the aggregate picture of **people's** needs/wants level, not other indirect and possibly inaccurate economic, social, or political indicators.

Institutions and Human Needs/Wants

Institutions of all kinds are human inventions
designed to optimally pursue human needs/wants.

Since Huntington (1965) posited that decay as well as development is a possible outcome of a nation's developmental endeavors, the idea of institutionalization has been an important

---

19 The NORC Scale is constructed by survey research of American national samples using a number of criteria including sense of job prestige, desirability, and material rewards.

concept for distinguishing the two sets of outcomes. A system that aspires to develop without this capacity is likely to invite decay. Development does not only require that the regime gain the capacity to respond to various types of demands. It also requires that these capacities become institutionalized as routine mechanisms for dealing with these demands. In this manner, government develops the capacity to handle a larger demand load, as most demands can be processed through routine procedures. Furthermore, popular perceptions of government capabilities are enhanced, leading to a sense of security among the population. Of course, it is not just any capacity that must become institutionalized, but the capacity to respond to specific types of substantive demands that is important. A government that has an efficient mechanism for regulating automobile traffic is not likely to survive unless it also has institutions that can guarantee sufficient gasoline to power those cars. What is needed, then, is some idea of what capacities must be developed and institutionalized.

In the context of our paradigm, a social institution is considered a human invention intended to provide a regularized, routinized mechanism for the satisfaction of a particular human need. It is the capacity to provide the goods and services necessary for the satisfaction of specific substantive needs that is the *raison d'etre* of institutions, and therefore, it is the nature of the needs that actually determines what regime capacities must be developed and institutionalized. In the same way, institutions can be expected to change in response to the changing nature of human needs. This is how they maintain their effectiveness in achieving institutional objectives. Thus, the sequence in which specific institutions emerge in a society should parallel the sequence in which the needs of their constituents emerge.

When the most prevalent need among the members of a society is that of survival or, more concretely, obtaining food, we can expect the regime to give primary emphasis to the development of institutions associated with agricultural production and distribution. Government efforts to mobilize resources for policy performance will center initially on such things as land redistribution. Such policies are often used as a means of gaining and cementing the support of the rural population for the new regime. This was part of the Chinese Communist Party's strategy for winning popular support prior to their takeover and for maintaining that base of support after the revolution. Such programs are pursued in the early stages of postrevolutionary regime formation not simply for the purpose of maintaining the political support of the rural population, but also to ensure a stable agricultural sector that can provide the regime with a steady supply of products needed to fulfill the survival needs of the rest of society as well. Only by gratifying the most basic needs of its constituents can the regime hope to maintain its tenuous hold on political authority.

Quite often, however, the reestablishment of agricultural production is insufficient to ensure the continued supply capacity of the regime. Related policies will likely emerge, aimed toward agricultural research and development, increased mechanization of the agricultural sector and adoption of the latest in agricultural technology, public works projects such as irrigation programs, and projects such as road and railway construction that are the requisites of an adequate distribution infrastructure. These are some of the policies a newly formed regime is likely to pursue, and each of them is an example of government mobilization of resources for the purposes of satisfying the survival needs of the population.

Of course, not all nations are blessed with the resources necessary to attain agricultural selfsufficiency. For nations whose ratio of population size to amount of arable land precludes self-sufficiency at a subsistence level, institutions aimed at enhancing that nation's capacity to obtain agricultural products from other nations will be emphasized in the regime's policymaking. This is the situation that Japan has traditionally faced because of its relatively large population concentrated on a small land mass. Since the end of World War II marked a regime change in Japan, the differing responses to this dilemma exhibited by the two historical regimes may be instructive. Under the Meiji regime (1968-1912), Japan became the foremost military power in Asia, and used this might to subjugate Korea and Manchuria. Hence, territorial expansion through the use of military strength brought considerably more land under the control of the regime and heightened its capacity to ensure the satisfaction of its constituents' survival needs. At the same time, Japan became increasingly effective in international trade. While the incursion of the West reduced China virtually to the status of a colony, Japan developed the institutional means to deal with the Western nations on a basis of equality in international trade. In this respect, its military might and trade capacity served as mutually reinforcing mechanisms to ensure its continued capacity to provide an adequate supply of agricultural products. Since World War II, with the abolition of the Japanese military, the institutions associated with its trade capacity have received increased emphasis. The result has been Japan's meteoric rise to second largest producer and exporter of manufactured goods for decades, ensuring it the resources necessary to be one of the world's largest importers of agricultural products. Given its relative paucity of domestic agriculture, Japan has proven capable of providing food in amounts far beyond what is needed for the physical survival of its population. It has done so by developing the institutional capacity to operate as an effective participant in international trade.

When security from violent threat is a central concern guiding the conscious behavior of people in a society, the regime's response must involve the institutionalization of internal security in the form of a police force, and external security in the form of an effective military force. Given the early and intense primacy of such needs, it should not be surprising that many newly independent nations soon come under military rule after a brief period of tenuous, unstable civilian rule. The military's *raison d'etre* is providing security from external threat and, along with the police, ensuring internal stability. Hence, the vacuum left by a civilian government that is unable to respond to the survival imperative will soon be filled by those who control the institutions specifically designed for such purposes: the military leadership.

In summary, then, in a society where survival needs are the most salient, we can expect government policymaking and institutional development to be centered on military and law enforcement, and the agricultural sector of the economy. These sorts of conditions prevail in a newly formed nation or, more generally, in one that has experienced the takeover of a new regime. In particular, when the regime change has occurred in a context of widespread civil and/or international violence, the survival needs of the populace will move to the forefront as civil violence and the absence of a stable regime increases the public sense of danger and deprivation. The contending political faction that can best demonstrate its capacity to guarantee survival will be the one that stands to gain the most popular support, and will thereby enhance its chances of gaining political power.

As society attains a reasonable assurance that its survival needs will be met through institutional mechanisms providing necessary goods and services, then, the population's emergent need level will shift to that of belonging. The emergence of such a need in a society on a broad scale requires an active, multifaceted program of socialization aimed at generating a sense of community and a measure of diffuse loyalty to the regime, or loyalty beyond what could be expected simply as a function of the tangible rewards provided by the regime. Institutions such as the family, religious groups, mass media, and the educational system, as the primary agents of socialization, will be the focus of government policymaking, as the regime attempts to harness the power of these institutions in such a way as to make them agents of political socialization. It is at this stage that the importance of ideology also reaches its height. Ideology becomes a mechanism by which government attempts to instill in the populace a belief system supportive of the regime and its goals. This belief system, then, is propagated by means of the various agents of socialization, especially those over which the regime can exercise some direct control, such as the mass media and the educational system. The family, religious groups and other more primary groups deal with belonging needs on a more personal and intimate level. They provide the individual with a secure, basic sense of belonging that can then be translated into more general (and politically relevant) attachments to the broader political community.

It is these latter sorts of attachments that are most important to the regime. To the extent that they can be fostered, the resultant diffuse loyalty allows the regime some flexibility in its pursuit of further policy objectives. Loyalty to the regime is less exclusively contingent upon the immediate material rewards the regime can provide. Therefore, policies with more longterm objectives, requiring some measure of delayed gratification by the populace, can be pursued without risking a critical erosion of popular support.

Ideology, then, is the institutional mechanism by which the basis for such loyalty is propagated. The ultimate goals of the regime are spelled out, which permits justification of current policies (and any sacrifices entailed therein) in terms of their efficacy in bringing about the ideal states spelled out in the given ideology. Ideology provides a common political belief system for the people. It spells out their place in the current society as well as in the promised utopian future state of the society. As such, the common basis for political community becomes internalized in the members of society, and a sense of belonging in the larger society is generated on the basis of this shared political belief system.

The American case provides a striking example of the sorts of conflicts that emerge in the early postregimeformation era and of the role an ideology performs in resolving these conflicts. While the revolutionary forces in colonial America were diverse and small relative to opposition, they managed to achieve a degree of ideological solidarity during the revolutionary years. In the name of liberating the colonies from British rule, the revolutionaries set aside regional and inter-colony rivalries in order to face the British as a unified force.

However, once the revolution ended and the British threat had been pushed off American shores, the tenuous unity of the colonies, formalized in the Articles of Confederation, became less than adequate for a nation suddenly lacking a unifying common enemy. The old rivalries and disputes resurfaced with increasing intensity, and the nation of thirteen states was in danger of disintegrating into thirteen autonomous nations.

The Constitutional Convention was an effort to construct a new institutional foundation for the unity of the states. The new constitution provided the formal basis for the strengthening of the central government, while allowing a measure of autonomy for the states. The individual liberties guaranteed in the first ten amendments became the basis for individual loyalty to the newly formed regime. These documents, supplemented by the elegant defense of this government contained in the Federalist Papers, came to represent the American political ideology. Herein are the defined purposes and limits of government as well as its structure, and more broadly, a conception of the nature of humankind in society and its appropriate form of government. As such, the documents perform the national integration functions of an ideology in that they spell out not only the formal basis of government, but the reasons this particular form of government is worthy of citizen support. The phenomenon that external common foes invariably help a political system solidify its power through overcoming factional differences is evidenced today in the Middle-East regimes in turmoil.

To the extent that institutionalization of the mechanisms that lead to such integration is achieved, we can expect subsequent needs to emerge in the population. That is, if the regime succeeds in generating and maintaining a sense of belonging and political community among its citizens, the members of the community will soon shift to the next level of needs hierarchy-the need for leisure. As the leisure lifestyle involves material consumption beyond what is required for survival, as well as free time in which to enjoy such consumption, institutions intended to promote automated mass production of consumer goods will be put in place. Thus, industrialization becomes the inevitable contemporary institutional concomitant of leisure's emergence.

Government response to these needs can take a number of forms depending upon the character of the regime established in the first two stages. Under a highly centralized regime with state control of the economy, government planning institutions will be instigated. These organizations perform the task of translating broad policy guidelines into concrete production programs.

Coordination of various industries and distribution of resources among them is undertaken with the goal of achieving an optimal return in terms of goods and services that satisfy popular leisure needs. In a market economy, institutions that regulate the market emerge in order to prevent any serious breakdowns in production or distortions in the allocation of resources to the several sectors of the economy.

An apparently universal concomitant of industrial growth is urbanization, or the increasing concentration of populations in urban areas. This in itself creates needs for government institutions, as public services must be provided for these populations. For example, whereas in a rural setting each farm unit can provide its own water supply with a well, it is impractical, if not impossible, for each family in a city to sink its own well. Hence, the government must provide such public services as a matter of both necessity and convenience. A whole series of public services-such as water, sewage treatment, public transportation, and environmental control-will be demanded as needed auxiliaries to the growth of the urban industrial segment of a society. Failure to develop the institutional means to provide these services will not only deter the growth and efficiency of the industrial sector, but will also eventually have a negative impact on governmental stability, as the regime's ability to provide for leisure needs fails to meet the level of popular expectation.

As industrialization progresses, a growing number of people, especially those in urban industrial centers, will be able (even forced) to join the crowd of mass consumers. Those who achieve this stage of leisure lifestyle will, unfortunately, not remain content with these fruits of industrial life. There will soon emerge among them the next level of needs, the need for social control.

Those who seek social esteem tend to compare themselves with others. They desire is "more" of the visible signs of status that would distinguish them as being more esteemed than other prominent members of society. They want more of everything, and the most significant "everything" is usually money. Politically, such things as power or the relative advantage of one group over a rival group will become salient goals. These types of competition have a zerosum character in that one competitor's gain necessitates another's loss. Hence, the dilemma facing the regime is that it cannot simultaneously satisfy everyone's needs in this area. Thus, conflict can only be managed it cannot be totally resolved.

At this stage, institutions designed to manage such zerosum conflicts emerge. Political parties attain special importance as channels of competition in politics. Interest groups emerge as institutional mechanisms to enhance the competitive advantage of their constituents. Labor unions develop from simple bargaining units to enhance workers' material lifestyles into political organizations that can make or break parties and candidates in an election. In short, the sorts of institutions that become ascendant at this stage are the ones designed to pursue power and influence that by definition cannot be possessed by everyone simultaneously.

In sum, members of a society pursue their needs by forming institutions, and the nature and type of prevalent social institutions at any given time can be described by observing the thenpredominant human needs. When physical survival becomes the most pressing need, institutions pertaining to police and military, as well as those related to food production and agriculture, are regarded as primary. The family, churches, mass media and schools surface as important institutions when people seek groups with which they can associate for a sense of belonging. Industrialization, urbanization, and a market economic structure gain cultural and social supremacy when people desire to consume more than what is needed for survival. Political parties and interest groups develop when people strive for social recognition and esteem.

Attitudes, Behaviors, and Human Needs/Wants

As people pursue their specific needs through institutions of a particular nature, their attitudes and behavior will be patterned in a changing, yet predictable, way. Thus, if we can tell the kind of need one is pursuing and the type of institutions with which one is likely to interact, we might be able to ascertain one's attitudes and behavioral predispositions at that point in time. As we now have postulated a set of relations between human need types and patterns of institutionalization, we can, with greater simplicity, specify some attitudinal and behavioral consequences of the various needs.

Obviously, when someone's minimum physical survival is threatened, any inconvenience imposed upon him or her will be accepted if such an imposition assures better chances of survival. Here, people will be inclined to be submissive and compliant-particularly to authorities who might offer them an improved chance of survival. We are reminded of the prevalent fact that when a government wants to raise a sense of patriotism and loyalty to the state, the notion of a security threat is invoked at times in a greatly orchestrated manner.

Lawrence Kohlberg (1969, p. 379) describes this level of "moral development" as a "punishment and obedience" orientation, where the consequences of an action determine the value of the action. When survival is the dominant motivation, attitudes and beliefs about any sort of behavior will depend on the efficacy of that behavior for survival. Hence, a person may have little or no compunction about stealing food when starving, whereas the same person, with a fairly comfortable material lifestyle, may not even consider engaging in such behavior. That is, institutions relying upon coercion, such as law enforcement and military agencies, can be most effective when the majority of the people in any given society are involved in survival-related activities and are therefore dependent on and submissive to such authorities.

However, in the subsequent stage, where humans desire a sense of belonging, attitudes and beliefs about behavior will be formulated with more of an eye to the response of "significant others." Initially, at least, one seeks the approval of those with whom one has immediate and frequent contact: family, neighbors, and fellow workers. Here beliefs are grounded in one's group affiliations and are as changeable as the groups. The task facing the regime at this point is to prevent this panoply of groupbased beliefs from becoming the source of excessive group conflict. Group diversity is bound to generate belief conflict, and government, through the educational and mass media institutions, must attempt to minimize the differences by providing some broad belief system that can accommodate the various beliefs and thereby minimize the importance of differences.

At the individual level, values and belief systems are articulated as an attempt to justify group affiliations and social behavior. Here, education and religious experience serve to enhance one's ability to justify a social existence in terms of more abstract principles and beliefs. At this point, one will develop a stronger sense of "us versus them" or "ours versus theirs," thus promoting the organizational mind or "associational sentiment."[20] It is the development of this psychological predisposition that facilitates the emergence and spread of ideologies, often serving a regime which otherwise might experience a severe setback in integrating the political community. The anticipated cultural and social fragmentation (a point we will elaborate upon further later) is mitigated by the regime's promulgation of a common set of abstract beliefs and ideologies.

---

20 Development theorists such as Daniel Lerner, Lucian Pye, David McClleland, and others who empathize with Max Weber adhere to this view.

When members of a community shift their need level to one of leisure life as a result of the successful gratification of belongingness needs, we can expect that social change will move in the direction of industrialization, urbanization, and market economy. As people attach themselves to the spinning wheels of industrialization and become "cogs" in the wheels of production, they claim a small area of expertise and develop a rather segmented view of life. As the structure of industrial society is largely bureaucratic, the industrial person will also exhibit what is commonly referred to as the "bureaucratic mentality," characterized by impersonal, formalistic, and segmented relations toward others.

Urbanization, on the other hand, is known to be destructive to traditional family and communal ties and social structure, and forces city-dwellers to become selfcentered and concerned with privacy. It is one of the great ironies of history that people find themselves more isolated in heavily-populated urban centers than in a rural communities where neighbors are often scattered miles apart from each other. It is quite common for an urban dweller not to know the people living next door to him, as he has little incentive indeed to know anyone with whom he or she has no functional interaction or economic interest.

Finally, market economy transforms human nature in a most powerful and profound way. In keeping with the dynamics of the market economy, people learn to be bargainoriented and economically rational, pursuing maximum payoff at a minimum cost. As the market transforms all values into the common quantitative yardstick of currency, people naturally seek more of everything, thus embracing the simple value equation of "the bigger, the better." At the same time, the industrial person becomes a slave of "convenience" and automation. Here commodities are designed and redesigned to be convenient and timesaving. In this process of innovation of commodities in a market economy, mass media become the means of promotion for mass consumption.

Once mass consumption becomes a necessary condition for a continuously prospering market industry, the consumer will be capable of buying just about anything that can be mass produced due to the inevitable development of banking and credit systems. Thus, people without the actual resources to purchase their commodities will still be able to maintain their consumption level by using "plastic money" (credit cards) which most major companies and banking institutions will grant to anyone with a job. These mass consumers will soon become psychologically uneasy as their debts accumulate thus they will become "precarious consumers" as well as "vicarious consumers."[21]

Most likely, the leisurelife pursuer in an industrial society will seek entertainment of all types. In fact, the options for entertainment and the selection of instruments to entertain become broad and diverse, ranging from social parties to sports. Even politics comes to be considered a form of entertainment.

Finally, the competitor, who seeks social recognition and esteem by winning competitions and conflicts, will surface. By the time the acquisition of massproduced commodities has made it difficult to distinguish the "winner" from the "loser," social recognition pursuers will look for those values, resources, and commodities that cannot be massproduced or possessed by so many as to become meaningless. People will seek such things as power positions, rare collections, and vaunted reputations. As discussed earlier, this stage of development is characterized by a high sense of competition and by a proliferation of gameloving personalities within a society. Games such as chess, bowling, baseball, horse racing, car racing and football are no longer for entertainment only at this stage. Participants in these games, either through actual physical participation or psychological association as fans, will become deadly serious about competitive outcomes. Professional institutions grow up around games in game-loving societies, and players within these institutions are rewarded with enormous recognition and material compensation. Rewards for winners, no matter how unreasonable the amount, are deemed natural, and the losers' sufferings are seldom seen as worthy of sympathy.

As games are played by rules rather than customs, gameloving people tend to maintain their lifestyles and sense of justice within a framework of detailed laws. It is not an accidental development that the court is becoming an integral part of life in America and other postindustrial societies. Every type of dispute is taken to court. Family disputes, educational disagreements, and even love affairs are arbitrated in court-the ultimate umpire in social competitions and human games. Increasingly, we see evidence of the belief that what is legal is also right.

In sum, by examining the needsstructure of individuals and the characteristics of corresponding institutions, we can ascertain

---

21 The "precarious consumption" is compounded by what Veblen called "conspicuous consumption" in which the consumer demonstrates his or her purchasing ability as an attempt to show off social states (Veblen, 1899).

behavioral and attitudinal characteristics at various stages of social change. Understanding psychological and behavioral predispositions becomes crucial as we attempt to discuss political characteristics and the policy directions of various political systems for the purpose of explanation and prediction, as well as the ultimate goal of problem solving.

Political Development Defined

Consistent with the spirit and principles of the discussion above, I now advance the theorem that *political development refers to the capacity of the political system to satisfy the changing needs of the members of the society.*[22] This definition satisfies the definitional criteria for political development as discussed in the previous chapter. First of all, the universal presence of human needs and the continuous effort on the part of mankind to satisfy these needs appear to be nonculture bound and nontime bound. More importantly, these phenomena are clearly common to members of the "underdeveloped" as well as the "developed" society. Furthermore, this definition captures the important qualitative dimensions of societal development within a framework of human needs progression. In other words, this definition is valid and useful for accurately assessing the true process of development. It lends itself to the crafting a theory that may be grand and comprehensive enough to begin a paradigm of social and political development.

Before I venture to face the task of building a paradigm, some semantic clarifications are in order. A paradigm is a system of theories; a theory is a system of laws; a law is a system of concepts. As such, concepts are the ultimate building blocks. A concept is a meaningful term, whereas the definition of meaning is a teleological construct in that it has a purpose inherent in it. Once a term such as development is defined, it attains a meaning. The word *development*, as it is defined in terms of human needs/ wants *satisfaction*, now becomes a concept with a clear meaning. When this concept is connected to other concepts in a logical and systemic manner, it becomes a part of a diverse set of laws. For example, the revolutionary paradigm known as Marxism consists

---

22 Eisenstadt (1968, p. 184) offers a similar definition in that political development refers to "the capacity of modern society to adapt itself to continuously changing demands, to absorb them in terms of policy making, and to assure its own continuity in the face of continuous new demands and new forms of political organization."

of multiple theories such as the theory of social class formation, the economic theory of capitalism, the psychological theory of class consciousness, and the political theory of class conflict. Each of these theories contains multiple laws, each specifying causal relationships between or among diverse concepts. The Labor Theory of Value is, strictly speaking, a law, rather than a theory, which in turn consists of multitude of concepts such as "values," "classes," "exploitation," "state," and even "utopia." A paradigm, then, is a complex and encompassing system of theories, laws, and concepts constituting an "ideal type" that is inferred from historical realities. It has explanatory and predictive power, and ultimately is useful in the challenge of problem solving. Whether the paradigm to be advanced through the remaining chapters in Part Two of this book will be useful for explaining and predicting political development cannot be determined until the paradigm has been formulated and applied.

The Theorems

A paradigm, like a law of physical science, can only claim validity when a certain set of assumptions are taken to be valid, as well. The proposed paradigm, as is the case with any paradigm in what Kuhn (1962) terms "normal science," presupposes a set of assumptions and conditions. The validity of these presuppositions may be debatable, and some may be timebound, thus necessitating the constant reevaluation of their validity. Nevertheless, they are theorems or assumptions necessary for the deductive structure of the proposed paradigm and are claimed to be valid in light of contemporary society and politics.

Theorem 1: Man behaves in such a way as to conscientiously and constantly pursue the optimum satisfaction of his needs.

This theorem is consistent with the much-debated yet widely utilized economic assumption of human rationality (Friedman, 1953). A more fundamental justification for this assumption might be found in the common definition of human behavior as a function of goaloriented action. In addition, however, we will need to assume the presence of some structure of human needs as being a specieswide characteristic if we are to formulate laws and theories explaining human behavior from a developmental perspective and at a crosscultural level. A further discussion on this assumed universality of the structure of human needs will be presented later.

Theorem 2: At any given point in time, a society's developmental tasks may be determined as a function of the thendominant needs of its individual members.

This theorem, in congruence with the perspective of "methodological individualism," defies any reification of a society or social institutions; the "whole" is explainable by its parts, and any emergent quality of the collective unit of society--such as General Will (Rousseau, 1762) or Social Fact (Durkheim, 1938)--is not given credence. This would also imply that the state of human nature, insofar as the pursuit of individual need satisfaction is concerned (Theorem 1), is considered constant regardless of whether one is an independent actor or part of a group.[23]

Theorem 3: The legitimacy of government (and politics) lies in its contribution to enhancing people's needsatisfaction.

Thus, a political system (in terms of regime type and institutional characteristics) changes, at least in the long run, in such a way that the emergent needs of the people (or, in practice, the ruler's interpretation of public needs) may be most effectively met.

This theorem seems plausible in view of the consensus among virtually all contemporary ideologies that the ultimate foundations of legitimate power rest in the consent of the ruled. Unlike the ancient and medieval doctrines in which different regimes sought different bases of political legitimacy-some in the virtue of the *Philosopher King* and others in the name of Divine Providence-all contemporary governments since the inception of the Lockean principle of the *Social Contract* have sought the consent of the people as the ultimate reservoir of political power.

This theorem is also consistent with some leading theories of politics, including Easton's view (1964, Chapter 8) that the system is sustained by its ability to respond to changing demands. In terms of the Eastonian systems model, we may posit that "support" as the basis of legitimacy is generated as a function of the regime's capacity to meet people's demands, i.e., the expression of their needs. Roland Pennock (1965, p. 420) has more directly suggested that the goal of government and the political system is the provision of political goods to satisfy human needs. It is the fulfillment of needs that makes the policy valuable to man and

---

23 For definitions of methodological individualism, refer to J.W.N. Watkins, "Methodological Individualism and Social Tendencies," and May Broadbeck, "methodological Individualism: Definition and Reduction," in May Broadbeck, ed., 1968).

gives it its justification in the eyes of the public. On this basis, we suggest that political legitimacy and, therefore, regime stability, are analytically determined by the difference in amount between support and demand. Thus, a legitimacy crisis occurs when the level of demand exceeds the level of support.

States and Political Development

We have established that certain types of human needs are likely to facilitate the development of certain institutions, and, as members of these institutions pursue their needs, certain attitudinal and behavioral traits will be formed. Assuming that styles of politics may be affected significantly by the nature of human needs and the demands placed upon the government, we can now infer political characteristics and policy preferences in different stages of social development by considering the human needs hierarchy and institutional formation.

Specifically, we have established that human needs have a systematic, ordered structure in which the unique characteristics of the different needs result in institutional diversity as well as structured behavioral patterns. With the assumptions that a society's need characteristics are defined as the aggregate of its individual members' needs, and that a regime is to maximize its efforts in responding to the prevalent needs of the members of the society, we now can propose the structure of the process of political development. By determining to what extent the political system has capably accomplished its function of meeting these needs, a systematic process of development can be identified. The process may be seen as occurring in four distinct phases, with the government's response to each progressively higher level of needs constituting each of the four phases. These stages appear to represent much of the process of developmental political change, regardless of the regime type (ideological and structural) directing the process in any given instance. These stages may be called (1) regime formation, (2) political integration, (3) resource expansion, and (4) conflict management. Just as human needs are hierarchically ordered, these stages of political development are incrementally and sequentially structured. I shall explore further characteristics of each of these stages in the ensuing chapters.

Chapter 6

Survival and Regime Formation

A new nation may emerge as a result of internal revolution, independence, or as a movement toward what Organski (1965) calls "primitive unification." By any of these channels, a regime comes to power by winning the competition between groups contending for political supremacy. This struggle for power may provoke large-scale forms of conflict such as civil wars, or it may provoke more focused forms of power conflict such as military coups. In either case, people will perceive a threat to their physical survival. In times marked by a crisis of physical survival, people naturally want political stability of any kind, irrespective of the type of government, as long as the emerging regime can assure their survival. The question of regime "legitimacy" in this initial stage is largely irrelevant or, at most, is only of secondary importance. The "legitimate" regime is quite simply the power group that demonstrates its ability to quell domestic conflict. Thus, a regime may emerge from a power conflict without any demonstrable evidence of popular support, an occurrence that would have been impossible within a peaceful form of political succession. However, once a regime is formed, it will attempt to solidify its power base and gain popular support. At a time when public needs are structured largely around priorities of survival, the regime is likely to adopt policies that will help restore social stability and facilitate agricultural production. As people's attitudes tend to be compliant and submissive at this level of need, the regime can easily develop a centralized form of leadership such as a military dictatorship. In a military government, the method of rule is not nearly as important as whether or not social and political stability is established and maintained. Such leadership can often be effective in generating public support insofar as the public desires a more secure and safe environment, but it tends to be overly simplistic when dealing with other policy considerations. Thus, it may experience serious difficulty in responding to conflicting public opinions and in accommodating diverse organizations when such pluralistic development inevitably follows a period of social stability.

All states seek legitimacy for power in the name of helping people satisfy their basic needs. The origin of the state dates back millennia. As a natural community is formed, the need for fulfilling a myriad of collective challenges emerges, such as protecting members of the community from external hostility, collecting and redistributing both tangible and non-tangible values and resources, and creating and legitimizing systems of governance. When a state is formed, it is bound to change over time, sometimes through a drastic and abrupt process known as a revolution. Regardless of the type, regime formation refers to the process by which a new political system emerges. In this process, new leadership will be identified, established, and defined. New rules will be promulgated to establish authoritatively which individual and group behaviors are tolerable and which are not. New political structures and institutions will be installed to replace the old, and above all, concerted efforts will be made by the leadership to solidify the populace in order to expand the scope of its capacity to control people and events, thus perpetuating its power position. A regime formation entails much more than a change in government personnel. It means a profound change in the nature of the political community itself.

Roads to Regime Formation

Regimes may be formed in a variety of ways. One of the earliest forms was "primitive unification" (Organski, 1965) in which tribal groups were consolidated under a common authority. Although all modern nations may have gone through this stage of primitive unification at one time or another, regimes are no longer formed in this way. Another type of regime formation, which was rather prevalent during the dynastic era of political history but is no longer common, is hereditary succession of power. Although there may still be some monarchs remaining in the world today, their roles are mostly symbolic and ceremonial, with the exception of a handful of systems such as Morocco, Syria, Jordan, Cambodia, Thailand, and Saudi Arabia. Even in those systems, the very *raison d'etre* of the monarchy is often challenged by mass dissention movements, as witnessed in the Arab Spring of 2010-2012. With reference to the present topic, however, we can say at the very least monarchy can no longer serve as the institutional channel for succession and change in political leadership.

Ever since the introduction and doctrinal acceptance of the social contract as defined by Thomas Hobbes (1588-1679), John Locke (1632-1704), and Jean-Jacques Rousseau (1712-1778), modern regimes have been formed through either *election* or *revolution*. As a common institution, the election often fails to produce a new regime, but some elections do lead to profound changes in the nature of the political system. Although mass revolutions have been rather infrequent, their impact on the course of history has been extensive indeed. Mass revolutions, like sleeping volcanoes, may not explode regularly, but when they do, their component behaviors and impacts become very difficult to assess scientifically. When a seemingly revolutionary change fails to shakeup of the political system itself, thus resulting in a leadership change only, such an event can be most appropriately characterized as a *coup d'etat*. Owing to its frequent occurrence, the *coup d'etat*, which is usually instigated by the military, has become an important mechanism of regime change in postWorld War II world politics.

In short, there are several different types of regime change in addition to primitive unification. Of these, hereditary succession and electoral transition of power are commonly considered "legitimate" forms, as they proceed through existing institutions and according to rules based on widely shared norms and values. On the other hand, revolution and *coup d'etat* are the extrainstitutional or "illegitimate" means of regime change, as they occur in defiance of such rules and with the expressed purpose of altering, among other things, the rules of succession.

In this chapter, we shall examine each of these types with a more exhaustive discussion on revolution. Additionally, we shall examine the nature of the newly emergent political system itself, as we seek to illuminate some characteristic features of newly formed social and political institutions and their relationship to the indigenous cultural configurations of a society.

1. Hereditary Succession

In the modern era, as the basis of all regimes' claims to legitimacy has shifted from such principles of Divine Right or the Mandate of Heaven to some form of social contract, traditional hereditary dynasties have been replaced by various manifestations of republican government and people's democracies, all of which claim legitimacy on the basis of some type of mandate of the governed. Yet, the reality is that some states still maintain a system of inheritance, and many demonstrate symbolic statehood around the institution of monarchy. Then, who and what might be the sources of empowerment for contemporary monarchs? It is obvious that all political powers originate from the consent and support of the ruled. Even a monarchy cannot legitimize its power without the support of the people. Why and how do the people support such a system that undermines all forms of values and premises underlying the concept of "consent of the people," the key of which is equality for all?

There could be a few reasons that people support monarchical institutions. First, there is the long-standing allegiance to the monarch, which has become a passive and habitual pattern of a way of life for the people. Second, there is the coercive capability on the part of the monarchy to impose its will upon the people. In this case, people submit themselves to the authority because the repercussions of disobedience are too dire to risk. Third, people may find that the system adequately provides for their needs, lessening the propensity toward revolt. Fourth, people may find, as subjects of the monarchy, a sense of belonging in association with a long cultural and political tradition. In this case, the culture is likely to embrace collectivism.

Different religious persuasions vary on the issue of collectivism versus individualism. Christianity of the West, for instance, places a high value on individuality and individualism, in comparison with Confucianism of Asia or Islamic persuasion of the Middle East. This may explain the historical fact that liberal democracy has found its nursing grounds in Christianity, whereas social collectivism and political statism have been more prevalent in Confucian Asia and Islamic Middle East. In any event, in modern times, hereditary monarchs rarely wield political power, nor do they personify public opinion or any popular mandate. In this sense, heredity is no longer a meaningful institution of power succession because political clout lies elsewhere within such systems. To the extent that a state needs symbolic authority and desires to induce pride among the people for the history and heritage of the nation, the royal institution may be desirable and even functional toward that end. Nonetheless, succession through inheritance is no longer used in itself as an institution of regime change.

This is not to disregard the fact that many reform movements and even revolutionary changes in the characteristics of political systems have evolved around replacement of rulers through the means of inheritance. The Meiji Restoration of 1868-1912 in Japan was an example in which political reform was carried out by a warrior class, as it attempted to restore the power and authority of the royal family. But even in this case, the reformists did not start the restoration movement just for the protection of the royal institution; rather, the warrior class (*Samurai*), disenchanted with the feudal social structure and political order, used the idea of royal restoration to justify the "modernization" of other social and political institutions.

2. Election as a Mobilizing Mechanism

As we noted earlier, since the inception social contract theory in the early 17th Century, governments of all types have sought legitimacy for their exercise of political power through the "consent of the governed." Thus, at least in theory, it would be unlikely that any government could prolong its claim to power without obtaining the continuous support, in some form or another, of its people. Although "popular support" and "consent of the governed" have been interpreted in a variety of ways by ruling elites of different political hues, no one would deny the importance of some minimal level of popular wellbeing as the ultimate basis of popular support and, therefore, of a regime's claim to legitimacy.

Thus, the popular election, as an institution by which candidates for positions of power are compared in terms of the levels of popular support each can generate, has become an effective, rational, and widely used institution for the orderly transfer of political power. In reality, however, a regime change does not occur in so orderly a fashion unless the politics is guided by some form of constitutionalism and certain "rules of the game" that are deeply imbedded in the culture and political experience of the society. In other words, orderly change through elections is not expected in those societies where such culture and political experience are lacking, or where the masses are struggling for satisfaction of the most basic needs of physical survival. In such a society, the elite's claim to legitimate authority is tenuous at best, and electoral mechanisms themselves do not have the legitimacy that makes them institutions of orderly personnel change. Social and political pluralism, as well as alternative parties and candidates, are lacking and may even be outlawed. Whatever opposition exists is likely revolutionary in nature, and seeks not only changes in government personnel from within a given elite group but replacement of the current elite group with an entirely different group. Under such conditions, those in power will use the election mechanism as a means to rubber stamp their own incumbency rather than a means by which to test the popular support for a set of policies.

Thus, it should be to no one's surprise that elections in such societies have seldom served as a means of personnel change, let alone change in the structure of the regime and the political system itself. Where elections are taking place in the Third World, patterns of electoral behavior are often strikingly different from those accompanying elections in more mature pluralistic democracies. In many incidences, elections are used by the ruling elite to mobilize votes and supports from the populace as opposed to having the institution of election as a mechanism of electing or selecting government.

As the records indicate, few regime changes have resulted from lawful elections in societies outside the Western Hemisphere. But the institution of elections has been employed in virtually every modern nation, including even totalitarian communist systems. This implies that elections serve some other purpose if not regime change. In countries experiencing difficulties in maintaining regime stability, often the occupants of the elite structure utilize electoral institutions for soliciting expressions of support for their claim to power or for expanding their power base. Particularly when the regime has just gained control over rival elite groups, it will need to prevent the possible resurgence of contending leaders. Thus, it is commonplace to find that purges and executions of opponents usually occur after a regime change, and elections that might lend popular legitimacy to the rivals' claims and aspirations to power are not likely to be permitted.

In examining the functions of elections in emerging and unstable societies in this way, it is safe to conclude that the electoral system as a mechanism for regime succession is not a viable institution in these societies. In fact, many studies on the social conditions of democracy have suggested that the democratic electoral system is unsuitable for economically and socially underdeveloped countries (Park, 1976).

3. Military Coup d'État: A Vicious Cycle

An overwhelming proportion of Third World nations have experienced frequent regime change at the hands of the military. Many of these countries do not seem to have any alternative but to remain in a vicious cycle of successive military *coups d'état*. For instance, Bolivia has experienced over 200 irregular government changes since the nation's independence in 1825. Most of these regime changes, instigated by the military, involve only the circulation of government personnel and have little if any impact on the distribution of wealth and power, or on the social and political institutions of the country. However, each time a society undergoes a military coup, the population must face a certain amount of political instability and uncertainty and often serious threats to their physical safety.

There are several characteristics of newly independent and previously colonial countries that render them susceptible to successive military coups, as the military enjoys an enormous amount of prestige and leverage for several reasons:

a) *The Military as a Symbol of Nationhood.* As a nation becomes politically independent from a colonial power, the first order of business tends to be the building of its own military machine. This is even more urgent when the people attribute the shameful experience of colonial rule to the former lack of military capability. Here, amidst the euphoria of independence, the people are often quite willing to give unconditional support to the building of the military. Symbolic features such as military uniforms, national anthems, and national flags are likely to reinforce and accommodate nationalist sentiments among the public. Thus, it is expected that in a newly independent nation, populist culture will be such that the institutionalization of the military will attain priority over the institutionalization of other political structures.

b) *The Military as Mobilizer.* Most Third World nations employ conscription as a mechanism for military recruitment. In such a system, the army comes to represent numerous segments of the society, and thus can mobilize mass public support.

During the early stages of political development, the military has a wide range of functions in addition to its primary role of national defense. These functions include generating public support, implementing policies by serving as a law enforcement agent, and even economic functions such as engaging in road constructions and other civil engineering projects. While performing these diverse roles, the military comes to command a great deal of power and authority beyond that which is associated with its defense function. This inordinate extension of the military's sphere of authority is facilitated further by the absence of any other large institutionalized political organization It comes to dominate civilian political institutions rather than simply serving as the enforcement mechanism for civilian policy makers.

c) *The Military as a Modernizing Agent.* In a society where a large proportion of the population is illiterate and has little motivation to train itself or to alter the lifestyle it has inherited, military personnel often constitute the most skilled labor pool. In fact, military draftees in an underdeveloped society are often taught to read and write and are provided with training in various technical fields which can be utilized in industrialization and other developmental social changes.

When a soldier is discharged from the military, he becomes an important opinion leader in his community and often exposes that community to information and ideas from outside the traditional community and its culture. Chances are that he himself will eventually migrate to an urban and presumably industrial locale and bring other members of his family to the city, thus contributing to demographic changes in the society. The extent of the military's contribution to social change is enormous when the military is the primary large-scale modernized state organization, as is likely to be the case in any new nation.

d) *The Military as an Egalitarian Institution.* The institution of the military, with its rigid hierarchical command structure, is commonly known to be undemocratic. But in a newly independent nation, the institution promotes achievement norms and provides a democratic experience, at least to a greater degree than other traditional social institutions.[24] Coming from a society that is primarily agrarian in its economy, feudal in its social structure, and authoritarian in its political culture, the new soldier will experience a clear departure from the structural and cultural norms of the society. Every draftee, regardless of his social and economic background, is to be treated equally in that all receive the same uniform, the same amount of pay, and have the same obligations and duties. This is a rather drastic and remarkable departure from their conventional social situation for the majority of the recruits.

When soldiers are released from their military duties and return to civilian society, they often find it difficult to readjust due to the new attitudes developed by their recent brush with egalitarianism. As discussed earlier, many of them will leave their home communities for this reason and seek alternative lifestyles in urban settings. With urban culture still in its formative stages, the migrant will find that there are few cultural conditions to which he must adapt. Rather, those newcomers who have had military experience will find that their shared values and attitudes, as well as job skills and experiences, will exert fundamental influence on the emergent urban culture, thus shaping the manner in which urban communities develop. Urban areas formed in this manner are more likely to adopt a generally egalitarian social practice, and

---

24 A rich body of literature is available on the nature and role of the military. For a concise discussion on violence, state formation, and the military, see Posen, Barry. "Nationalism, the Mass Army and Military Power" *International Security* 18 no. 2 (1993), pp. 80-124.

their new norms and values will be fundamentally inconsistent with the traditional rural and agrarian culture in this regard.

These and other features of the military institution in many newly emerging countries contribute to making that institution a pivotal developmental organization. All other institutions are likely to be centered on the military. Even in educational planning, national defense and the role of military will be given the highest priority. The economy will be decidedly affected by military needs and capabilities. Every family will have someone serving in the army. Popular culture in the form of folk songs and stories and arts of all kinds will, in some way, promote military heroism. In such a society, it would be highly unlikely for anyone who does not have military leadership to emerge as a national political leader. This helps us understand why Third World military behavior often has such a political overtone, and why military leaders are most likely to dominate political proceedings.

However, this still does not answer the puzzling question of why some societies have more stable military leadership than others. Many militarybacked leaders around the world have enjoyed relatively stable and prolonged occupation of leadership positions, whereas many more have experienced short terms, and even shortened lives, as a result of their inability to control recurrent military coups. A cursory observation of regime changes around the world would suggest that there are some common characteristics among the more stable military regimes, and that these characteristics have helped the leadership in prolonging its power position. Among them we can cite (1) perceived or actual threat from outside forces; (2) the maintenance of a closed political system by controlling popular access to the outside world and by controlling communication among the domestic population; (3) creating an air of charisma for a leader through politicization of the masses around a cult of personality.

The crucial parameter for an effective military is its coercive capability, and, accordingly, the primary instrument for military control of political decisionmaking is its use of physical coercion. In domestic politics, however, coercive measures will not be effective for long unless their use is seen as legitimate. In other words, in order to crack down on dissent and government critics, while at the same time building a stable foundation of popular support, the regime needs to employ some sort of justification for repressive action. Such justification is often found in claiming a threat to the nation's very existence, thus making compliance with government policies a necessity for the nation's survival.

Arousing the perception of threat from without in order to solidify power within is hardly a novel strategy for a government or any other organization. Georg Simmel's study of organizational behavior espoused the thesis that organizational solidarity is likely to be enhanced when the environment is perceived to be hostile (there is also experimental evidence from small group psychology confirming this same phenomenon).[1] Given the potentially severe consequences of a foreign military attack, governments can generate considerable national unity by creating even a minimally credible perception of foreign hostility. The actual probability of conflict is less important.

Shielding information from outside and controlling information flow within is essential to maintaining a stable military dictatorship, if for no other reason than the aforementioned purpose of perpetuating a sense of national crisis. To this end, a military regime imposes tight censorship on the media by allowing only a limited number of channels to serve as official, or functionally official, government organs. Keeping the public selectively informed, misinformed, or completely uninformed about world affairs is a common strategy of repressive regimes seeking to prevent riots and demonstrations or other antigovernment activities. By keeping the public incapable of comprehending public affairs and world politics the regime effectively maintains a closed society, and therefore is able to control people and events. It is often in the interest of the regime to retain the underdeveloped conditions of low literacy, governmentally constrained mass communication, and nonparticipatory political culture. In this sense, an ideal policy for perpetuating a military regime is to adopt a totalitarian form of government, since the most enduring military leaderships are found in totalitarian countries.

In the foregoing discussion, we identified a few bases upon which a military regime attempts to prolong its political incumbency. Implicit in the discussion were the converse: namely, the causes of unstable military leadership. From this discussion, we might be able to discern a few propositions to help us answer the crucial question of why some regimes never seem to escape the vicious cycle of military coups. Even with strong charismatic leadership in a tightly controlled, closed society where people are politically inactive and non-participant, a regime can experience instability if its people are living in a state of extreme poverty without any alternative but rebellion. When a people's survival is threatened and the government is held responsible, the regime may be unable to prevent riots and uprisings.

Based on the paradigm being proposed in this book, we can postulate a dilemma facing all military regimes, one that might be a key to explaining the phenomenon of successive military *coups d'état* in societies where the government is performing its role efficiently. The dilemma exists in that people in first stage societies will shift their emphasis to other needs once they are reasonably assured of food, shelter, and protection from lifethreatening conditions. A society with a military government that can assure satisfaction of these most basic needs will move into the second stage of political integration, when people's needs shift to belonging. In this case, the regime will lose its foundations of popular support not by being incapable of gratifying survival needs, but rather because of a failure to address the newly emergent need for belonging. When the regime is inappropriate or incapable of adjusting its policy priorities to corresponding changes in popular needs and demands, it cannot retain the some level of popular support it generated in the first stage even if it continues to be effective in delivering the basic services necessarily for physical survival.

The military institution cannot easily adapt its policies to accommodate people's desire to enhance their social and psychological belonging. The military is an institution where values such as uniformity rather than diversity, command rather than compromise, and physical control rather than psychological comfort are given distinct prominence. It is said that there are three ways of doing things in the world: the right way, the wrong way, and the military way. As such, professional militarism and military organization usually constitute a barrier to the second stage of social development. When a regime suffers a low level of public support, it becomes vulnerable to power conflict, and a likely form of power conflict in this early stage of development is one occurring within the military itself. In the course of personnel shakeups in the government, which are to be expected when eroding government support leads to antigovernment activity in society and power conflicts within the regime, the once-secure basis of the people's physical survival will be threatened. As a result, the prevailing popular needs and demands will revert from the level of belonging to the more basic needs of physical survival. A new military government, which can successfully seize power in a coup, is bound to gain some support from the people simply by returning political stability and reestablishing the capacity to ensure survival needs.

However, as soon as a new stability is achieved and the basic needs are assured, people will once again prioritize the need to belong. This leads to another legitimacy crisis for the new regime if it fails to adapt its policy priorities accordingly. When the effects of the power struggle are so extensive that the capacity to ensure survival needs cannot be revived easily and quickly after the coup, the government will enjoy a relatively prolonged period of minimal support for its rule, as the people's wounds from political turmoil and the struggle to survive gradually heal. A country like Bolivia, which has recorded perhaps the greatest frequency of military coups, is not a country whose people live precariously close to starvation, desiring merely physical survival. Rather, it is a country capable of providing basic services through its bureaucracy. For this reason, ironically, it might be more vulnerable to frequent coups, especially if these events leave the bureaucracy relatively intact. Indeed, a great military involvement in politics exists in countries with relatively higher rates of economic growth, rather than the poor and stagnant countries. In short, what causes regime stability is not merely the efficiency of the government, but to a large extent, the degree to which it can anticipate and adapt to the changing needs of the public. This conclusion is not to suggest that all governments are inclined to respond to people's needs but rather that a government must adjust to the changing characteristics of popular demands if it is to draw public support. It is the people's support that ultimately justifies political power. The military's rigidity, limited vision, and a narrow range of capacities may thus be an important contributor to the phenomenon of vicious cycles of *coups d'état*.

4. Revolution: the Ultimate Change

A revolution represents the most traumatic and extensive form of regime change in that it affects both the political system and the lifestyle of the masses. A change in governmental structure or its personnel may be an important outcome of most revolutions, but it alone cannot constitute a revolution in its entirety. A government change, in fact, is not only insufficient for a revolution, it is also theoretically unnecessary. At times, we use the label "revolution" for any extensive social change forcing alterations in societal structure and lifestyle, but such changes do not always demand governmental reorganization. The Industrial Revolution would be an example of this. In most cases, however, a revolution does involve governmental reorganization and overthrow of the incumbent regime through mass violence. A revolution, then, can be defined as a type of social change in which profound institutional upheavals force members of the society to drastically alter their lifestyles in a relatively short period of time.

In such a revolutionary process, it is expected that many vital institutions will be dismantled and new ones formed. At the same time, a major proportion of the people find themselves socially dislocated and preoccupied with the tasks of relocation and readjustment to the new emerging institutional reality. Thus, political and social instability are typical symptoms of any revolution. In this section, we shall briefly examine the causes and dynamics of revolutionary social change as espoused by different authors, and attempt to synthesize their views while refining some theories for a more comprehensive analysis of revolutionary phenomena.

There are a good many theories of revolution and revolutionary activity. While there are varying views as to conditions for revolution, they all seem to agree that men rebel when they feel unhappy to the extent that they are willing to risk personal injury to affect a drastic alteration of the existing power and authority structure. What facilitates this psychological dissatisfaction may vary, as evidenced in the economic determinism of Marxist theory, the political determinism of Lenin, and the psychological determinism of Davies (1971). The immediate cause of any revolutionary activity, however, has to be the individual actor's attitudes and behavioral predispositions. One cannot explain revolution in any causal sense by direct use of aggregate social or economic variables, since a society or even a class as such cannot have a motive for taking an action. Only individuals have motives. This is not to suggest that we can or should deny the importance of social and economic conditions that are likely to produce a revolutionary state of mind among individuals, but our immediate analytical concern should be with the kinds of mindsets that might be conducive to engaging in revolutionary behavior. Social and economic conditions may be found to be the ultimate source of psychological discontent, but, in particular, certain social and contextual conditions cause revolutionary behavior through their impact on individual psychology and/or behavioral tendencies.

We shall examine a few premises and theoretical concepts that have been proposed as being valuable tools for the explanation of revolutionary behavior.

a) FrustrationAggression: A basic premise in the frustrationaggression model is that revolutionary activity will occur when there is widespread frustration of some felt need or needs in society, and the government is viewed as being in some way responsible for this frustration. This premise is grounded in two psychological theories: frustrationaggression theory and the general theory of human needs as the motivating forces of individual behavior. Frustration, following Gurr's discussion, "can be regarded simply as interference with goaldirected behavior" (1970, Chapter 2). Aggression, an activity designed to injure the frustrating agent, is the individual's usual response to intense frustration. When the government is blamed for the frustration of large numbers of people in a polity, violent action aimed at the current regime will result. Thus, it follows that by knowing what needs are held in common and are prevalent at a given point in time, we can determine better which societal conditions are likely to produce such frustration.

For theoretical purposes, we maintain that all humans share the same basic needs, which dictate behavioral goals for the individual, though what counts for satisfaction of a given need may vary across cultures. All behavior is a means for the fulfillment of these needs and desires, which acquire or assume a hierarchy of importance. Thus frustrations can occur at any level of social development since individuals may be frustrated for different reasons. A person can be frustrated, for example, because he or she is deprived of the basic needs of food, shelter, and security. Others can be equally frustrated because of denial of freedom or belonging. Still others can be discontented because of continuous failure in their attempts to secure greater share of power and influence.

As Davies correctly observes, this model requires "the assessment of the state of mind of a people" to predict the source and level of frustration and, hence, the probability of revolutionary activity (1970 p. 146). While it is possible at times to actually collect information on an individual's state of mind through the use of interviews, an extensive direct inquiry into the "state of mind" would be impractical. Furthermore, levels of frustration in the populace would be changing their needs and desires change and as societal conditions change necessitating constant reassessment of the situation. It would therefore be desirable to determine what social conditions lead to frustrations in regard to individual needs.

Obviously, the most basic need of humans and other organisms is the need for physical survival. But in individual terms, satisfaction of this need is not necessarily related to the level of aggregate or average wealth in the society. We would not want to say that the poorer a society is, the more likely there is to be frustration of basic needs and therefore the more likely the occurrence of revolutionary activity. While the frustration statement might be true enough, revolutionary activity is actually unlikely to take place in the most economically backward societies. As Davies notes, in such societies the physical and mental energies of people are totally occupied with the tasks of

106

merely staying alive (1970, p. 136). Starving people do not join guerrilla armies, nor can they afford to take time out to throw rocks at government officials. On the other hand, in advanced societies with considerable wealth, the great majority would not risk losing physical comfort by engaging in revolutionary activity. Therefore, it is in transitional societies that we are more apt to find the types of political strife typically subsumed under the term "revolution." It is these societies that are undergoing the socalled "revolution of rising expectations." Hence, it is in the context of transitional societies that we shall examine two alternative theoretical frameworks of revolutionary causation: the J-Curve and the U-Curve.

b) The "JCurve" and the "U-Curve" In his seminal work "Toward a Theory of Revolution," James Davies proposed a conceptual framework based on the psychological concept of rising expectation and the social variable of declining achievement (Davies, 1963). He postulated that human discontent will be intensified as one finds a growing discrepancy between his expectations, which tend to increase constantly, and one's actual achievements, which tend to lag below the expectation level. The gap between the two levels will not necessarily lead to a revolution as long as it remains within a "tolerable" range. However, when uncontrollable changes in the society, such as economic recession, cause a rapid decline in the level of one's perceived achievement, the result is a dramatic increase in the gap between expectations and achievements. When people find that the gap cannot be tolerated, a "revolutionary state of mind" emerges among members of the society, inevitably leading to an actual revolution (Figure ?). In an effort to demonstrate the applicability of the "J-Curve" theory of revolution, Davies cites three cases, including Dorr's Rebellion, the Russian Revolution, and the Egyptian Revolution of 1952.

While, as a conceptual model, this theory is both intuitively appealing and apparently rich in potential explanatory power, Davies acknowledges that his "J-Curve" model cannot explain all instances of revolution. And while he does tentatively limit its applicability to so-called "progressive revolutions," nowhere does he specify what is meant by the term progressive, nor does he examine why his theory should be limited in applicability to revolutions of this type. This limitation seems based upon commonality in the espoused goal of the three revolutions that Davies uses as test cases of his model's validity (Davies, 1971).

In order to more fully realize the explanatory potential of Davies' model, we must first specify the "type" of revolutions – in terms of the social preconditions and psychological causes – to which the Davies model is applicable. Toward this end, we shall examine the assumptions–both implicit and explicit–of his theory in order to more precisely deduce the scope of this model's empirical applicability.

Figure 1. J Curve.

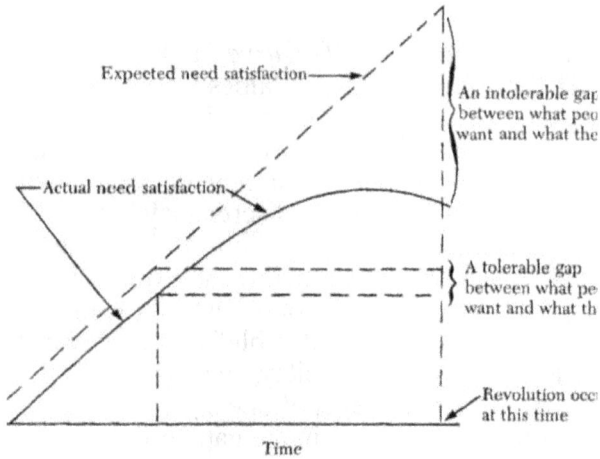

Expected need satisfaction ⟶

An intolerable gap between what peo want and what the

Actual need satisfaction

A tolerable gap between what pe want and what th

Revolution occ at this time

Time

Source: Davies 1971, p. 135

Subsequently, we shall propose an alternative explanation of the causes of revolution that, in terms of the scope of its applicability, will stand as a complement to the Davies theory. That is, rather than a denial of the Davies "Jcurve" thesis, this alternative explanatory model will be applicable to certain types of serious civil disturbances that, while definable as revolutions, are not within the empirically specified domain of the Davies model. What, then, are these assumptions, and how do they limit the applicability of the Jcurve model? As alluded to earlier, Davies' central thesis is that "revolutions are most likely to occur when a prolonged period of objective economic and social development is followed by a short period of sharp reversal" (Davies, 1971, p. 136). This proposition is deduced from the contention that the former period (of socioeconomic development) will solidify a public expectation of continued ability to satisfy their needs, even as those needs rise and expand. The frustration of these expectations that occurs in the latter period of decline will give rise to a revolutionary state of mind.

Thus, according to Davies, a certain trend in socioeconomic conditions is assumed to engender in individuals feelings of dissatisfaction and, in the absence of complete socioeconomic deprivation, collective dissatisfaction will find social expression in revolution. However, several scholars (most notably Ted Gurr[25]) have identified at least one other variable that is relevant to determining whether the dissatisfied state of mind, even when generalized into the requisite "social mood," will seek overt social expression in the form of revolutionary behavior. Even if the general state of life conditions is such that, for the population as a whole, minimum physical survival is assured, dissatisfied people are less likely to revolt if they perceive the government as having the capacity to put down the rebellion. If the probable costs of a revolution, in terms of human lives, are perceived as being extremely high, the masses may develop serious doubts about their chances for successful revolution and, consequently, not attempt such an uprising. Thus, the government's "coercive potential" is of relevance to the last link in the causal chain between the social mood of dissatisfaction and its overt expression as revolutionary behavior (Gurr, p. 1968).

A second and perhaps more crucial assumption in the Davies model is that expected need satisfaction will continue to rise even after there has been a sharp decline in the level of actual need satisfaction. The validity of this assumption is essential to the logic of the model since it is in this manner that the frustration necessary for revolution is created. Frustration is here conceived as the gap between expectations and achievement. The contention that expectation or aspiration will continue to rise even after a sharp decline in actual need satisfaction can be problematic. People might adjust the level of expectation downward in times of a sharp downturn rather than keeping the level of rising expectation. Thus the gap between achievement and expectation may not increase following a sharp decline in achievement. This view was depicted by the theory of a "U-Curve" as shown in Figure 2.

---

25 Ted Gurr's numerous works on revolutionary causation began with *Why Men Rebel* (Princeton University Press, 1970).

Figure 2. U Curve.

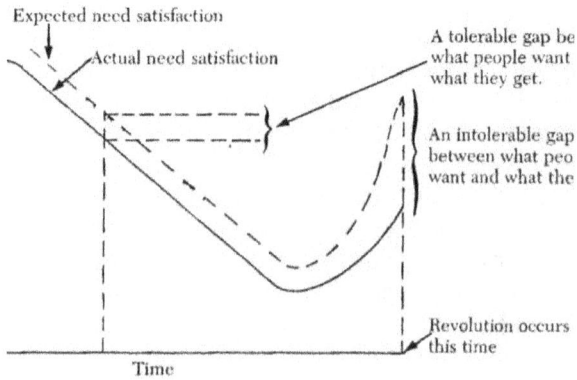

In the case of the U-Curve, the maximum level of frustration or dissatisfaction is likely to be when the downward adjustment starts to rebound following a brief period of decline. Thus, the intolerable degree of frustration and the "revolutionary mind" could be formed at this time. The downward adjustment of the aspiration level is not expected to continue if the worsening of need-satisfaction involves qualitative change in life style. For example, people may consider driving less or even switching to a smaller automobile to cope with economic downturn but they would be extremely reluctant and refuse to switch to a bicycle or walking on foot.

Putting the two curves (J and U) in the framework of our stages of development, it is obvious to suggest that if the decline in achievement threatens spiraling down to cross a line of development stage where members of the society are forced to compromise and give up what they already accomplished needs/wants satisfaction, the unacceptable "gap" may lead to a "revolutionary mind." However, if a downturn of achievement remains within a stage line, the revolutionary state of mind will not materialize as illustrated in Figure 3.

Figure 3. J and U Curves in Stages of Development.

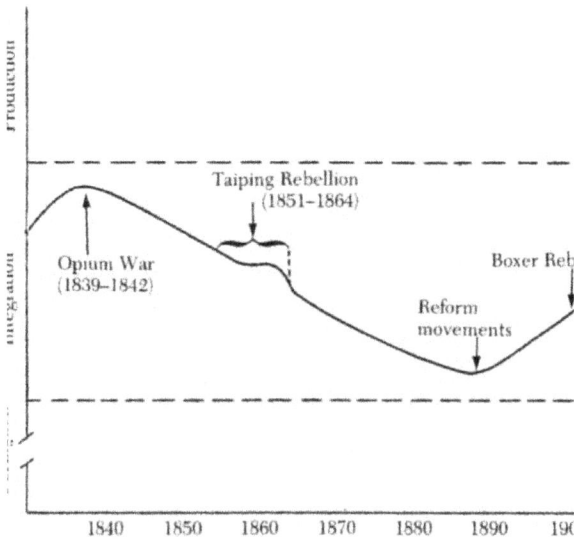

Thus far, we have discussed extensively what appear to be promising models for explaining revolutionary behaviors in various societies in differing stages of developmental change. Both the "Jcurve" and the "Ucurve" theories combine the psychological factor of aspirations and the societal dimensions of achievement. Now we will introduce another set of concepts that have been used extensively in the literature of revolution. These use the societylevel premise that revolutionary behavior originates from the actor's relationship with the society.

C) Relative Deprivation: Relative to What? While the concept of relative deprivation is germane to almost all theories of revolutionary activity, its operational definition is seldom agreed upon. Following the orthodox definition of relative deprivation found in the Marxist tradition, Davies (1959, p. 283) defines the term as "when a deprived person compares himself with a non-deprived person, the resulting state will be called 'relative deprivation.'" In this case, the person compares himself with others.

Ted Gurr (1970, p. 24), on the other hand, suggests that "relative deprivation is defined as the actor's perception of discrepancy between their value expectations and his value capabilities." Thus, one's status in the social hierarchy becomes significant.

Several meaningful definitions, each depicting important aspects of the revolutionary state of mind, deserve our attention. Analytical distinctions between these definitions and their implications for the study of revolutionary behaviors are discussed below.

C-i) Social Comparison: Marxist and NonMarxist Perceptions. As described above, relative deprivation is commonly conceived of as one person comparing his situation with that of another individual he considers to be significant in some way. Thus, a person's sense of deprivation or gratification is entirely dependent upon how he compares himself with others. Similar dynamics are implicit in Marxist theory in that the proletariat derives its sense of deprivation from observing enrichment of the bourgeoisie.

This sort of social determinism has been the foundation of Marxist and other socialist revolutions throughout the world. An application of Marxist theory to European history demonstrates how the thesis of "relative deprivation" has gained traction as the sole theoretical basis of revolution.

Among other phenomena causing extensive social change in the eighteenth and nineteenth centuries, the Industrial Revolution forced the European economic structure to undergo dramatic divisions of labor. Despite all the moral ills, including the "alienation of man from things," the new division of labor did contribute to productivity increases and eventually mass production. While this was going on, the capitalist economic system, governed by its laws of supply and demand, compelled those who did not own the means of production (the laborers) to rely totally on the mercy of those who did own and control them. Since the laws of supply and demand determine the value of commodities in capitalist economies rather than by the amount of labor invested in their production, the people who were in a position to control the means of production were able to accumulate what Marx referred to as surplus value (market value minus labor value). This unwarranted profit, according to Marx, inevitably enriches the "haves" by means of impoverishing the "have-nots." This process leads to an unbridgeable polarization of social classes. On the premise that economic structure is the basic framework that determines the nature of all other social and cultural superstructures, Marx predicted that the class polarization would necessarily lead to the development of distinct and mutually incompatible relations between the two classes. As a result, in a mature capitalist system where the "haves" are profitmotivated and the "havenots" are impoverished to the extent that they can no longer tolerate the injustice, a proletarian revolution will occur. As the iron law of history indicates, Marx was naive in believing that when such a rebellion takes place, the small number of "haves" will be helpless in defending themselves against the huge masses.

History did not follow the path of Marxist projections. In the process of modern industrialization, a large middle class emerged which did not belong to either of the two polarized classes. The social class structures in both transitional and postindustrial societies were more open to class mobility than Marx had anticipated. Also, technological development provided the oppressors, in some societies, with highly mechanized and sophisticated weapons with which they could easily suppress mass rebellions.

It would be unrealistic not to recognize the impact Marxist views have made on the course of history. Marxism and its variations have caused more revolutionary social changes throughout the world than any other single idea or theory. The Russian, Chinese, and Cuban revolutions as well as numerous rebellions in Asia, Africa, and Latin America have indeed been Marxist revolutions of sorts. Ironically, none of the revolutions occurred in a mature capitalist country, contrary to Marx's expectations. In fact, no revolution has occurred in any society as a result of capitalist maturity. However, the humanist message condemning the social and economic inequality inherent in capitalist systems appealed to "relatively deprived" masses in the underdeveloped and developing regions of Russia, China, Eastern Europe, and the Third World.

Extending the premise of "relative deprivation" by social comparison, one might attribute global insecurity and international conflict to the disparity and inequity among nations. Authors such as Johan Galtung have long adhered to the view that world peace cannot be maintained as long as we fail to bridge the gap between rich nations and poor nations. This view seems to be at least intuitively plausible and appealing when we consider two facts: (1) rich nations are maintaining their affluence in this deeply integrated global economy at the expense of poor nations who are compelled to supply raw materials and cheap labor, and (2) due to the development of worldwide communication networks and the increasing communicative capability of Less Developed Countries (LDCs), poor countries are keenly aware of their situation and are increasingly determined to protect their national interest. These factors will undoubtedly spur the sense of "relative deprivation" on the part of LDCs. In fact, the emergence of a New International Economic Order with a potentially explosive NorthSouth confrontation has just about replaced the conventional ideological axis of the EastWest competition. Revolutions in the LDCs, still poor and struggling in the Southern hemisphere, are more likely to be nationalist in their motivations and are more likely to target entities outside their domestic borders. The recent revolutionary movements in Iran, though religious in appearance, was indeed a nationalist revolutionary uprising against U.S. interventionist policies. The Maoist revolution itself, and revolutions in Southeast Asia, such as those in Vietnam and Kampuchea, can all be best characterized as nationalist movements rather than Marxist revolutions.

As evidenced in many revolutionary phenomena depicted above, the concept of relative deprivation through social comparison helps us understand many revolutionary activities in different societies. It is not only theoretically appealing but analytically very useful. However, the social comparison does not fully account for the basis of relative deprivation, as one's comparison of himself with others is not the only basis for comparison.

C-ii) Temporal Comparison: While one may feel deprived or gratified relative to other people, one also may feel deprived or gratified by comparing the present situation with a past situation. One may find it gratifying to have made a big improvement over a period of time even if one's present situation is still worse than that of others. By the same token, one could surely be unhappy and feel a deep sense of deprivation when one's present situation shows little improvement over time, even though one's situation is currently better than that of others. For this reason, steady improvement in the form of pay raises and other rewards is necessary to keep people happy and to maintain a stable political system regardless of the level of affluence in a particular society.

In a developing society where people experience rapid improvement in their lifestyle, we often find mass support for the regime based on its effective role in bringing about such improvements. This often occurs even if the people still are far from affluent and even if the regime fails to promote social and economic equality within the country. In fact, a rapidly developing transitional country with selfsustaining economic growth is most likely to have increasing disparity between the rich and the poor, and yet the regime may enjoy widespread support, as has been the case in South Korea since the 1960s. Anyone who visits China today will find the rural Chinese to be very poor, their living accommodations marginal, recreation facilities virtually nonexistent, and the mechanization of agriculture almost invisible, yet he will he struck by their genuine sense of happiness, particularly on the part of older people. It will only take a cursory conversation with a Chinese citizen to figure out why they are happy: they still remember those bad days before the revolution.

The two bases of comparison, social and temporal, are not mutually exclusive. On the contrary, one may be able to explain the revolutionary mind more completely by combining these two bases. One may compare himself with others by comparing his rate of social and economic improvement with that of others over the same period of time. For instance, the rate of pay increase might be a basis for social comparison, although the rate itself is a temporal (timeembedded) concept. This kind of comparison will expand the explanatory power of the concept of relative deprivation itself.

C-iii) Spatial Comparison: In addition to the social and temporal comparison, social psychologists, notably Brickman and Campbell (1971), introduced yet another basis of comparison that may explain some cases of relative deprivation. This kind of comparison is referred to as *spatial comparison*. In this case, one compares some areas of one's achievement with other areas of one's own achievement. Relative deprivation will result when one dimension of achievement is seriously lagging behind other achievements. For example, a welleducated American with a highly-paid and prestigious job who was somehow compelled to live in a poor housing project would feel dissatisfied due to the gap in his areas of achievements.

This basis of comparison may be particularly useful in studying the attitudes and behavior of people who have discrepancies between their achievements and ascriptive statuses, such as a racial and ethnic minority that has succeeded economically but still faces sociocultural discrimination in the United States. The status of minorities in this regard is surprisingly similar throughout the world. We find many situations analogous to the African American minority in the situations of minority nationals in China, Japan, and ethnically heterogeneous African nations.

In fact, the state of mind with respect to relative deprivation is rather complex in this case because the "spatial comparison" is often combined with the other two bases, social and temporal. Thus, a black American may find himself experiencing a perplexing mixture of relative gratification and relative deprivation: he feels gratified when he compares himself with his

115

own past, and deprived when he sees himself in spatial comparison terms. In this case, whichever may prevail in a given situation at a given time will dictate his pattern of behavior.

In this section we have discussed some bases of relative deprivation and relative gratification. We suggest that the state of mind behind rebellion is a complex thing, and numerous bases of comparison are necessary for its synthesis.

iv) The Tunnel Effect: Alternative to Relative Deprivation. In a fascinating analysis of "tolerance for income equality in the course of economic development," Albert O. Hirschman (1973) proposed a concept that questions the basic premise of relative deprivation. According to this concept called the "tunnel effect," a person may find himself happier when he sees other people making progress. Thus he will allow himself to remain behind so long as he expects that their progress will someday lead to his own improvement. To elaborate this concept further, Hirschman uses an analogy:

> Suppose that I drive through a twolane tunnel in the same direction, and run into a serious traffic jam. No car moves in either lane as far as I can see (which is not very far!). I am in the left lane and feel dejected. After a while, the cars in the right begin to move. Naturally, my spirits lift considerably for I know that the jam has been broken and that my lane's turn to move will surely come any moment now. Even though I still sit still, I feel much better off than before because of the expectation that shall soon be on the move.

The "tunnel effect" thesis seems to be particularly applicable to a society where class mobility is possible, and people are achievement oriented. If McClelland's (1961) observation is correct and people in economically developed countries are likely to be more achievement oriented than people of less developed countries, the tunnel effect thesis may be more useful in studying economically affluent nations, whereas the relative deprivation thesis would be more valid in poor countries. The transitional developing nations with a capacity for rapid economic growth are those that usually experience income inequality, however. Yet, as Hirschman observes, people in such nations tend to have a greater tolerance for inequity because of the tunnel effect. Consequently, there seem to be conflicting views as to what kind of society is more likely to be subject to the premises of the tunnel effect.

Nevertheless, the thesis of the tunnel effect offers a significant validity and explanatory utility for certain people who are achievement oriented.

In this section, we have discussed some of the social and psychological bases of revolutionary activity, and concluded that assessing the "revolutionary mind" requires a careful analysis of its referents from premises of relative deprivation and tunnel effect. The state of mind conducive to revolutionary activity is the result of an extremely complex mental process. To understand it, a genuinely interdisciplinary analysis is imperative, as the "revolutionary mind" is likely to be a product of a wide range of variables at all levels of social complexity.

Institutionalization and Cultural Formation

We have discussed that the process of regime formation can be achieved through various channels such as hereditary succession, election, military coup, and revolution. Once a regime is formed and a ruling elite is identified, the political system will undergo a process of institutionalization intended to solidify the power base. In this process, some institutions are given more emphasis than others based on the degree to which an institution is vital to generating the necessary resources and values for the survival needs of the people.

In this initial stage of development, three institutions are likely to be considered vital, and institutionalization or institutional rehabilitation will be centered on them: the agriculture, the military, and the police. They are crucially important as they generate food, protect the society from external aggression, and maintain internal stability. All other institutions such as education, the family, manufacturing, and political parties will have only secondary significance as they seem to be designed for "living well" rather than "living" itself. As we shall discuss later, different institutions will be assigned varying levels of significance (centrality) as the society makes its developmental shifts.

In the agricultural sector, one can see almost invariably the practice of land reform as early as possible after the formation of a government. This phenomenon is clearly not bound to culture or ideology. We saw a massive land reform and "land rehabilitation" after Mao's revolution in China. Japan was no exception as it introduced extensive land reforms following the Meiji Restoration. Most new nations of the Third World have introduced measures

117

intended for the redistribution of land and revitalization of land use at one time or another. Particularly when the new regime comes to power as a result of revolution, the extent of these practices will be far reaching. As these measures are intended among other things to increase agricultural productivity, there will be some attempts to induce agricultural technology. Caution will be taken, however, not to destroy the existing production mechanism. Preserving productivity is the case even under a new regime with entirely different ideologies. In China, for example, Mao and his government were determined to uproot corruptions and contradictions of the Nationalist regime and introduced land reform policies and agricultural rehabilitation measures with extreme caution. In fact, in the early phases of the new socialist regime (1949 1952), they did not introduce the ideas of collectivization and socialization. Under the slogan of Mutual Aid, which had been the practice throughout Confucian China, they emphasized the increase of production. It was not until the mid 1950s, when the Agricultural Producers Cooperatives were formed, that private land ownership was gradually replaced by collective ownership.

Considering the fact that an overwhelming majority of the population is likely to work in agriculture in this stage of development, the government cannot afford to disturb the agricultural community through land confiscation and redistribution to such an extent that production capability is impaired. Farmers and peasants are basically manual laborers, and their primary need level seldom exceeds the basic need of securing physical survival. Any drastic structural changes in the production mechanism could easily bring about a serious threat to their wellbeing. They are not expected to be ideologically oriented as long as they are struggling to feed themselves, nor are they expected to enjoy much leisure.

In such an agrarian society, people will have little exposure to the world beyond their own community. The community's authority structure is likely to be little more than an extension of that of the family itself, which is essentially parochial rather than contractual. The location of authority and responsibility is readily identifiable and each member of the community will know exactly where he or she belongs and will have no ambiguities as how to behave properly. This kind of life environment will force community members to develop submissive attitudes and learn the virtues of obedience. Challenges to superiors and even disagreement with them will be entirely unacceptable regardless of the issues involved. This absolute *obedience* is reinforced by the state and *fate accepting* agrarianism from farmers who submit themselves to the law of nature in the practice of cultivation. Their lifestyle, even their existence itself, depends entirely upon the mercy of nature.

The police, another prevalent institution in this initial stage of regime formation, would have an extensive role in maintaining the stability of the social and authority structure. In fact, in most societies at this stage of development, an individual's only contact with political authority beyond the community would be through the police distributed widely throughout the country. More police forces would be appropriated where social unrest and political dissension are most likely. In this context, the police force would be viewed as a source of sanction and will be avoided. People would be in fear of the police and would tend to comply with orders and directives given by authority. In this way, the function of the law enforcement agency goes beyond maintaining law and order; it often includes mobilization of support for the regime.

For a cultural system in which submissive and authoritarian attitudes prevail, the police institution serves as a facilitator with its authoritative method of operation. In the absence of due process, people are inclined to conform to orders, as it is certain that disputes with the police will invite trouble. The same can be said about the military. In the absence of any other large organization whose membership represents the whole society, the military institution enjoys an exclusive position in which it can mobilize the masses and exert absolute power and influence over the people. It is common in this case that the military and militarism enjoy a widespread reputation and prestige. It would be considered an honor to be able to enter the military academy and become an officer, and young people usually compete for such honors, particularly in times of peace.

Style of Politics: Rule Characteristics

People at this stage of political development will look to the government as the provider of their needs, and will give their absolute support for what it does in guaranteeing food, shelter, and security. Support for the leadership in this case is for what it does, rather than what it is. The basis of legitimacy will have little to do with values or ideologies that the government may uphold. A bowl of rice is a bowl of rice to a hungry stomach irrespective of whether it is from a collective farm or the black market. The issue of ideological legitimacy becomes trivial and largely irrelevant. The sole consideration in politics is the effective and swift delivery of the needed resources and services. Naturally, the government will be structured in such a way that decisions can be made quickly and policies implemented without delay.

No known style of politics is more effective in this regard than a centralized totalitarian form of government with a clear position of authority and responsibility in the power structure. The government will be more paternalistic and thus rule responsibly, and obedience with reverence will characterize the political dynamics. A pluralist democracy or even a bureaucratic autocracy is not likely to develop in this initial stage. As discussed earlier, institutions adopted from more advanced societies, such as electoral systems, are likely to deviate from their original functions. Notions such as interest articulation and aggregation are almost entirely alien to this stage of regime formation and politics will not be conducted based on public opinion.

Ironically, the greatest danger to this kind of regime is its own success in raising people's perception of need by satisfying the most urgent need of physical survival. On the other hand, if such a regime is incapable of becoming an effective provider, an alternative regime might be invited without changing the style of politics. The regime in this case may avoid mass starvations and absolute deprivation of human basic needs, but it typically suffers from distributive injustice and structural violence to which the masses may respond with violent means of their own. When this happens in our globalized world, foreign intervention often occurs, as seen in the Arab uprisings in Egypt, Tunisia, Syria, and other places. This further complicates the already complex political dynamics. We will address this issue later in Part Three of this book.

Chapter 7

Political Integration and the Need to Belong

The needs/wants hierarchy we postulated in Chapters 4 and 5 indicates that as soon as people find their survival needs are comfortably attained, they will shift their needs focus from survival to belonging. In order for the leadership to effectively respond to this shift of needs, it will be forced to develop new policies and institutions designed to respond to this new level of needs and demands. Not all systems are prepared to face this challenge.

In such a case, there are three alternative courses for the nation's development. First, the regime may be replaced by another via legitimate or illegitimate means. Second, the incumbent leadership may remain in power by creating a sense of emergency. This can be done either by inviting conflict with other nations or by creating lifethreatening social and economic conditions within the nation. In either case, people will be reduced to desiring nothing more than survival, and thus the regime will, at least temporarily, stave off instability caused by the rising need to belong. Third, the government can adopt or develop a political ideology under which newly emerging value orientations and existing social groups and institutions can be used as channels for socializing the populace into proregime values or orientations. When the government is capable of opting for the third course, we will witness the beginning of the second stage of the political integration paradigm.

The state of political integration, then, is characterized by the flourishing of ideas and cultural activities on the part of the masses. Often, the government finds this state of affairs detrimental to political stability, particularly to the stability of the regime itself. As we saw in the case of the Chinese "Hundred Flowers" campaign, the unfettered expression of new ideas and political views inevitably leads to criticism of the incumbent government, sometimes to the point of necessitating a forceful crackdown on dissidents. If this crackdown is sufficiently severe in its intensity and pervasive in its scope, the society may revert to a situation where people's life environments become unpredictable, and physical survival itself may be threatened. In this case, progress to the next stage of needs will be delayed.

However, the regime can be effective in persuading the masses in such a way that this flowering of cultural and social expression may remain within the boundaries of acceptable diversity. For this, the leadership will need to define the limits of such expression through its own ideographic program of political socialization or public indoctrination. This can best be achieved through the use of educational institutions and communication media as instruments of government persuasion. To effectively socialize or indoctrinate the masses, the government will need the services of intellectuals and other cultural elite groups. The ability and willingness of the ruling government to recruit and mobilize intellectuals into the mainstream of politics and decision-making is crucial to the regime's ability to survive the transitional period of political integration. If the intellectuals are not actively recruited, they may form a counterculture with a counter ideology that will pose a persistent impediment to the regime's indoctrination efforts, and therefore to its political integration strategy. Intellectuals mobilized by the regime will be expected to develop a new political ideology or to justify and elaborate one imposed upon them by the political leadership. An ideology will be defined and refined in such a way that the goal of national and political integration can be achieved most effectively. The goal here is to encompass conflicting values and belief systems into an integrated political community, one to which everyone can feel a positive sense of attachment. In this sense, their belongingness needs will be satisfied by the nature of the political sphere.

Thus, political ideologies may be viewed from the functional perspective as institutional means employed by political leadership for the purpose of politically integrating the nation and legitimizing the regime. The nature of an effective ideology will be determined by the contextual factors of the society, such as culture, social and ethnic characteristics, and level of economic development. To the extent that no societies are exactly alike in terms of their respective sociocultural and economic characteristics, the ideologies of different countries are expected to differ from one another even if they pay homage to the same intellectual ancestors. Differences in socialist ideologies manifested in Marxism, Leninism, Maoism, and Third World socialism in Africa and Latin America can best be explained by the contextual differences to which they were applied. The same can be said with respect to capitalist democracies in Europe, Japan, and smaller Third World nations such as the Philippines and South Korea. When social and economic conditions are similar, ideologies originating from different philosophical convictions may become quite similar, as we see in the socialist systems and democracies of economically underdeveloped countries.

In this chapter, we shall examine the thesis that political ideologies are intended to perform the role of legitimation and political integration, first by looking at the spectrum of ideological changes as they evolved over time, and then by comparing and contrasting some selected political ideologies witnessed in the postWorld War II period. Later in this chapter, we shall examine the nature of mass belief systems in an effort to illuminate the process by which political culture is integrated.

Ideology as Instrument

In the political integration stage, ideology emerges as an important mechanism by which the basis for mass support is generated and propagated. Ideology is especially useful when diverse and competing belief systems proliferate and political culture disintegrates, indicating a crisis of national identity and regime legitimacy. In such a context, an ideology presents the populace with a comprehensive political belief system enumerating the ultimate goals or endstates of that society and the legitimate means by which these goals can be achieved. As such, it provides the individual with a vision of his political society, his place in it, and a set of reasons why this system, and not some other, is worthy of his loyalty. It is only in this sense that we can understand why political ideologies have actually emerged at times of crisis of regime legitimacy and national identity.

Throughout the evolution of political ideologies, we have seen a number of belief systems and philosophical configurations employed by various regimes in order to legitimize certain power positions and justify the suppression of others. When possession and exercise of power needed no justification in premodern times, philosophical ideas never coalesced into a political ideology for the regime. Throughout ancient and medieval times, power was taken for granted as the possession of the ruling elite who were regarded as superior to the ruled, and thus needing no persuasion or justification for their ownership of power. The Platonic idea of the "philosopher king" was intended to define who should rule and who should be ruled. As long as the rulers showed that they were philosophers, i.e., knowledgeable, it was taken for granted that they were qualified to rule the masses. In this situation, the ruling elite do not need to worry about the legitimacy of their power.

This point was elaborated on in the discussion of the "sociology of knowledge" in Chapter 1.

With the spread of philosophical individualism and the *laissezfaire* economic doctrine, however, legitimacy based on human inequality became subject to criticism. The notion of legitimacy by the governed ascended, thus paving the way to the theory of social contract as advocated by John Locke. The emerging social contract theory became a powerful ideological doctrine embedded in classical liberalism, challenging the preceding capricious social and political order. In this sense, the emergence of liberalism was a response to the failure of medieval and early modern doctrines of human inequality as a means of legitimizing political power. Since the introduction of the social contract, political ideologies have emerged competitively, with varying perspectives as to the proper relationship between the ruler and the ruled- a question of legitimacy.

Classical liberalism, with its doctrine of civil liberties and the reinforcement of economic capitalism, advocated that the greatest collective good could be served by minimum governmental intervention in the private lives of citizens. Thus, a government that exercises the least amount of power was regarded as the best form of government. But it did not take long for the liberalists themselves to realize that freedom from governmental constraint did not necessarily make one free: in order to exercise the right of freedom, one must have the necessary resources and values with which to obtain and maintain freedom. The ensuing ideologies, under the rubric of socialism, were designed to remedy that situation which, to the growing number of impoverished people, the right to freedom meant only words written on a legal document. In this sense, the Marxist denunciation of capitalism can be viewed as a humanist effort to guarantee a better distribution of resources at the expense of property rights and freedom, if necessary. In fact, Leninist socialism called for maximum government intervention in creating and protecting resources and opportunities that the masses were lacking under a capitalist structure. The success of the Bolshevik revolution in Russia and the Maoist revolution in China can be attributed to widespread disappointment at classical liberalism's failed promises in those nations. In this sense, we can say that socialism, too, was a means for political regimes to broaden their legitimacy. The fact that Lenin's version of socialism was not consistent with orthodox Marxism was undoubtedly due to the indigenous condition of Russian agrarian feudalism that would not have been "ripe" for a Marxist proletarian revolution.

Of all variants of socialism practiced in history, Maoism has affected the most people in a profound way. Mao Zedong, unlike Karl Marx, was not a theoretician but a politician. What he needed was not a flawless theory but a workable doctrine for his attempt to win public support at a time when the existing liberal ideology was experiencing a serious crisis of public confidence. In a semifeudal, agrarian, and Confucian society, Mao's forces needed a doctrine that would accommodate the salient social and cultural features of China, yet effectively challenge the Nationalist government and its attendant ideology.

Even a cursory examination of Maoism will show that Mao's socialist ideology is fundamentally different from Marxism, and the difference can be explained by the unique nature of the Chinese social and cultural milieu, as well as by the particular economic imperatives of twentieth century China. If an ideology that does not recognize the process of class polarization and fails to take into account the centrality of class consciousness and class struggle cannot be called a Marxist ideology, then Maoism certainly is not one. Mao saw in China a diverse array of economic classes, not a simple capitalistproletariat polarity. Consequently, he sanctified the "peaceful resolution" of societal conflicts through the means of self-criticism. In this way he could broaden his base of appeal and build a revolutionary class that will be united not by its common relationship to the means of production, but by its shared opposition to the Nationalist regime. These revolutionaries intended to accommodate Chinese indigenous conditions about which Mao himself was so emphatically concerned. For the same reason, socialist leaders in the Third World, such as Sengor, were never in line with orthodox Marxism due to the semifeudal social system, colored by colonial experiences, in which they operated.

Tracing the ideological spectrum in the liberal tradition will also lead us to conclude that political democracies have exhibited a variety of belief systems and policy priorities. Democracy in America today is clearly different from what the Founding Fathers once envisioned, especially in the explosive growth of federal power and welfare policies. Smaller democracies around the world have shown a number of deviations from the classical liberal tradition, as we have witnessed in Sukarno's "guided democracy," Marcos' controlled system, South Korea's oppressive regimes, and many other systems where social and political stability is constantly threatened. In accounting for the economic boom of the Asian Tigers, the key is "state capitalism," which is far removed from liberal democracy.

The repeated failure of nonwestern democracies, with political institutions originally developed in western industrial societies, has led serious students of social change to question the applicability of democratic institutions to those foreign lands. The general view is that political ideology, like any other institution, cannot be transplanted without modifications and, often, drastic changes. This is due to the fact that political ideologies are intended to be useful to the regime in its effort to generate popular support, and this effort will not be effective unless these ideologies address real needs in the indigenous social and cultural context. In this sense, we might conclude that political ideology is not a commodity that can simply be imported from foreign countries.

Contextual Correlates of Ideology: Conditions for Democracy, Autocracy, and Communism

Some societies are more successful with any given ideology, such as democracy, than others, implying that there might be a set of socioeconomic and cultural characteristics that are more conducive to that ideology. In fact, several major studies have been done on the very question of "requisites" for democracy. If a political system is going to achieve the goal of political integration, based on the attainment of ideological consensus, it is essential for the regime to have some knowledge of the conditions and correlates of the particular ideology that will be used by the regime in its efforts to integrate the political culture.

On conditions for democracy, a number of studies have advanced with empirical documentation a set of such conditions. Since Lipset's pioneering work, "Some Social Requisites of Democracy," numerous studies have inquired into the role of socioeconomic development in democratic performance.[26] While some studies, such as Neubauer's and Jackman's, questioned the validity of the theory that democracy has a certain prerequisite level of socioeconomic development, most studies appear to at least suggest a positive association between the indicators of democracy and those of socioeconomic development. These earlier studies of democracy led to a set of conclusions with regard to conditions for liberal democracy, and they include the following:

---

26 Seymour Lipset, "Some Social Requisites of Democracy," *The American Political Science Review*, Vol. 53, No. 1 (1958), pp. 69-105

- Advanced level of economic growth facilitates democracy (Lipset, Cutright, Neubauer)[27];

- The rate or pace of economic and social change is negatively associated with democracy (Park)[28];

- Advanced level of education is needed for democracy (Lipset, Neubauer);

- Urbanization is positively associated with democracy (Lipset);

- Industrialization is positively associated with democracy (Lipset, Cutright)

- Civil society leads to vibrant democracy (Verba)[29];

- Stable society is necessary for democracy;

- Some cultural attributes are conducive to democracy, including civic culture (Verba), achievement orientation (McClelland), mobile personality (Lerner), and empathy.

Yet, in contemporary democracies, especially in the United States and Western European systems, the idea of liberal democracy is not closely consistent with the reality. It is the idea of participatory democracy that carries greater validity, and needs greater attention.

What Makes Participatory Democracy Work?

We conceptualized democracy in terms of "governmentbythepeople" and the mutual adjustment policymaking mechanism. Thus, democracy is characterized in terms of certain behavioral attributes. To the extent that behavior can be explained by contextual factors, we see some validity in the relationship between socioeconomic conditions and the behaviorallydefined concept of democracy. As a way

---

27 For Neubauer and Jackman's findings, see Deane D. Neubauer, "Some Conditions of Democracy," *The American Political Science Review*, Vol. 61, No. 4 (1967), pp. 1002-1009.

28 Han S. Park, "Socio-Economic Development and Democratic Performance," *International Review of Modern Sociology*, Vol. 6, No. 2

29 Sidney Verba and Norman Nie (1972), pp. 125-137

of establishing the analytical context in which socioeconomic conditions may be assessed, we will formulate a conceptual framework within which we can account for the phenomenon of participatory democracy. Political participation may be viewed as a direct consequence of citizens' attitudes and the "behavioral context," both of which are affected in turn by the contextual conditions subsumed by the socioeconomic variable. Most scholars agree that for participatory and competitive attitudes to emerge in a people's political life, the citizens need to be politically motivated and feel efficacious in the political realm. We could also argue that, since we define democracy in terms of participation and mutual adjustment policymaking mechanisms, the cognitive capacity and rationality of the citizens should be included as an essential factor in a democracy.

a) Democratic Personality:

Democracy can best be characterized by the process in which political decisions are made through the decisionmaking mechanism of mutual adjustment, and political legitimacy is based strictly on the contractual right by which the government is expected to represent the will of the people and to comply fully with their articulated and aggregated demands. In this, we are assuming a great deal of capability on the part of the people in that they should be capable of defining their demands and of directing such demands to the government in exchange for their support of the regime.[11] Thus, a democratic actor needs to be receptive to and provided with political information relevant to his position and role in the political system. In this, education contributes decisively to the formation and development of such political attitudes necessary for political participation, particularly those of political efficacy and civic responsibility.

It is an established fact that persons with a high level of education are more likely to be politically efficacious than persons with less education. This has been confirmed in virtually all countries studied so far, with the exception of some cases where highly-educated persons have developed cynical attitudes about their potential for political influence, becoming more apathetic than efficacious.[12] Persons with poor education, particularly rural residents, tend to be more politically passive. Furthermore, an educated person is believed to be openminded and to have the ability to systematically organize his opinions, and thus is more capable of articulating his demands. A person with these characteristics, essential to the "democratic personality," appears to be more active in group endeavors which, in turn, increase his motivation to become involved in political affairs in general.

For these reasons, it is essential for a democratic system to have a population that is well educated, and, as a result, imbued with the democratic personality traits needed for effective political participation.

Once we have met the cultural requirement for fostering "democratic personality," we can say that the most salient precondition for a viable democratic system has been met. However, even if you have the desire and propensity to have democracy, other factors are necessary for the realization of such desires. Some of these factors might be identified when we define the democratic process as a choicemaking process.

Once we define democratic processes as participation or choice-making behavior, we need to ask the question of what it takes to make a rational choice. Choicemaking of any kind has a set of requisites necessary for such behavior that include a "rational mind," the presence of alternatives, the availability of information about the alternatives, and preference ordering on the part of the choicemaker.[14] These factors necessary for choice making should likewise be present for a participatory form of politics. We shall discuss the implications and significance of each of these properties as we attempt to specify the conditions conducive to the adoption of democracy.

b) Rational Mind:

This notion of rationality is derived from the field of political economy and was adopted by Anthony Downs for an analysis of choice making behavior in democracy.[30] Downs, inferring from Arrow's earlier work, *Social Choice and Individual Values*, defines rational man as one who behaves as follows: (1) he can always make a decision when confronted with a range of alternatives; (2) he ranks all the alternatives facing him in order of his preference in such a way that each is either preferable to, as desirable as, or inferior to each other alternative; (3) his preference ranking is transitive; (4) he always chooses from among the possible alternatives the one that ranks highest in his preference ordering;

---

30 For an earlier statement of this notion of rationality, see Milton Freeman "The Methodology of Positive Economics," *Essays in Positive Ecominics*(Chicago: University of Chicago Press, 1953).

and (5) he always makes the same decision each time he is confronted under the same conditions with the same alternatives.[31]

As the definition clearly implies, a rational man is one who knows what is good for him and behaves in such a way as to maximize his interest. This would mean that democracy requires its citizens to be what may be called "economic actors." For this, we might assume that the market economy would be conducive to the development of such an "economic mind" and rationality. In a market situation, one is expected to be a bargainer in that one wants to pay less for more. Furthermore, the purchaser is likely to be provided with alternatives from which to choose, and the very presence of alternatives will enhance his bargaining strength and the desire to make the best deal. The seller's position is exactly the same as the purchaser in that the former's bargaining strength will be enhanced when more buyers compete with each other to buy from him.

As we can assume that the market situation is characterized by a choice making mechanism, we could contend that a democracy will enhance its chances for success when a market economy prevails in the economic system of the society. Here, we must emphatically point out that it is the functioning of a marketbased economic structure and the related social phenomena that is helpful for the growth of democracy and not industrialization itself, even though the latter is usually accompanied by the former. The apparent association between industrialization and democracy that we presented earlier might be attributed to the fact that industrialized societies happen to more frequently exhibit the kind of economic and social structures subsumed by the concept of a market economy. If a society can retain an agricultural economy while manifesting a sound marketbased economic system, it could certainly develop the type of social and cultural environment conducive to democratic development.

c) The Presence of Possible Alternatives:

When a political actor participates in the process of politics, either in the direct form of participation (election) or in an indirect way through interest group or political party activities, he is essentially expected to make choices from alternatives. The alternatives may be in the form of candidates, issues, or parties. Without the presence of alternatives for the choice maker, his decision cannot be called choicemaking. Thus a clear distinction

---

31 Anthony Downs (1957), p.7

between alternatives and the presence of a wide range of alternatives are features essential to choicemaking behavior.

Studies on participation have presented substantial evidence as to the facilitating role of the presence of alternatives and clear distinctions between them in increasing participatory behavior. As Milbrath and others have long held, "people are more likely to turn out for an election when clear differences are perceived than when alternatives are unclear."[32] This phenomenon may be attributed to the fact that when the alternatives are clear, the costs of collecting information and making decisions are reduced.

This phenomenon seems to suggest that the presence of alternative parties and competing candidates is needed for participatory democracy. Thus, discouraging the growth of a competitive party system and political competition between individuals and groups would be detrimental to democratic development.

d) Information Availability:

As alluded to earlier, for one to make rational decisions, the choice maker should have all possible information about the available alternatives in order to make a comparative assessment of them.[18] Political parties should fully communicate their policy positions and candidates should provide the citizens with information concerning their positions on policy areas as well as other pertinent issues. This would suggest that a fully functional mass communication system might be essential to a democratic society. It is in this sense that we could rationalize the empirical studies in which a high degree of association was established between democratic performance and communications development. It also suggests that freedom of communication needs to be maximized.

e) Cognitive Capacity (Political Sophistication) of the Citizens:

Even if there is a widespread mass communication network and guaranteed freedom of communication, participatory democracy will not be facilitated by this if the people are not capable of comprehending political communications. The degree to which a person is capable of political communication depends on two actors: cognitive capacity and the complexity of political issues. A person's cognitive capacity is believed to be enhanced by education.

---

32 Milbrath, Op. Cit., p.105.

Education, here, is expected to provide him with not only new information but also the ability to evaluate issues and events and to think logically.[19] The high association between educational attainment and political democracy that was found by the empirical studies discussed in this chapter is naturally to be expected when we conceive of the function of education in this way.

Perhaps one of the gravest problems with contemporary democracy is the fact that all societies are facing increasingly complex social and political issues. Furthermore, most of these issues can have a multiplicity of alleged solutions, and the public is likely to be either deceived or blindfolded with respect to which solution is best. It is in terms of this complexity of issues and problems that political power everywhere becomes more and more centralized, and the public gradually more alienated from the process. Some critics of contemporary society have even coined an alternative concept to democracy that they cynically refer to as "technocracy." Thus, for the public to comprehend political issues, the issues need to be clearly interpreted by the government as well as by the mass media.

f) Allocation of Values Over Production of Values:

The democratic process is not very efficient. It is a process designed to produce an optimal level of popular satisfaction in which every individual is reasonably content rather than to produce the maximum outputs on the part of the total community. As such, democracy will be more functional in a society where there are sufficient values and resources to be made available to its members. However, in a society marked by scarcity, the expectations of maximum production tend to generate public support for the efficiencies of centralized control, and some sort of socialist form of economic structure is likely to emerge. Thus, socialism is often regarded as a preferable ideology for planning and implementing developmental programs in economically underdeveloped nations.

However, as a society attains sufficient resources for its citizens to maintain leisurely living, socialist arrangements will experience serious setbacks due to the increasing desire of the public to own private property and maintain an unconstrained (by government) lifestyle. This development may have explanatory persuasiveness for the demise of the socialist bloc following the collapse of the Soviet Union itself in the 1980s.

Autocracy or Illiberal Democracy

Autocracies come in a number of different forms, but they all share one trait: they do not rule by people's participation and consent. A participatory democracy is not expected to be formed in this political integration stage because the people and the society would not be equipped with the necessary conditions for democracy as discussed previously. On the contrary, a political system that has just achieved a stable, secure society with the provision of food and shelter for the masses is likely to be still struggling with wide-spread illiteracy, absence of civic culture and civil society, and potential political unrest, thus lacking every condition that is viewed a requisite for democracy. This environment is ripe for and can easily be subsumed under autocratic rule.

An autocratic or dictatorial system is likely to emerge when the requisite conditions for democracy discussed above are absent or inadequately presented. As people living in a life-threatening environment with shortages of food and unstable security conditions are likely to be authoritarian and submissive in their political propensity, the institution of democracy in such a life environment such as electoral system is not going to work as it should in a more developed society. Even with proper education, the electorate can be more authoritarian and submissive in some countries than others depending on the more salient context of certain civilizations and religions. When a large proportion of the people are unable or disinclined to acquire "democratic personality", such a system can struggle with democratic political system. By the same token, when the electorate is under-educated, unable to comprehend political information, and unable to make rational choices, such a system will also find itself struggling with the institution of participatory democracy. As the United States and Western systems have attempted to transplant their institution of liberal democracy in the social and cultural context that is unprepared for democracy, the institution is likely to become illiberal and autocratic. There were a great many such systems in the Third World during the Cold War era ranging from Marcos of the Philippines to Hussein of Iraq. Almost all "democracies" with the electoral system in the underdeveloped world are illiberal democracies.

Can illiberal democracy be called a variation of democracy? It certainly cannot be called participatory democracy or government by the people. But one can postulate that, as long as benevolent dictatorship may be seen as a form of government FOR the people, illiberal democracy could also be a form of democracy. That is why Communist China calls itself the People's **Democracy** and even North Korea is named as the **Democratic** People's Republic of Korea. Are we willing to stretch the meaning of democracy that far? If not, one should refine the meaning of liberal democracy as governance **by** the people.

Paternalism

Of illiberal systems, there is a unique variation that may be called the paternalist system as evidenced by Mao's China, Ho Ji Min's Vietnam, and Kim Il Song's North Korea. The leader of a paternalist system attains an absolute charisma comparable to the benevolent father of a family in a traditional society. In fact, each of them has been referred to as "the father" by the people. The relationship between the leader and his people is seldom perceived as being contractual but natural. The farther can make mistakes but his "fatherhood" will remain. Mao was such a figure, and is still regarded as the "founding father" of the nation. Kim Il Sung was such a leader. When this happens within the civilizational context of Confucianism, the institution of family is so central that loyalty to the father and the family is regarded as more important and more virtuous that loyalty to the state. The father is not only a source of authority and power but is burdened by heavy obligations to protect, educate, and show loving care to the rest of the family. He is expected to be a role model for the children. They are and should be differentiated from typical autocratic dictators like Saddam Hussein of Iraq, Ghaddaffi of Libya, and Chacesque of Rumania. We might note that neither Mao nor Kim nor their family members nor relatives have been found guilty for crimes of smuggling national treasures out of the country for personal gains at the expense of the people. These paternalistic leaders are respected, revered, and loved by the people. North Korea represents a truly intriguing case where the paternalist system has continued through generations.[33] Until Western scholars and leaders succeed in comprehending the paternalist nature of North Korea, the handling of that country's nuclear conundrum is not likely to be resolved.

---

33 For an insight into this aspect of North Korean system, refer to Han S. Park (2002 and 2012)

Communism

A communist system is a system that does not allow private ownership of any kind; everything belongs to the collective community so as to guarantee absolute equality by the same zero ownership by each and every member of the community. This ideal is appealing to a society that is radically impoverished where any degree of skewed or unequal distribution could invite mass starvation and deaths. The Marxist dictum of "distribution by need" was designed to ensure the optimal chance for maximum number of members of the community to sustain their physical survival. Historically, poverty has been the nourishing ground for communist revolution and communist rule in many countries including China, Vietnam, and Kampuchea. However, when a country gets out of the state of absolute poverty and the people begin to seek economic prosperity, a normal communist system will lose its authority and power.

If and when communism is combined with paternalism, the system and leadership can be uncommonly stable as evidenced by China, Vietnam, and now North Korea. One should realize that there is a close affinity between paternalism and communism in that both institutions are built on collectivism and they defy contractual relationship and private ownership.

Thus far in this chapter, we have discussed the nature and types of ideology and the contextual conditions that are conducive to the realization of various ideologies. Each of the ideologies does have a system of norms, values, and beliefs, but the fact that all the ideologies have been the instrumental means to help the system and leadership to legitimize power remains constant.

Institutional Development

Once a new regime is in command and the members of the society are sufficiently certain of its institutions' capacity to provide the basic need of physical security, their need level shifts to that of belonging. This necessitates a new emphasis on social institutions such as the family, churches, local communitybased group affiliations, and educational systems that function as mechanisms for the individual's gratification of these needs on a more intimate facetoface basis.

As the initial need of physical survival might still be on the minds of many people, even if the level of urgency has subsided to the extent that they now are predisposed to the belonging need, the institutions of agriculture, police, and military remain of central importance to the community. However, these institutions will expand their functions to include activities that might promote a sense of belonging and mutual affiliation. At the same time, as pointed out above, a series of other institutions intended for generating the belonging need will attain saliency in the community. More often than not, the second stage institutions will gradually take over the functions of the first-stage institutions, creating a phenomenon of institutional malfunction, thus changing all institutions in their functional boundaries.

The family, for example, which developed an extended family structure, as discussed in the previous chapter, for the necessity of securing household labor power, is now becoming a community social unit while still performing the same economic function of agricultural production. Thus, the meaning of the extended family system has changed from an economic unit to a social unit. There will be more cultural and social activities that the family could not afford in the initial stage. There will be more emphasis on mores, customs, and norms without which family bonds may be weakened as the old basis of economic necessity is felt as being less than imminent.

The other two institutions, the police and the military, will also modify their roles significantly and in an expected direction. When a regime seeks to prolong its power incumbency, as it usually does, the police will become an agent of the incumbent leadership in its effort to gain the support of the masses. It is well documented that voters in underdeveloped countries have often been subjected to political mobilization by agents of the regime. Often it is the police force that becomes the effective "campaigner," as we can easily see in numerous autocratic democracies in Africa, Asia, and Latin America. In this stage, the military itself often becomes massively politicized and is utilized as an agent for the indoctrination of the masses. Even a cursory examination of the role of the Red Army in the course of socialist national integration will testify to the political role of the army, once national security is sufficiently assured.

Education is an institution whose primary function is to help people expand their knowledge, skills, and social frame of reference so that they can establish a broader and richer context in which to seek out and establish their social affiliations and, hence, satisfy their belonging needs. Students meet other students and later become members of alumni groups. Furthermore, they learn ideas and beliefs with which their value positions can be defined, thus providing ideological affiliations. They also learn about other people, thinkers, philosophers, and leaders, and establish intellectual and philosophical associations that will help them promote their sense of belonging. At this stage these types of intellectual affiliations might be more salient than many other more physically proximate facetoface associations.

In this sense, it is expected that educational curricula in preindustrial societies will emphasize liberal arts and philosophy rather than science and technology. When we examine countries that have undergone the stage of political integration, such as the United States and Japan, we can easily observe that liberal arts and philosophical fields had their heydays in the preindustrial times of the American postcivil war and the preMeiji Japan. Many Third World countries such as Mexico, Israel, the Philippines, and Korea have consistently demonstrated that liberal arts education has been given greater emphasis at times of nation building and political integration and has weakened in the process of industrialization.

The concept of compulsory citizen education will be introduced and implemented, as it presents the regime with an opportunity for political socialization. In fact, at this level of development, the government not only makes public education compulsory but it often dictates educational curricula with uniform official textbooks and other curriculum requirements. Politicization of education is seldom viewed as improper; the appearance of politicians on campuses is even fashionable and schools often compete to invite political leaders to their campuses. Students are also frequently mobilized by the government for political rallies and demonstrations, although antigovernment demonstrations are not infrequent when the government fails to satisfy them. In any case, education in the second stage of social development becomes highly politicized and students become highly political.

The phenomenon of student politicization leads to an active role for students in the process of political change. In the absence of largescale organizations and mass media in many preindustrial societies, students as a group can be very effective in aggregating public opinion and mobilizing mass movements. We have seen many instances of studentengineered political turmoil and regime turnover in places such as Turkey, South Korea, the Philippines, Mexico, and Iran.

As an ultimate source of psychological belonging, religious institutions will be more meaningful to the seeker of belonging. At the same time, the ruling elite will see the utility of harnessing religious institutions for the task of regime legitimation and political integration. It is for this reason that the notion of state religion as an officially approved religion has been quite prevalent in the course of nation building in virtually every country, be it in the form of Christianity, Islam, or MarxismLeninism. This assessment of religions is not meant to undermine the theological importance of particular religions to various individuals, but rather to illuminate the commonality of the social and political functions of religion as a human institution. No one can deny the massive political and military role of the church in medieval Europe and in contemporary Middle East as well as in Japan. Perhaps more wars have been fought in the name of God and more bloodshed has been justified by the Church than for any other reason. The "militaryreligious complex" has often provided massive forces for a "just" destruction of political enemies, defined publicly as religious heretics. Furthermore, religion can be an integral part of education itself as the "school prayer" was a legitimate function of education in the United States. Many Third World societies at this level of development tolerate extensive interplay between education and religion.

Cultural Change and Behavioral Dispositions

As members of the society experience a series of institutional changes and as their behavior is altered with these changes, new value systems and behavioral predispositions will develop. We have pointed out that through the institutions of agriculture, military, and police, the regime formation stage facilitates such value orientations as authoritarianism, submission to external forces, and fateaccepting norms, as opposed to egalitarianism and selfdetermination. However, in the course of the second stage of development, we might expect the emergence of a new set of values and norms that may well be considered to be the antitheses of the value sets engendered in the regime formation stage.

Groupism or Collectivism:

The very desire to belong implants the importance of group membership in the minds of people. They desire to identify with other people who share common views, goals, or simply achievement orientation or ascription attributes. Family and ethnic groups maintain internal homogeneity in terms of the common ascriptive attributes of their members. Alumni groups and other educational organizations provide the members with common achievement attributes. Cultural groups may have common orientations and values. Religious organizations unite their members with common spiritual perspectives and worldviews. The belonging experience is a sharing experience; it is an experience in which one projects oneself into others. Thus, one will be inclined to be more empathetic toward other people. One will think in terms of "us versus them" rather than "I versus you," the latter having been a prevalent orientation in the survival stage.

This group orientation makes people easily susceptible to political socialization and ideological indoctrination. Ideologies that emphasize collectivism, such as socialism and communism, are usually more appealing to people at this stage of development, as newly independent nations of the Third World have demonstrated.

Altruism:

Relatively speaking, the regimeformation stage marks the height of hedonistic individualism, at least in the sense that Hobbes and Machiavelli once envisioned in the context of transitional periods of turmoil that accompanied political change. By contrast, the second stage is characterized by the growth of altruism. The three main institutions -- the family, school, and church - uphold the virtue of altruism. Uncalculated sacrifice within the family is always considered virtuous, regardless of structural characteristics of that institution. No religion will advocate hedonistic selfishness in the religious socialization of its members, although not every religion will sanctify nondiscriminatory love and understanding. The same can be said with respect to educational institutions.

In fact, in this stage of development, individuals become virtuous by sacrificing their personal interests, including even their lives, for the wellbeing of their associated groups. It is not unusual to place the highest respect in human sacrifice and martyrdom for religious persuasions and ideological convictions. Such acts are regarded as the ultimate manifestation of altruism. A comparative study of religious life in societies experiencing different levels of social development will most probably show the pervasiveness of the sacrificial virtue at this stage.

Egalitarianism:

Another norm expected to develop in this political integration stage is egalitarianism. As in the case of altruism, the egalitarian orientation also represents a sharp contrast to the submissiveauthoritarianism of the first stage society.

As public education spreads, more pupils will be subjected to a new social context in which every one is presumably viewed in terms of "fellows," irrespective of their family background. Children use the same facilities, study the same material, eat the same food, and spend the same amount of time at school. This is a remarkable experience for those who have been subjected to social inequality, authoritarianism, and the capriciousness of the social order in the first stage. This explains at least in part the almost fashionable phenomenon of student demonstrations against the social and political establishment in societies where such an establishment is still autocratic and authoritarian. This explains at least in part why a majority of college students in Japan are attracted to socialist ideas while they are on campus, only to become assimilated into the establishment itself after graduation. It also helps explain why socialist movements in China, Germany, Japan, India, Pakistan, Great Britain, and the United States are started by college students. They are the ones who see the discrepancy between what they learn and experience on campus and what they see in the community. What they learn and experience is shockingly egalitarian and leads them toward socialist ideas.

Idealism:

As religion provides one with transcendental experience, and education fosters abstract thinking, people in this stage become more metaphysically oriented in their thinking, especially in comparison to their cognitive orientation in the first stage. Particularly when philosophical education and liberal arts and humanities are emphasized as much as they are in this integration stage, members of the community are expected to become idealistic in their attitudes and values. Indeed, those who are more idealistic and philosophical tend to enjoy a prestigious reputation in the cultural system, as witnessed in the relatively high social position of intellectuals in this stage. "The learned" in such a society refers to intellectuals with ideas rather than the scientists with technologies. The ageold Confucian ideas in which people who work with their minds have always been regarded as superior to those who labor with their hands should be understood in light of this perspective of the sociology of knowledge. An examination of intellectuals in the postindustrial societies of Japan and the United States will reveal the trend that the reputations of

140

intellectuals in the humanities and philosophy have progressively diminished as societies transition from the integration stage to the industrial stage.

This second-stage idealism, however, prompts people to orient toward political ideologies, and behavior is dictated by ideological persuasions rather than pragmatic interests.

Universalism:

As Talcott Parsons correctly juxtaposed in his "pattern variables", value systems in more primitive societies tend to be universalistic rather than specific, indicating that people at this early stage of social development are inclined to maintain synoptic views of the world. When they assess an object or a person, they think in simple terms of good or bad rather than being able to clinically examine both good and bad aspects. This is attributable in part to the excessive ideological orientation of their value systems and attitudes in this stage. Universalism combined with idealism will lead the actor to exhibit extreme forms of behavior, seeking 'all or none" without compromise.

Furthermore, people who seek belongingness are afraid of being isolated or alienated. They want to be in the mainstream of society. This tendency would discourage the development of minority group based identity and a pluralistic style of politics, as we will discuss later. Decisions in the group setting are most likely to be made by the convention of unanimity rather than the majority rule; unanimity is created by the predominance of the need to conform for gaining a sense of belonging.

With these attitudinal and behavioral dispositions, government and politics will exhibit a new set of styles different from the initial stage of regime formation. I shall discuss some prevalent political characteristics in the following section.

Rule Characteristics

Charismatic Leadership:

Most societies experiencing the diversification of ideas and views on public issues at this stage of development tend to be unstable, as the sheer coercive capability of the first stage regime is not capable of accommodating the newly emergent need of belonging. Some societies have managed to avoid the dissolution of the regime through the charismatic qualities of their leaders. Here, the masses will render uncalculated support and loyalty to the regime, personified in the public perception of the charismatic leader.

Charismatic leaders have emerged in many societies that have gone through a period of colonialism and the struggle for national independence. Most charismatic leaders were people who had been known as heroes to the masses for their leadership in independence or revolutionary movements. In this sense, we can say that charisma is born in times of national crisis. Thus, efforts to generate charisma for a leader in times of peace and prosperity are doomed to fail. By the same token, we can say that charismatic leadership cannot be inherited from parent to child.

Under a charismatic leader, the leadership style is expected to be that of mass leadership, prohibiting the development of an entrenched bureaucracy or any other form of intermediary power groups. In fact, for the sake of solidifying and stabilizing his power base, a strong leader will not promote or encourage any other leadership. Indeed, a successor to a charismatic leader will not likely be designated before his or her death. As a result, a period of extreme turmoil will often follow the death of such a leader, usually culminating in collective leadership.

Doctrines and Extremism:

As expected in this stage of political integration where ideologies are extensively utilized for power consolidation, politicians will associate themselves with legitimizing doctrines. Policies with strong ideological objectives will be formulated and implemented, which sometimes may be counterproductive for practical purposes. Power conflict is to be maintained in terms of ideological confrontations. Social and political organizations will likely be justified in terms of ideas and values. In fact, people with stronger value positions will be more likely to be leaders of various organizations and institutions.

When politics is guided by ideological considerations, it will become more oriented to the extreme rather than to compromise. Sometimes, violent means are employed to convey political views. Mass demonstrations are often mobilized by politicians and the government for political purposes. Under these conditions, the

142

presence of divergent political groups will most probably lead to social turmoil and instability, resulting in either a repressive dictatorship or continuous political instability inviting successive regime turnovers. If a charismatic leader emerges, the society is likely to have a repressive dictatorship. If not, it is headed toward the vicious cycle of military coups.

Thus, when a society has builtin social and cultural diversity and pluralism, the political task of achieving national integration is most demanding and difficult. However, when integrated social and cultural forces are already present in the society, this second stage of political integration can be expeditiously achieved. Japanese nationalism and the Shinto culture made Japan's postwar integration rather easy, even with a foreign ideology at its base. By contrast, the Indian case represents a situation where indigenous social and cultural conditions are not conducive to national integration, even with a longer period of political socialization with a similar political ideology.

Politicization of the Public:

For the purpose of legitimizing leadership, the government needs to facilitate the political education of the masses through various mechanisms. For one thing, it will expand the public school system and ensure that children get the necessary ideological education, endorsing the ruling elite and their official doctrines. The government usually writes textbooks for all public schools in the country. When regimes change, the new leadership customarily rewrites textbooks that may be pertinent to ideological education. We see this in changing societies such as China, where there were sharp contrasts in the content of public education before, during, and after the Cultural Revolution.

Also, the regime will attempt to censor and control mass media to ensure that only the "right" information is promulgated to the masses. Surveillance and intelligence activities will be stepped up, and possibly among the public widespread fear of government sanctions will become an effective instrument for maintaining order and stability. Because the role of intellectuals is vital to successful politicization, the regime will attempt to gain the support of intellectuals, particularly wellrespected national spiritual leaders. If intellectuals are not readily manipulated, they can be subjected to harassment or subtle pressure.

However, mass culture at this point is more sympathetic to intellectuals, and the suppression of intellectuals can generate massive disenchantment with the regime. Thus, the government can face a serious legitimacy crisis when its policy toward intellectuals fails.

Mass Participation:

As a result of increasing politicization of the public, levels of political participation can be extremely high in preindustrial societies as witnessed in Third World democracies such as the Philippines, South Korea, Mexico, and India. These Third World nations have consistently recorded high participation rates in public elections and other forms of participatory mechanisms, considerably higher than their industrial counterparts in the United States, Great Britain, Canada, and West Germany.

There may be different explanations for active political participation on the part of people in preindustrialized societies, but the fact that they do participate more actively than industrial citizens remains undisputed. In explaining this phenomenon, some suggest that people in underdeveloped societies, especially those in the lower socioeconomic stratum, are easily mobilized by the incumbent regime in its effort to generate mass support. Others maintain that there are unique social and cultural characteristics that prompt the masses to invoke greater political interest in politics. The inference here affirms both of these explanations, as we maintain that people in this second stage of development are being actively politicized and they have the predisposition to be indoctrinated readily. They become more politically oriented and thus participate more actively. At the same time, the government's efforts to mobilize their support can be effective in the context of the hyperpoliticized culture.

In short, based on the assumption of this present paradigm that people's needs shift from survival to belongingness when they are assured of their physical subsistence, we have discussed a series of new developments in a successful regime. Among them is the emergence of political ideology as a vital institution for the regimes seeking to legitimize the power base and establish political consolidation at a time when the masses are more inclined to seek associations with one another. Whether the regime is going to stay in power will largely depend on its ability to integrate the political community without causing serious dissatisfaction on the part of belongingnessseeking masses. In order to analyze the process of political integration, we suggested that understanding the nature of mass belief systems is essential. Further, we attempted to investigate the structure of mass belief systems when we generated a sixteenfold typology of belief systems. With the typology we might be able to assess the extent to which a nation is culturally integrated and to be able to compare different political communities in terms of mass belief systems.

In this chapter, we also examined the likely direction in which institutional changes may occur, particularly in the form of new emphasis on socialization agents such as family, education, and religious institutions. Finally, we observed that a series of sequential cultural changes and evolutions in political styles might follow. On the whole, the process of political integration will mark a style of politics markedly different from the initial stage of regime formation.

Chapter 8

Leisure Need and Resource Expansion

As observed thus far, the structure of human needs is such that when people are assured of physical survival and of sufficient levels of psychological and social belonging, the need for leisure will emerge as the most imminent need in determining their patterns of behavior. In this chapter, I shall examine the structure of leisure itself as a psychological and sociological concept. Subsequently, I shall elaborate on the thesis that industrialization was initially instigated and has since been advanced because of the human desire for leisure. Finally, the impact of industrialization on cultural and social change will be closely examined.

The Psychology and Sociology of Leisure

"I never met a blacksmith who loved his anvil."

Kurt Vonnegut

Though there is some question as to whether man has the inherent desire to work, human history tells us that his more consistent desire has been to avoid work rather than to look for more.[34] Worker demands for longer vacations and fewer working hours in all societies are unmistakable indicators of the human desire for more leisure time. This is not to suggest that a person without work is in an ideal situation. What is being suggested here is that it is not work itself that one desires when and if one does work. Rather, it is what work brings to the individual by

---

34 To the Greeks, leisure was concerned with those activities that were worthy of a free man, activities we might today call "culture." Work, on the other hand, as an instrumental and productive activity, was regarded as below the dignity of free man. Since then, the work ethic may have changed significantly but the unmistakable fact is that it is leisure, not work, that man has sought and largely earned in the course of human history. For a concise discussion on this thesis, see Bennett M. Berger, "The Sociology of Leisure," in Industrial Relations, Vol. 1, No. 2, February 1962.

way of securing survival and social belonging that is the source of his motivation.

The needs for physical survival and social belonging may be more urgent and basic than the leisure need; thus, the former are expected to be pursued at the expense of the latter if necessary. In any event, the present analysis is based on the assumption that man pursues leisure as soon as he is assured of more basic needs, and that this characteristic in human beings may well be universal and unrestricted by cultural norms, ideologies, or social differences. As discussed in Chapter 5, the desire to play with toys on the part of a growing child is a universal indication that leisure is an inherent desire of any ordinary person. For the child to play with toys, two conditions are essential: time and resources.

In line with the definition offered by Weis (1964, p. 21), leisure time is defined as "that portion of the day not used for meeting the exigencies of existence." Those who just manage to live on a subsistence level or those who are seriously ill, thus devoting all their energies to the task of staying alive, cannot be said to have leisure time. As Weis clarifies, leisure time is time made available by work, not time in which work is made possible. It is, therefore, different from time for relaxation or rest to recover from work and for more work. In this sense leisure involves the consumption of time, energy and other resources. Leisure is a commodity whose value is measured by the amount of free time available and the amount of nonessential commodities available for enjoyment during that time.[35]

Man's desire for a more leisurely lifestyle has been an important driving force in the invention of tools. Tools help one finish one's work in a shorter period of time and with less energy. The more efficient use of both time and energy is vital for leisure as well as increased productivity. As the agricultural sector's share of total employment decreases (or the share of the work force engaged in industrial and service activities increases), the typical number of work hours will be reduced. This trend is expected to be the case in all industrializing societies, as laborintensive agriculture is replaced by capitalintensive industry.[36] According to one study, leisure time for Americans has increased steadily since 1900, whereas their work hours have declined over the same period of

---

35 For a further analysis on the measurement of time allocation, refer to Gary S. Becker, "A Theory of the Allocation of Time," *Economic Journal*, September 1965.

36 In this respect, the author of this book challenges the Marxist contention that human efforts to eliminate labor is not to increase leisure but to maximize profits and opulent of the capitalists.

time, indicating a close link between industrial development and the amount of leisure time.

Elsewhere, I made a concise assessment of the structure of leisure time in American labor forces where I noted that the amount of leisure time in the United States coincided with the expansion of the post-industrial economy following the conclusion of the Vietnam War in the late 1970s. In this period, the service sector replaced the manufacturing sector as the most voluminous employer in America. At the same time, foreign laborers immigrated in mass numbers to the new land of opportunities and concurrently American suburbanization became a trend: Refer to Han S. Park (1984, p. 190).

A grand total time of 1,329 billion hours for 1950 was computed based on a total population of 151.7 million people in the United States, each of whom had twentyfour hours a day for 365 days a year. Based on numbers of people in each age and occupation group and on the typical pattern of daily activity, a total budget of time was prepared for 1900 and 1950, and estimates were made for 2000. The amount of leisure time increased from about 27 percent in 1900 to 34 percent in 1950, whereas work time decreased from 13 percent to 10 percent during the same period.

At the same time, as industry expands, there will be a greater demand for new laborers, enabling previously employed or seasonably unemployed workers to find more secure and better-paying jobs. As a result, family income will increase, and the additional income will help them use available leisure time in more efficient and enjoyable ways. In order to expand leisure activities, workers will demand material consumption beyond the level of basic needs, and industry will respond with the production of goods designed to enhance a leisurely lifestyle. For example, in a typical family in a nonindustrial society, one or more members of the family may spend an entire day out of each week washing the family's laundry by hand. This is a highly laborintensive and timeconsuming activity, yet it produces virtually no increase in the family's wealth. By contrast, a factory worker in an industrial society may buy a washing machine that will do the family's laundry with less human labor and in less time. Thus, the family members whose time and energy were once consumed in washing clothes now can invest that time and energy in other activities, some of which may well be leisure activities such as playing tennis or watching television. Automobiles perform the same function: they reduce the amount of time and energy consumed in various activities, thus creating additional time and energy to be invested in productive or leisure activities. The growth in the proportion of women in the work force and of twoincome families has been made possible in part by the proliferation of such products of the industrial society. The same can be said of the growth of the "leisure industry" which produces such things as televisions, sports equipment, movies, video games, and a myriad of other nonessential leisure goods. The increase of leisure time is not limited to the United States. All industrialized countries share the similar trend.

The shift from an agrarian economy to an industrial one will eventually generate a more complex class structure organized around individual command of skills and technology. Those who have skills and technological knowhow will enjoy more leisure time, and those who do not will continue to be engaged in laborintensive occupations, thus having less leisure time. It is expected that unskilled laborers in industrializing societies will struggle at the bottom of the social strata for little more than physical subsistence, whereas skilled technicians and white collar workers will seek out the kind of culture and lifestyle that are suitable for satisfying the leisure desire, as they attempt to ensure what Lenski refers to as "creative comfort" (Lenski, 1966, p. 38).

When a society consists of a larger leisure class, or at least, leisureseeking class, the production of commodities in the areas of laborsaving appliances, hobbies, and recreation will increase. At the same time, technological innovations and modifications will be designed to make them even more convenient and efficient. The "industrial man" will eventually become totally dependent on machines, and by this time the age of "push buttons" and "disposables" will be imminent.

Industrialization and Social Change

Leisure and Division of Labor

As Durkheim observes, "an industry can exist only if it answers some need. A function can become specialized only if this specialization corresponds to some need of the society." The emerging imperative for the industrializing society is in the expansion of commodities designed to make more leisure time available for the consumer. Thus new specializations are aimed at increasing and improving productivity so that more goods can be made with fewer manhours (Durkheim, 1933, p. 272).

Division of labor in a sense can be viewed as a social expression of "simplifying work" when work is unavoidable. By engaging in only limited segments of production, one expects to make the work routine and easy to perform. As a result, the division of labor facilitates role specialization and professionalization. Acquiring role expertise is viewed as highly desirable in a society where its members are appraised by the performance of their functions. This is especially true in a new urban community where its members are assigned their relative status not on the basis of their ascriptive characteristics, but by virtue of their achieved positions.

Industrial growth in turn led to extensive social and cultural change, directly in the forms of role differentiation and functional specialization, and indirectly in a number of other, more profound ways. One area that was affected by the industrial division of labor was the institution of higher education, which became compartmentalized into specialized disciplines, crippling scholarship (this issue will be depicted in the next chapter).

Social change involving industrialization tends to be most drastic and is likely to unravel the very fabric of the traditional cultural structure. Industrialization is inevitably accompanied by urbanization and the expansion of market system, and eventually the growth of a middle class. Furthermore, as the industrial economy crosses national boundaries and penetrates into the world market, a global community will emerge with a patterned network of economic interaction. In this process, world cultures will become increasingly similar and integrated as traditionally different peoples on this planet come to experience similar problems. In this process, the "rational man" will be born, and he will become the typical personality type. We shall discuss some dynamics and implications of these aspects of social change, since they are ultimately responsible for many of the emerging global problems.

Mass Consumption and Marketing

The desire for leisure and "conspicuous consumption" (Veblen, 1931) on the part of the consumer is an effective impetus for continuous industrialization. The industrial economy is fundamentally different from the agricultural economy in that it possesses the capability for virtually unlimited production of consumer goods, and these goods, unlike most agricultural products, are usually not essential for physical survival. Rather, industrial goods are intended for the more leisurely living desired by the consumer who has already secured survival.

For the survival of industry itself, manufacturers will strive to sell new products to the leisureminded conspicuous consumer. This, of course, requires advertisement and marketing. At this stage of social change, huge amounts of resources are invested in market expansion. The survival of an industry will depend on its ability to sell what is already produced, and to make "better" products continuously so that "old" products can be replaced and rates of mass consumption maintained. The automobile industry, for example, will not survive unless the consumer is after new models coming out every year. It is not in the industry's interest to encourage the consumer to retain his present automobile for a prolonged period of time by making them durable. The same logic is applied to a number of other consumer goods, ranging from appliances to clothing fashions.

In an attempt to induce the masses to consume, a variety of marketing strategies will be devised. We could point to coupons toward the purchase of goods, rebates, trading stamps, discount sales, catalogue sales, allowance on tradeins, and using price tags deceptively marked $9.99 instead of $10. Advertising techniques are extremely sophisticated in all industrial societies where marketing is an integral part of economic and social life.

Since mass consumption necessitates advertisement in such a way that the public can be reached most effectively, mass media will become a powerful instrument for the expansion of demand for industrial products. Commercials dominate newspaper pages. Radio broadcasts programs with a multitude of sponsors. Indeed, the mass media themselves are completely reliant upon advertising sponsors. Although the mass media have always carried advertisement, the extent to which the advertising of consumer goods overwhelms the media is a relatively recent phenomenon, expected only in mature industrial societies.

I have made a comparative examination of the Sears Roebuck Catalogue in selected years of 1900, 1920, 1940, 1960, and 1980 in an effort to observe the pattern of emphasis on consumer goods as society moved to the pinnacle of industrialization. In the 1900 catalogue, there was virtually no item that we might identify as being leisure-oriented. The closest thing was fishing equipment, which might not have been for leisurely fishing alone. In 1920, however, some sporting items such as baseball equipment and archery appeared, but only in a few pages of the catalogue. By 1940 we see considerable emphasis on domestic commodities such as furniture, rugs, refrigerators, stoves, washing machines, and kitchen accessories, but in limited variety. A major change in consumer goods was observed in the 1960 catalogue where a variety of sporting goods are listed, including golf, billiards, weight lifting, croquet tennis, badminton, basketball, baseball, and of course fishing. There were even a variety of children's toys. In addition, there were, for the first time, fourteen pages of camping equipment, indicating that an increasing number of people by then had the time and resources to enjoy leisurely camp-outs. Commodities geared for convenience and saving time were prevalent in 1960 book, such as vacuum cleaners, rug shampooers, washer/dryers, freezer/refrigerators, electric kitchen appliances, dishwashers, electric stoves, and even adding machines. Some eight pages were devoted to items for pools and accessories. The 1980 book is distinctly characterized by electronic and computerized consumer goods. The appearance of the microwave oven in this book indicates the importance of saving time. It might be noted that these commodity items have new looks and more sophisticated features in each of the subsequent volumes.

Credit and the "Precarious Consumer"

By the time society is deeply into the process of industrialization, the masses are likely to have jobs with limited and fixed incomes. Here emerges a social dilemma: the masses are attracted to consume a wide variety and larger quantities of goods, yet their income may not warrant such consumption. At the same time, the industry needs to sell commodities in volumes that the consumer cannot afford.

To ease this dilemma, banking and credit systems develop to allow the consumer to spend with credit and loans of all types. Due to the relative stability of this stage of society, the creditor can extend loans to be repaid over an extended period of time. Buying a house on a thirty-year loan, which is a common practice in the United States and other industrial nations, is something unheard of in many countries, particularly those in the developing areas.

The magic of credit buying induces the consumer to seek newer commodities and more convenient items. Consumer debt in the United States, and probably in all industrial countries, has been steadily rising in the aftermath of the "buy now, pay later" syndrome.[7] By making credit easily available in large amounts, banks and other lenders offer additional purchasing power with which one can buy and enjoy now. To the fashionminded consumer, it is difficult to refuse such an offer, for among other things people prefer to have goods now rather than later. Their propensities are, of course, to go the quick route, the easy route to consumption. Coincidentally, government policies at this stage of social development encourage credit use as a way of stimulating buying power and higher levels of economic activity.

Bank credit cards, "plastic money," offer safety and convenience for consumers who are attracted to the temptations offered by the credit companies. To the business world, the simple fact is that debt is profitable— an end in itself to the businessmen and bankers. Indeed, in a mature economic environment merchandise and service sales have become a means to sell debt. In this credit economy, one can live rather comfortably, even consuming far more than one's income or social status warrants. When the commodities one uses are acquired through credit buying, and thus not truly "owned" by the consumer, one's state of mind must be different. At the end of each month, when the consumer is forced to pay his bills, he is reminded of the fact that possessions are not truly his. This could have profound psychological implications for the credit buyer in that he might feel uneasy and uncomfortable, although his physical comfort may appear to be secure. Thus, as the consumer becomes addicted to convenience and to the relaxed use of credit that lenders are eager to offer, he will become psychologically uneasy. This is termed the "precarious consumer," because his state of mind would be precarious with the fear of default and the burden of debt.

Money Addiction

With the expansion of the market culture, in which every commodity or every service is translated into a single yardstick of money, people's aspirations center on enriching themselves. Unlike smoking or drug addiction where health warnings and societal sanctions work as prohibitive forces, money addiction is virtually unchecked. In fact, a unique feature of money addiction is the fact that more money is always looked at as something to be desired, whereas the other forms of addiction are not usually admired or desired by the nonaddict. People get addicted to drugs because it does "wonders" which only the addict knows, but one does not have to be an addict to know what wonders money can do in the industrial market society. It is hard to think of anything that money cannot buy.

In this third stage of resource expansion, however, money is not earned for accumulation but for the consumption of industrial commodities that are designed to appeal to the leisureseeking consumer. Indeed, the consumer rarely makes enough money to accommodate his desire for the conspicuous goods that are constantly being replaced by newer patterns and more convenient models.

I once asked the college students in my classes in late 1980s to make a list of consumer goods that they thought were designed primarily for convenience and for the expansion of leisure time. The following were some of the most frequently mentioned items:

electric garage door

hair appliances blow dryer, curling iron, rollers

hot shaving machine

sun lamp

electric can opener

dishwasher, dryer, washing machine

garbage disposal

automatic nail buffer

drivethrough window (banks, restaurants)

microwave oven

automatic ice maker

electric toothbrush

"insidetheegg" egg scrambler

automatic telephone dial

remote control television

electric knife

moving sidewalk

cruise controlled car

power windows

electric trunk opener

riding lawn mower

digital watch

golf cart

super glue

treadmill

tennis machine

shower massager

In light of the fact that consumer goods are subject to constant refinement and "improvement, keeping up with the current fashions requires an enormous amount of money. Furthermore, the industry has by now acquired a lifestyle of its own, where its survival depends on its ability to innovate more appealing products, thus continually promoting sales. In addition, the leisureseeking consumer is attracted to timesaving and convenient commodities.

Bureaucratization and Alienation

The process of industrial production, with its foundation in the division of labor, forces social institutions to transform their organizational structure from a hierarchical structure, which is typical of agrarian communities, to a pyramidal structure. In the pyramidal structure, as typified by bureaucracy, social interaction is compartmentalized and peer interaction is restricted.

Such an industrial bureaucracy will spread to all other social organizations and political institutions where roles become specialized and performed by line experts. This phenomenon of role specialization will contribute to the development of a "diffracted" society, to use Riggs' metaphor, as the previously "diffused" society will undergo a structural and functional transition analogous to the prismatic effect, whereby a ray of light breaks up into a series of discernibly different rays as it passes through a prism (Riggs, 1964). In this kind of organizational structure, we would expect an incremental process of decision making in which synoptic or innovative decisions on the part of the organization as a whole will be unlikely. This will affect the practice of government bureaucracy in such a way that its role can be limited to caretaking and maintenance. Any kind of drastic change is likely to provoke serious dissent and turmoil, as witnessed in the industrial societies where sweeping government organizational changes are highly impractical and improbable. Government authority at this stage will experience a transformation of its basis of legitimacy from traditional or charismatic persuasion to rational persuasion.

In the operation of a bureaucratic organization, work performance will be rewarded on the basis of *efficiency* in terms of tasks defined in a job description, rather than on the basis of *effectiveness* in meeting broader objectives for the organization as a whole. By working on an assembly line, one is not expected to comprehend the entire process of production or to appreciate its final output. On the contrary, the assembly line worker tends to dig a small hole in which he finds peace and privacy, although boredom may prevail. "Industrial man" thus becomes gradually alienated from other members of his own organization as well as from his product. As Berger (1962) suggests, alienation would seem almost complete when one can say with honesty and moral conviction, "I am not what I do; do not judge me by what I do for a living," and when one turns to a non-working life for values and identity. If workers in industrial and commercial bureaucracies are indeed psychologically alienated, the Marxist indictment of capitalism as an alienating agent of human beings from things is indeed applicable to bureaucracies.

Tyranny of Technology and New Victims

Schumacher (1973, pp. 116-147) in his seminal work, *Small Is Beautiful,* lamented that "technology, although of course the product of man, tends to develop by its own laws and principles… (It) recognizes no self-limiting principle." As individuals become helpless cogs in a machine, they lose control over the machinery. Furthermore, when the machine gets more sophisticated, the workers are compelled to adapt themselves to it by obtaining new skills and technical know-how, or they will lose their jobs. Thus, as ironic as it may sound, man becomes subservient to machines, and technology controls man rather than the converse.

Technological sophistication is assumed to be unlimited because without it, industry cannot survive. Unlike agriculture, industry was made to expand, and industrial expansion is possible only by an increasing demand for industrial products. As discussed earlier, technological innovations on a continuing basis are necessary for producing commodities that will appeal to the eyes of the leisure-minded masses and the "precarious consumer." The growth potential of technology itself is virtually unlimited and, more importantly, there are no checks in place to hinder its progress. Technology transcends national boundaries or ideological differences. There is no such thing as capitalist technology as opposed to socialist technology. For that matter, there is no American technology that is repudiated in the Islamic world because of its origin. In this sense, as Boorstin (1971) observes, we may be drifting into the "republic of technology," where civilization will become increasingly homogenous and humankind will experience common problems of a common life environment. In the triumphant march of technology, all humans may end up as the victims, subservient to machines.

In a society where technocrats prevail, and new technical innovations are so swift that no one can acquire sufficient skills to enjoy competence throughout his life, the elderly will be sure victims because they are not as able and motivated as younger people to retrain themselves. As a result, older people will be largely eliminated from the work force, and those who remain will be discriminated against.

Industrialization also brings an irreversible change in demographic structure: the birth rate in the industrialized affluent societies has declined below the level of sustainment and population increase has been on the rise in the less developed world; the median age for the world and practically all countries are on the rise suggesting that world population is steadily becoming older. This trend of aging population in the advanced industrial societies affects a number of economic, social, and political life situations not only for the elderly themselves but the entire political system.

In the United States in 1976, there were 22 million adults who were 65 or older. One out of every ten persons in America belonged to this group, which has been rapidly increasing due to the prolonging of life and the declining birth rate. Not only will the elderly population keep growing, but it will become more concentrated in the upper ages of that segment, exacerbating the problem further.

Historically, the elderly were dependent on the family for survival. But the spread of industrialization and urbanization changed the institution of the family so that the place of work and home were separated, leaving fewer roles for the elderly. The extended family system was replaced by the nuclear family.

Houses became smaller, women worked, mobility increased and family care for the elderly became more of a burden. The elderly became marginalized. In a typical industrializing society, the increase of the aging population leads to a transfer of functions from family to government, thus, the government moves toward a welfare state. This trend will become more pronounced in post-industrial and global societies.

OverUrbanization

While urbanization is a natural outcome of industrialization, some cities increase their population without the accompanying increase in industrial development, exerting a destructive effect on social stability.

Hauser (1964) characterizes "overurbanization" as a situation in which "a larger population of people lives in urban places than their degree of economic development justified." As implied here by Hauser, the concept of overurbanization is defined only in relation to the level of economic development, rather than the sheer number of people residing in a city. Breeze (1966, p. 6) directly relates "over-urbanization" to the gap between urbanization and industrialization that makes it possible to provide employment to all persons coming to urban areas.

Many other authors advanced the notion that overurbanization can occur when the size of a city is unrealistically large, as though there is an optimality in city size. According to this view, the relation between the efficiency of a city and the size of its population is curvilinear; in other words, a growing city is expected to contribute to economic development and social stability only up to a certain point. An overly grown city would have an adverse effect on its socioeconomic and political development. Estall and Buchanan (1961, p. 107) assert that:

> At some time or other most of the world's great industrial complexes have been thought to be beyond the point where economics are offset by the extra cost incurred in various ways.

Still others maintain that the phenomenon of a primate distribution of cities will be harmful to the society. The primate

159

distribution phenomenon will occur when one or a few core cities grow rapidly, thus slowing down the growth of smaller and middle-sized cities. This will accelerate the core cities' modernization at the expense of the rest of the country. This trend has accelerated in pace with globalization. It is believed that a tendency toward the primate distribution of cities is not only destructive for the balanced growth of the cities themselves, but also harmful to the political stability of the nation. Conversely, this would mean that having a "rank distribution" of cities of varying sizes simultaneously would be conducive to the nation's development.

In any case, mechanization of agriculture, combined with the apparent promises shown by new industrial jobs, facilitates the process of overurbanization of one sort or another, contributing to urban unemployment and other social dislocations. Massive influxes of population are difficult for the government to manage effectively, and such cities will become subject to increasing urban crime and violence.

The Rise of the Middle Class

As a direct consequence of industrial development and urbanization, one should never forget the emergence of the middle class, a class that was not foreseen by Karl Marx when he so penetratingly evaluated the process of social change accompanying the market economy. What made the middle class different from the proletariat was its ability to influence the mechanism of production without owning the means of production. The middle class person is by and large a selfsupporting person with job security and a constant, fixed income, usually working in salaried position. This worker would have been labeled as a proletariat who would have no way out of endless exploitation by the ownership. This once-helpless member of the proletariat has now gained significant leverage in generating higher pay, and is now a part of a true middle class. There are three distinct sources of increasing the leverage:

1. The industrial worker had to constantly upgrade his skill level to be more competitive as required by mechanization of the industry and market demand. Once the worker is equipped with skills and technical know-how, he cannot be easily and readily replaced. Thus, the Marxist premise of an abundant pool of proletariats turned out to be false. In other words, industrial workers managed to develop their expertise and claim their fair share through collective

bargaining and strikes. Thus, the blind exploitation on the part of the capitalist did not happen as Marx had predicted;

2. As the worker realized that he had more bargaining leverage, he was able to join with other workers to form labor unions and institute collective bargaining, a fact that Marx did not foresee. It is the collective bargaining empowered the salaried workers to more forcefully negotiate the terms and conditions of their contracts with the bourgeoisie class. In industrial societies, collective bargaining is leveraged with the instrument of labor strike, accounting for the enhancement of economic condition of the workers;

3. The salaried workers themselves became mass consumers with formidable purchasing power. As mass production requires mass consumption, the ownership and industrialists realized that impoverished working class would work against their interest, and needed to keep the working class as a source of healthy consumption. The volume of consumption on the part of the middle class could be so large that the industrial sector becomes completely dependent upon it. It is by its collective purchasing power that the middle class gets appropriate recognition, which will help it improve its social and economic position. We discussed earlier how dependent the industry would be upon continuous consumption by the masses, and it is the middle class that has the purchasing power to fuel the trend of mass consumption.

These three phenomena contributed to the formation of a middle class, which would have prevented class polarization as envisioned by Marxist socialism. Indeed, such a middle class may have prevented the articulation of class-consciousness as a necessary condition for a proletarian revolution, which Marx would have expected to witness. The middle class person is likely to be socially and psychologically alienated from others, as we see in a typical urban worker residing in an apartment cell. The middle class, however, develops its own set of unique psychological dispositions and cultural orientations, such as reverence for privacy, the lack of public-regard, selfishness or self-centeredness, alienation from the community, and laziness. These symptoms will increase systematically as the stage of development shifts toward post-industrial society, as we will discuss in the next chapter.

So far, we have discussed the idea that the human desire for leisure may have paved the way for technological development and industrialization, and subsequently for behavioral and social change. We shall now examine the impact of such development on societal institutions.

Institutional Changes

It has been maintained that industrialization is a comprehensive process of social change in which the traditional community is rapidly dismantled. In this process, some farmland will be destroyed and converted into industrial parks, highways and parking lots, resulting in a sharp decline in farm population, although not in agricultural productivity. The military will undergo a process of declining relative importance as it becomes subservient to industrial pressures, and yields to the broader "Military Industrial Complex." The family as a primary institution will experience a profound transformation endangering the very foundation of its existence. Education will have to adapt itself to the new cultural and societal demands and even religious organizations will become more secular and commercialized. We shall examine some of these changes in more detail.

Agriculture: A Loser

It seems as though farmers are the perennial losers in all societies. Since what the farmer can do is limited to the production of food and basic necessities, his function will be appreciated less and less in societies where people's imminent needs are beyond those necessities. Furthermore, as agricultural productivity is restricted in part by the amount of arable land and other natural conditions, agriculture can offer little competition to industry in generating an expanding national product for society. Industrial output is relatively free from national boundaries, so long as market expansion accompanies this process.

As the farmer's function becomes more peripheral to the nation's economy, agriculture also suffers in its relative importance within the changing culture. Many farmers in agrarian societies enjoy their prestigious position in a culture where farming is regarded a sacred job, only to find that the wave of industrialization overwhelms them with social change.

Unlike urban industrial workers, farmers are tied to their land and have little mobility. They lack bargaining power because they seldom have alternative employment. Work boycotts are not realistic tools for bargaining because farmers cannot afford to lose a whole year's crops, since most of them are already impoverished or at least deeply in debt. Furthermore, since farmers are more individualistic than group oriented, they are not motivated to organize collective bargaining. Thus, they eventually are absorbed by industrial expansion.

The Military Industrial Complex (MIC)

Once industrialization gets underway, it is difficult to contain its expansion because industry has its inherent dilemma of "growth or death." Industrial economy is such that firms cannot accommodate any reduction in their operation. As such, the forces of industrial expansion are fierce, and they will spill over into every other aspect of the society. The military can hardly be an exception.

The institution of the military, despite its sacred and exclusively assigned function of territorial defense, will be impaired by industrial intrusion. Realizing the fact that the military is a unique institution for which there can be no economic recession, industry will be eager to benefit economically by penetrating into the operation of the defense apparatus.

The phenomenon of the Military Industrial merger is more apparent in capitalist industrial societies where weapons are manufactured by industry upon terms of contracts. In this case, the parties in the contract represent two different behavioral entities: while the government is a publicly-funded organization that does not have to be "rational" or profit motivated, the industry is a profit maximizing institution. This would lead to terms of contract favoring the industry without personally costing the government personnel making the agreements. Given the magnitude of the cost for developing and building sophisticated weapons such as bombers, missiles, and tanks, we can easily imagine the magnitude of economic interest on the part of the industry.

Military buildup, in collaboration with industry, is not subject to innate limitations, as we witness in the unending process of the arms race between industrial giants. As a way of promoting the endless process of military buildup, military super powers are often compelled to become merchants themselves when they cannot consume all the hardware the industry wishes to produce. This involves selling arms to surrogate countries and even enemies of the surrogates. Indeed, it often appears that it is in the interest of the super powers to facilitate conflicts and wars around the world so as to meet domestic industrial demand. We

163

should not be misled into believing that the arms race toward the alleged balance of power has necessarily contributed to global security. In fact, many wars and regional conflicts during the Cold War era were "sponsored" by the super powers themselves, and many of them for the domestic reasons of the Military Industrial complex. One need not be a critic of the United States to be able to see the formidable role of the industry in shaping American military policy. As we will revisit this issue in the post-Cold War and globalization era, the military–industrial complex became contagious and spread to most political systems of the world.

The Family: A Last Resort Threatened

The extended family system was commonplace in agrarian communities, for it was conducive to organizing and mobilizing the labor force, and the practice of uncalculated mutual aid within the family was beneficial to laborintensive farming. As the community opened up its door to industrialization and urbanization, the institution of the extended family system was the first to be affected. As youthful members of the family were attracted to urban centers, their allegiance and loyalty to the extended family came to a gradual end. At the same time, the new young members of the city were left with the awesome responsibility of forming a new family without the close guidance and protection of the more experienced members of the extended family. The trend in advanced post-industrial societies is that societies that

As Mead observes in the American context, young couples are living together in some arrangement outside the traditional families and are wholly dependent on their private, personal commitment to each other for the survival of the relationship.

In the urban setting, where there is little social interaction and communal congeniality, the nuclear family becomes the sole source of psychological comfort for individuals who seldom find a sense of attachment to their work environment. Thus, the socially isolated and emotionally lonesome "industrial man" seeks and expects the psychological comfort of belonging in the small nuclear family. But in the industrial society, both spouses are likely to be providers, though often failing to become mutual providers. This and other complications contribute to the endemic popularization of divorce epitomizing a crisis in the institution of the family in industrial society.

Additionally, even families that manage to avoid breaking up through divorce face challenges in protecting their children and satisfying their need to belong. It is no longer shocking news that children are breaking away from homes. What is shocking is the fact that a majority of these children are from relatively welloff families, by economic and social standards. The soaring suicide rate among young people in relatively affluent societies may be attributed in part to the breakdown of the family support system.

Industrial development has changed the nature of the family institution in a number of ways. Among others, the relative roles of men, women, and children have undergone a profound transition. In the preindustrial society, many men worked a craft or farmed in or near the home. They were nearby to eat all meals with the family and share their workload with other members. This contrasts with industrial men who are expected to work away from home and whose work is in isolation from the family.

The role of women has changed perhaps more than that of men. In the past, housewives' tasks included the manufacturing of clothing, soap, bread, and other staples. Additionally, they were expected to educate children when public education was limited. In the industrial society, women's jobs at home became somewhat easier and less time consuming thanks to automated appliances and readymade food. As a result, they could go out and become wage earners.

The role of children has also changed drastically. Instead of being babysitters and helpers around the house, they now spend long hours away from their families, and often become wageearners themselves. Indeed, in the early expansion of industrial work demand, children became a part of the labor force, as we witnessed in the United States and Great Britain, where the government had to intervene with child labor laws to curtail the unjust exploitation of children.

In industrial and postindustrial societies, compensating children for their daily chores and other household work is common. Keeping separate banking accounts and legally defining property shares between husband and wife are no longer considered unusual. In fact, the family has, in some ways, ceased to be a natural social and human group. It is a contractual and legal association that is commonly subjected to the intervention of the court.

Education: An End to the Total Personhood

With the necessity to respond to industrial demand, educational curricula will gradually do away with liberal arts and philosophy and incorporate technical and scientific training. This trend is rapidly reinforced by the ascent of the technocrat in the community power structure. As Bell (1973, p. 78) observes, "With the rise of the technician has come the belief that advanced industrial society would be ruled by the technocrat." In response to the changing status of the technocrat, education as training for the total person will be replaced by technical training, and education will be viewed as a tool for obtaining more attractive (better paying) jobs, which tend to be in the technical area. Whereas fields such as philosophy and ethics lose popularity and in some cases vanish for lack of student interest, new fields and disciplines emerge for areas dealing with technology and management.

Traditionally, in societies at the second stage of development, education's primary function was to teach children the norms and beliefs predominant in the society, so that they could join the mainstream of the cultural system. But industrialization has completely altered the meaning of education. Education here is little more than vocational training intended to prepare the student for a particular job. Going forward, technical schools and vocational junior colleges will draw more students, and only a small number of "deviant" people will still take liberal arts and humanities courses. A layman's observation of educational institutions in developing countries will convincingly testify to the shift to technocratic training there, as well.

Religion: Secularization

As with all organizations, religious organizations are expected to have the social function of providing a sense of belonging to their members. In this respect, religion has secular functions. Nevertheless, the religious organization is different from all others in that its primary raison d'étre lies in its pursuit of visions beyond worldly affairs. Yet, churches in the industrial and postindustrial society tend to become profitseeking enterprises themselves, and many members profess to be "believers" on utilitarian grounds alone.

Furthermore, thanks to the failure of the family institution and problems with education in the industrial society, the masses are easily attracted to religious sects that appear to be more paternal and foster close relations among the members. These sects have proven to be as much business organizations as religious entities, as we have seen in many cases ranging from Jim Jones to the Unification Church of Rev. Sun Myung Moon.

The story of Reverend Moon is a truly unbelievable one. With a limited education, Rev. Moon tried to establish a Christian denomination of sorts in his own country, Korea, but never succeeded. His church was merely one of many frequently emerging religious sects. Unlike most of his competitors, Moon had a strong nationalist appeal to the Koreans, in that he proclaimed them to be a chosen people. This aspect of his religion helped him gain lukewarm political support from President Park, who was himself an ardent nationalist.

Rev. Moon's success in the United States, Japan, and Western Europe was indeed an unexpected surprise, even to the church leaders themselves. The fact that young people, many of whom were of a rather affluent social background, were helplessly and passionately absorbed into the Family of Rev. Moon remains a mystery. One most plausible explanation is that the social context of the industrial societies is such that many young people develop a deep sense of alienation, especially from their family. The Unification Church, with its doctrine that all members are brothers and sisters and belong to the same Family, is easily appreciated by the lonely youth. They find the rare opportunity to show their devotion to altruism by living together, working together, and sharing. Altruistic and brotherly living is much discussed in conventional churches, but idealistic youth may never find the preaching convincing. Thus, they become highly suspicious of the religious associations that the industrialized and "rationalized" Church offers. In this sense, we might even say that if someone is responsible for what has become of the religious sector, it is the society, the broken family institution, and the inhumane industrial culture that are liable more than anyone else.

This analysis is not to condone and sanctify the religious sects we have witnessed in recent years. In fact, churches themselves are failing. Of all conceivable deceptions, deceptions in the Church may be most grave. Despite making claims of brotherhood and equality before God, how many churches in the United States make serious efforts to have a racially-integrated membership? Indeed, few social groups are as segregated and closed as churches. In order to belong to a certain church, you have to belong to a certain secular status group in the first place. How can one justify this in the name of God?

Cultural Change and Behavioral Dispositions

When people are swept by the wave of industrialization and urbanization and the accompanying social changes, they are forced to alter their attitudes, values, beliefs and even behavioral patterns. In the previous chapter, we identified a cultural system indicative of the second stage of political integration as having values such as collective orientation, altruism, egalitarianism, universalism, and idealism. These values and beliefs will undergo a profound transformation in the resource expansion stage, in that nearly all the norms observed in the process of political integration will be replaced by a set of antithetical values.

Individualism

With the breakdown of traditional social systems, members of the newly-formed urban society will lose a sense of communal bonding and experience social and psychological alienation. The new life environment will eventually force them to develop a reverence for privacy and individualism.

Furthermore, the worker's job environment is such that reward is in proportion to individual achievement, and his work relationship is limited essentially to the employer, curtailing his group orientation and collective behavior. When the worker participates in some sort of collective bargaining or strike, he does so not do so for the purpose of promoting collective interest but for calculated selfinterest. Thus, mass movements cannot expect to succeed when such movements involve a high degree of risk to the participant, and the payoff is not readily translated into tangible individual gains for the present. This may be a partial explanation for the lack of mass political organizations and revolutionary social movements in industrial societies. The group-oriented phenomena of mass movements were most prevalent in the political integration stage where individuals in sufficient numbers were willing to sacrifice their individual interests for the collective good.

Rationality: The Birth of Economic Man

The concept of human rationality has evolved in a most intriguing way. Following the dark ages of the medieval times when legitimacy of power had little to do with people's consent, and with the introduction of "social contract" along with the concurrent development of philosophical individualism and *laissezfaire* economics in the ensuing decades, philosophers and political thinkers raised the issue of the state of human nature as the ultimate source of justification for different types of politics. Machiavelli, Hobbes, Locke, and Rousseau, to name only a few, had varying perceptions as to the state of human nature, and hence, different views of what constitutes a legitimate form of government. Nevertheless, they all agreed that "rationality" is virtuous and desirable, although they interpreted the degree of human rationality differently. Further, they had a consensus on the meaning of "rational man" in that he is benevolent and altruistic. Selfishness was regarded as "irrational," and it laid the foundation for tyrannical theories of political order as espoused in *The Prince* by Machiavelli and *The Leviathan* by Hobbes.

As the industrial economy with its market culture swept western civilization, the economic conception of "rational man" overpowered the traditional philosophical version of human rationality. The economic "rational man" was ironically considered the "irrational man" in the traditional sense. A man who is motivated to maximize benefit by minimizing cost is defined as "rational," and this very man would have been regarded as being "irrational" for his selfish motivation. In the mature industrial society, "selfishness" disguised as "rationality" is hardly considered a vice. Thus, hedonistic utilitarianism is accepted as a norm and anything unselfish is typically viewed as being "irrational" and abnormal.

In short, the industrial society made man not only selfish but justified his selfishness as being moral and natural.

Particularistic Values

In contrast to the value orientation of universalism in the previous stage of political integration, for reasons germane to the phenomenon of industrialurban development, people will gradually become oriented toward particularistic values. Here, man will develop an evaluative form of mind analogous to the clinical assessment in which an object is sliced into various parts for examination and treatment. The society is viewed as a system of parts, and it is the parts that make the whole system meaningful, thus rejecting holistic views as well as universalistic values. Accordingly, as every object in the market has a separate price tag, every part of the society has its own value and meaning irrespective of its relationship to the whole.

An individual's ability to evaluate issues and people will be greatly enhanced by a particularistic value orientation. Thus, public opinion can be articulated on the grounds of greater rationality and careful deliberations. Perhaps it is for this reason that participatory democracy is commonly regarded as being more suitable for industrial societies than agrarian societies.

Realism

Unlike the idealistic cultural norms and values that were prevalent in the political integration stage, people now become preoccupied with realistic values and tangible accomplishments. The age of ideology, as Daniel Bell (1960) observes, may be coming to an end as the society enjoys the fruits of industrial advancement. As we discussed earlier educational programs and the commercialized mass media will promote realism and pragmatic behavior to the extent that men with ideas will be put in the hands, and at the mercy, of men with matter.

Styles of Politics

The extensive social and cultural change expected in the process of industrialization and urbanization will profoundly affect the nature of politics and style of government. I shall point out some major characteristics of politics one might expect in the stage of resource expansion.

Technocrats and Managerial Leadership

The autocratic leadership of the firststage society and the charismatic leadership of the secondstage society will no longer maintain their popularity in the stage where "money does the talking." In industrial and postindustrial societies, leadership groups will center on industrial elites such as capitalists and managers. In addition, government bureaucracy will become stabilized, and professional bureaucrats will be established just as technocrats are finding their stable positions in the industry.

An essential requirement for any aspiring politician is the ability to ally himself with business and secure its support. As such, there will be an intimate functional interaction between the business circle and politics. Just as in the case of the Military

Industrial complex, the demands of business will spill over the entire spectrum of politics. In fact, it is highly likely that many political posts will be occupied by business executives, and many politicians will take business posts after retirement from political life. This phenomenon is quite evident in postwar Japan where government retirees have usually been invited by big businesses. When business personnel become an integral part of politics, the leadership style will be patterned after the managerial and technocratic mode of industrial operation.

Priority for Economy

With the imminent need for resource expansion, governments of all ideological hues will place top priority on strategies for economic growth. Quite often, they install development plans with specific growth targets, and their implementations are engineered by government initiation. Some governments exercise greater amounts of control than others but government intervention in the economic sector tends to be quite extensive in all cases. Government monopoly of major industries is instrumental in tight regulations, sometimes with quotas imposed by the government.

All major industrial countries such as the United States, Great Britain, and Japan, had a period of growing governmental intervention in the national economy. After the Civil War, the U.S. government expanded its power over industry with new fiscal policies and regulatory measures intended to control business, as well as direct intervention in the areas of railroad construction, metal and mining industry, and transportation.[37] Japan was not an exception. Since the Meiji restoration in 1868, concerted efforts have been made by the government to formulate policies to encourage capital investment in industrial production. The extent of government involvement in resource allocation is demonstrated by Rosovsky's study which points out that the mean government share of gross domestic fixed capital formation from 1887 to 1896 was 42.5 percent.[38] Allen (1946, p. 30) points out that "there was scarcely any important Japanese industry of the Western type during the later decades of the nineteenth century which did not owe its establishment to state initiative." A similar pattern is found in the experience of British economic growth where the

---

37 For government regulations and development subsidies in the process of economic expansion in the United States, see John M. Peterson and Ralph Gray (1969), especially Chapter 10.

38 Henry Rosovsky, *Capital Formation in Japan (1868-1940)*

government initiated economic programs and policies intended to protect and expand the industry.[39]

Industrialization for the "late comer" has shown a unique pattern in that it benefits from technology available in advanced societies and the international market in which it can compete favorably with industries of the laborscarce advanced economy. Thus, a large number of countries managed to achieve economic growth in relatively short periods of time.

Explosive expansion of the Third World countries was seen in the United States and advanced industrialized Europe during the 1960s and 1970s, while the First and Second World remained unchanged.

Growth over Distribution

As alluded to earlier, many developing countries have made rather effective efforts to industrialize the economy due to technology transfer and the international market. However, industrialization is often marked by seriously inequitable distributions of income, to the extent that the masses come far short of enjoying the leisure mode of life. It is not until the process of industrialization reaches its optimal point where the purchasing power of the masses becomes imperative for continuous industrial prosperity that the mode of income distribution will shift toward a more equitable form. Even then, if the domestic market is not vital for industrial growth due to the vast reservoir of the international market, domestic income distribution could be unaffected, leading the political system to become even more repressive and protective of the establishment. This perpetuation of gross inequality and capricious control by the ruling elite have paved the way in many potentially stable countries to mass revolts and political turmoil, as might be the case in Iran, South Korea, and El Salvador in the late 1970s and early 1980s, and the phenomenon became more prevalent the Middle East and North Africa in the first two decades of the 21st Century.

The government will attempt to justify the inequitable distribution of income in the name of economic growth, and there are a good number of theories to rationalize such an attempt. However, the public, to whom leisure is a most imminent need,

---

39 For a further discussion on the role of government in economic development in Japan and Britain, see Robert Holt and John Turner (1966).

will not tolerate a situation where their needs are continuously and indefinitely denied in the name of the nation's economic growth. A nation's growth may mean much to a person who is desperately demanding the need for belonging, but it may mean little to the leisureseeking consumer.

To sum it up, in this chapter, we observed various aspects of social and political change that are likely to result during the process of industrialization and urban development. We maintained that the invention of tools and the subsequent development of technological growth and industrialization were all to be expected, as they were necessitated by the emergence of new human needs and wants, which, in this case, are leisure and comfort.

In the resource expansion stage, certain aspects of that which were achieved and developed in the previous stage will be altered or replaced by something antithetical to what was. This is particularly the case with changes in cultural and behavioral characteristics, as an emphasis on "matter" overtakes an emphasis on "mind."

Once a society reaches the stage of resource expansion, it has begun a journey that, once embarked upon, is irreversible. Industrialization and market expansion are here only to expand, and as the globe offers limited resources with which to satisfy everyone's wants, the postindustrial era signals warnings that can no longer be ignored, as we will discuss more fully in the next chapter.

Chapter 9

Control Want and Conflict Management

Man is never content with what he has, at least not in the political arena. Human desire knows no limit. With all the fruits of mature industrial society and the material prosperity of an affluent society, we find that man's desires are still not satisfied. He remains unhappy because, once he has achieved the material comfort for leisurely life, he must have "more," not just of these same goods and other resources but more than other people. The desire for status, prestige, power, and control over others - all manifestations of this desire to have "more" of social values than other people -- gives rise to the central political dilemma facing regimes in this stage: how to satisfy the demands for control by one group without alienating, and thus losing the support of, those groups that must inevitably lose control in this reallocation of fixedsum social values. The ultimate political manifestation of this basic human want is the desire to have some measure of control over the decisionmaking process by which all social values - including control, prestige, and power -- are allocated.

Thus, the very search for satisfaction of this desire will inevitably lead to social competition and conflict of a type that cannot be totally resolved. After all, to satisfy one person or group's demands for control over the decisionmaking process necessarily means reducing some other individual, group or groups control over that same critical process. As conflict during the technologically advanced stages of social and political development could have devastating effects (after all, there is much to be lost at this point in a society's development), the regime must develop the capacity to manage such conflict in order to maintain the continued stability of the society and, thus, the continued sustenance of the regime itself.

The Need for Control and the Zero-Sum Society

In a society where a substantial portion of the people have attained an effective and reliable means for satisfying their survival, belonging, and leisure needs, the need for "social control" will begin to emerge. The satisfaction of this need is determined by an individual's position along certain dimensions of achievement, relative to the position of their significant others.

When people formulate their demands by comparing what they have with what others have, government must serve as a "peacekeeper" of sorts by facilitating a "just" distributive system. It must provide the mechanisms by which people can take steps to remedy what they see as an unjust distribution of value and at the same time provide mechanisms by which those who lose in the reallocation of relative amount of social control can be persuaded not to withdraw their support from the regime. In short, a successful political regime at this stage must be capable of managing social conflict of a zerosum character. This stage of political development involves aspects of what Daniel Bell has described as the politics of postindustrial society, where increased production is no longer the central goal of society or of government policy.

In order to clarify the zerosum character of politics in this stage, we can compare the nature of the needs characteristic of this stage of development (and the valued objects which serve for their satisfaction) with those characteristic of the earlier stages of development. In an agrarian society, where popular needs center around survival and are met through the production of food and other necessities of human existence, social conflict is not necessarily of a zerosum character. Under some circumstances, people can increase the amount of food and other goods available for consumption. More generally, the supply of the goods that serve for the satisfaction of survival needs is not necessarily fixed. Increased food production combined with the control of population growth would mean that over the long term, and even in the short term, one person's satisfaction of their own survival needs would not necessarily reduce the ability of others to satisfy their survival needs. Similar arguments can be made for the subsequent two levels of needs and stages of development. The satisfaction of one person or group's need for belonging does not necessarily reduce the ability of others to satisfy the same needs. Indeed, it may even enhance the ability of others to satisfy such needs, since the larger the group to which one seeks to belong, the more easily that individual can be absorbed into the group without posing any threat to existing patterns of relationships within the group. Similarly, the satisfaction of one person's leisure need does not reduce the ability of others to satisfy their leisure needs. In an expansionary economy, such things as wage increases, shorter working hours, and the availability of leisure goods and activities are not necessarily of a fixedsum variety. Thus, one person's satisfaction of these needs need not necessitate some other person's dissatisfaction with respect to the same needs.

Where people compete for the sake of "winning," such a competition cannot be resolved without the loser's loss. Thus, the winner's satisfaction will be offset by the loser's suffering. Social and political competition in the mature industrial societies is generally of this kind, namely, a zerosum game. It is for this reason that societies that may have reached a mature stage of industrialization tend to shift their policy emphasis from production to redistribution.

In this regard, it is not surprising that definitions of politics offered by scholars of western postindustrial origin tend to focus on the function of redistribution, as we witness in the instances of Easton's "authoritative allocation of values" (Easton, 1953), and Lasswell's "who gets what, when, and how" (Lasswell, 1958). These definitions presuppose the existence and availability of values to be allocated and resources to be acquired by someone in the first place.

Post-Industrialism: The Threshold to Conflict Management Stage

Daniel Bell in his seminal work, *The Coming of PostIndustrial Society*, defines the postindustrial society as one that emphasizes "the centrality of theoretical knowledge as the axis around which new technology, economic growth, and the stratification of society will be organized" (Bell, 1973, p. 112). With the presentation of a comprehensive schema of social change, Bell contrasts the postindustrial society with the industrial and preindustrial societies in terms of various dimensions of social life. Here, using the United States as a sole example of such a postindustrial society, he maintains that "the concept of a postindustrial society is not a picture of a complete social order; it is an attempt to describe and explain an axial change in the social structure..." (1973, p. 119). Thus, the central criterion for a society to be called "postindustrial" is the place of "theoretical knowledge" as the axis around which patterns of social life revolve. While much of his analysis coincides with the empirical reality of America, the question of what makes postindustrial development necessary does not seem to be sufficiently addressed by Bell. It seems to be true, however, that the role of theoretical knowledge has a far greater potential and actual impact in human lives than the mere technical skills that the industrial society once revered so highly, as is exemplified by the development of nuclear science. At the same time, it is difficult to follow Bell's contention that the primary institutions in such a postindustrial society are universities, academic institutions, and research corporations, although that appeared to be the case when the Americans sought to catch and surpass the Soviets in scientific research in the decade following the Sputnik shock of 1957. This is not to undermine the pioneering work that Bell has made in defining postindustrialism as being uniquely different from the industrial society.

As an alternative conception of the postindustrialism, the present paradigm suggests that *a society enters the threshold of postindustrial society when its primary social and political issue shifts from the task of resource expansion to that of "just" distribution.* A society in this stage will force the government to shift its policy orientations toward issues of distributive justice, which can no longer be obscured by the existence of further economic growth and development. Following a period of industrialization and resource expansion in which the masses are told to wait for the arrival of the more affluent society that industrialization will bring, the consumer will reach a point where he can no longer tolerate the inequitable structure of social and economic life, particularly when further growth is not seen as necessary for him to claim a comfortable share of the existing resources. When the political system is insensitive to this rising expectation of the consumer, social and political unrest may result.

In the course of industrial development, the economic structure will reach a point where industrial expansion will become stabilized, as the United States and European nations have experienced invariably in recent decades. Most industrial societies passed the peak point of industrialization where the percentage of the work force employed in industrial sectors starts to decline. Interestingly enough, no society has reached the point where a majority of the population has ever engaged in work in the industrial sector. The industrial societies have generally passed the threshold point into post-industrialism sometime in the early 1970s when the economically active population declined, while such a population continued to grow in the less-developed countries.

Concurrently, the postindustrial society will see the expansion of the service sector, including a dramatic surge of whitecollar workers such as brokers, lawyers, accountants, and managers. Furthermore, service oriented institutions will become prominent in controlling more resources and social values than the industrial sector itself. This sector is centered on allocating resources than producing resources. The newly surfacing service sector includes banking institutions, insurance companies, trade firms, real estate, transportation, and communications. Just as the industrial sector was the axis locus of social structure in the resource expansion stage, the service sector will now become the primary force in the management of class stratification and social change.

Discontent of the Middle Class: A New Source of Social Unrest

In the previous stage of resource expansion, industrialization and urbanization reshaped not only the demographic composition of the society but also the structure of social class. Throughout the resource expansion stage, with the emergence of skilled workers and technocrats, social class structure underwent a profound change in which the traditional aristocracy had to yield their preeminent social position, and the new industrial middleclass gained social and political leverage.

But as industrial maturity reaches a peak point, stabilizing social and class mobility, members of lower social and economic classes have more difficulty moving themselves up the ladder of success by conventional means. Industrial and urban jobs no longer provide the kind of rewards sufficient to improve one's social position in a postindustrial environment. Instead, people engage in the service sector as opposed to the manufacturing or production sector will acquire the power to influence decisions in the social distributive system. Here, without government protection, people of lower socioeconomic status can easily fall victim to their own lack of influence over the distributive process. While they are likely to receive government protection (for reasons that we will discuss later when we examine the nature of the welfare system) these allocations are of a maintenance level at best, a do little to alter their relative lack of influence over the allocation process itself.

The middle class that emerged with the expansion of urban industrial jobs now becomes most vulnerable to manipulations of the social and economic establishment. In the process of industrial maturity, the middle class, who were basically wage earners, surfaced as the mainstream of the society with their distinct psychological and behavioral characteristics. They were the people who were more rational, consumer-oriented, private, and politically apathetic. With the expansion of the market economy, these fixed-income wage earners are faced with no other alternatives but to maximize their share of resource allocation by managing their spending. They all become bargainers and bargain hunters, a behavioral pattern common in the postindustrial era. As was discussed in the previous chapter, industry, for its continuous survival and growth, will make its products more appealing to the massconsuming middle class. In this course of development, the middle class becomes exceedingly selfish and oriented toward the private sector.

One consequence of this is that they will be unwilling to pay for the expansion or maintenance of public goods. They will be private-oriented because they are rational. Since they are rational, they will be unwilling to pay for public goods because so long as these goods are provided, they will enjoy their benefits regardless of whether they assume part of the goods' cost. As a result, public institutions and services will face an inevitable deterioration of public support so long as the government fails to intervene. Services such as defense, maintaining law and order, upgrading public parks, highways, and other public facilities will become totally dependent upon the government because, to the rational private sector, they are "someone else's problem." Ironically, it is the very rational middle class on whom the government will dump the burden without facing much resistance. A cursory observation of the American taxation structure, for example, will confirm the fact that it is indeed the middle class, especially the lower middle class, who assume heavier tax burdens, while upper-class Americans escape the tax burdens.

Realizing their deteriorating economic status, the more affluent middle class who were property owners, as seen in California, decided to cry out by calling for a referendum intended to lower the property tax. They succeeded with their campaign known as Proposition 13.[40] This event in an affluent state of America epitomizes the middle class's response to what it perceived as an intolerable deprivation. As we discussed in the previous chapter, these people are by-and-large salaried workers who were sufficiently isolated and unorganized politically as to make any organized collective bargaining against the government extremely difficult. However, as their lifestyle has become threatened by allocation decisions that shift social costs onto them as a group, we have witnessed the proliferation of organized political activity

---

40 For an early exposition of this reality, see *Taking Sides: Clashing Views on Controversial Issues, edited by George McKenna and Stanley Feingold (1982).*

by the middle class aimed precisely at avoiding these costs and shifting the burden to other groups.

As Parker observes, it was as early as in the 1950s that the United States experienced a transition from the primacy of bluecollar work to whitecollar work. Such a transition was considered "the harbinger of a great social revolution, the movement to the 'postindustrial society'" (Parker, 1972, p. 9). As automation increases, the number of bluecollar jobs will continue to decline, and the service sector will continue to grow.

By 1975, when the United States moved securely into the post-industrial stage, 46 percent of all American women 16 years of age and over were in the labor force. Fiftyeight percent of them were married and living with their husbands. Approaching the mid-to-late1960s, it was almost impossible for a family to live as freely and as comfortably as they wished on a single income. Salaries were not rising as quickly as prices in the late 1960s and were almost at a standstill compared to the spiraling, double-digit inflation of the 1970s. Wives and mothers were freed from the home by the many innovations that accompanied the later stages of industrial development. Convenient, timesaving devices such as the microwave liberated women from the kitchen, just as washing machines freed them from the laundry. The cultural liberation of the woman from domestic responsibilities, coupled with the expansion of the service sector and new job opportunities open to women through new policies, left but one logical alternative: a job outside the home.

The economic demands that push both parents into the full-time workplace contribute directly to the social and psychological dislocation of family members in such a way that the very foundation of that institution itself can become unstable, leading to another prime source of frustration and discontent on the part of the middle class.

Urban Decay and Suburbanization

As members of the middle class undergo economic hardships and lose their clout in the political system, the same people who made the emergence of the city become a liability to the city, rather than an asset, due to the increase of welfare spending and public expenditures. The middle class became dismantled by the fact that the more affluent white color middle class urban dwellers will decide to move away from the inner city to the suburb in search of a better quality of life. Thus, all large cities became metropolitan areas where suburbanites managed a drastically different life style from the urban populations: larger, better, and fancier single homes located some distance away from their job sites, necessitating the use of automobiles that forced the working members of the family, usually the parents, to spend more time away from home.

The suburbanites continue to prosper at the expense of inner cities. With super shopping centers and upscale residential communities, suburban residents enjoy their conspicuous consumption. These newly affluent people become the center of attention and political leverage. After all, they own the resources. On the other hand, the inner city carries on at the mercy of the government. Members of the city become disorganized, lose their sense of identity, and feel powerless in dealing within their own lives. The result is the emergence of urban ghettos.

The Rule of Law and Social Justice

To the extent that the fixedsum conflict is prevalent in a society, survival of the society will depend on the extent to which it is maintained by the rule of law, quite analogous to the playing of an actual game such as chess, where the functional stability is managed by the players' observance of the law. When there is disagreement or conflict, the ultimate reservoir of settlement lies in legal authority. The court as the interpreter and adjudicator of laws will intrude into all spheres of life, including the primary institution of the family. It is perceived to be quite natural in the context of the American society that family disputes are brought to court to decide who will get what and how. Perhaps it is no exaggeration to say that the majority of families in America end up in court over some matter, as we are reminded by the statistical fact that six out of ten marriages end in divorce.

The sanctification of laws in some cases paralyzes the function of secondary social institutions such as schools. When teachers are preoccupied with lawsuits that might be brought against them by their students, education is invariably hampered. Educators in America are competitively challenging the school administration for a larger share of resources and values, a challenge for which an optimal solution is rarely found in any redistributive model due to the zerosum nature of the competition. Here, again, the court is the authority and the ultimate peacekeeping agent.

For a society at the stage of conflict management, a bad law is still better than no law, and a bad interpretation of law is more desirable than no interpretation at all.

The Advent of the Advocate

In a society in which winning is all that matters, there must be arbitrators. It is in this context that postindustrial societies come to depend on lawyers and managers to resolve conflicts. As the locus of social interaction moves to legal solutions for social and human problems, the social status and prestige of the profession that is authorized to interpret the law is necessarily elevated. It is not a historical accident that judges and lawyers in the United States enjoy higher prestige and social status, as studies on American social stratification have consistently revealed. In fact, the American political arena and, for that matter, its business arena, today seems to be dominated by lawyers, a condition which is quite unique even compared to industrialized societies in Europe. An examination of the 97th U.S. Congress that convened in 1981, when post-industrial development was at its peak, indicates that 202 of its 535 members were holders of law degrees (JD or LLB). This is due to the simple fact that lawyers are the champions of advocacy. Indeed, a good lawyer can overrule common sense decisions concerning controversial issues, sometimes justifying the unjustifiable.

Virtually every public issue in the United States maintains two sides at the same time, the pro and the con: abortion, same sex marriage, global warming, immigration, tax systems, intervention in foreign wars, school busing, school prayers, the military buildup, and affirmative action programs, to name a few that characterize the controversial nature of the American political system. It should also be noted that these issues, involving the allocation of wealth and of opportunities, are zerosum conflicts in nature. Corresponding to the society's increased reliance upon and, indeed, reverence for the legal profession is the preeminence of the laws themselves.

What is Legal is Also Just!

As laws come to govern people's lives and fortunes, people eventually begin to "worship" laws. Because laws have the power of enforcement embedded in them, it does not take much for people to forget about morality as a means of regulating behavior. They come to think that what is legally justifiable is also morally correct. This confusion of legality with morality is further facilitated by the lack of a consistently propounded ideology. In the age of advocacies and confusion, the concept of justice is constantly defined and redefined by conflicting interests and by masters of advocacy. Thus, social justice, to any degree of objectivity, is inexistent at least in the mind of the postindustrial public. What is just is what was last affirmed by the courts. Since the time of Plato, law has always been only the minimum device for maintaining an orderly society. Laws, as such, are intended to draw a boundary between what is allowable and what is not, rather than what is morally desirable or undesirable. As the question of what is just and desirable becomes an issue subject to interpretation and determined by advocates, the society at this stage of development is not likely to demonstrate an objective (or even inter-subjective) notion of social justice. Thus, legality remains the only tangible yardstick by which to evaluate behavior. The rule of law is indeed the only insurance for the precarious maintenance of social stability and communal integration. If this last resort is threatened, the society itself will break down as unwritten morals and ethics, to the extent that there are such things, are no longer the effective means of conflict management.

Social justice as a concept stems from a philosophical conviction as exemplified by such norms as equality and individual autonomy as the guiding principles for human relations. As such, the concept of social justice should precede legality in that its appeal is toward specific normative prescriptions. Obedience to laws cannot be a value in itself, although it could be an instrument to safeguard other normative values. Even in the case of safeguarding other values, however, the rule of law is implemented through the negative means of punishing the violator rather than the positive means of rewarding the promoter. Thus, members of the society will be preoccupied with what they should not do, rather than what they should do for the betterment of society.

Equitable Distribution versus Distribution for Equality

Human equality as an ideal is hardly challenged. But as a practical policy guideline, equality is seriously hampered in this advanced stage of conflict management. As each member of the society is inclined to think he is more valuable than his rewards indicate, devising a formula for the allocation of values and resources will always be problematic. This is true even in socialist systems where the Marxist formula of "from each according to his ability, to each according to his need" is practically unrealizable.

To rationalize non-egalitarian distributive justice, the notion of "equity" is introduced. An equitable distribution could be any or any combination of the following: (a) according to their needs; (b) according to their ability; (c) according to their efforts; (d) according to their accomplishments; (e) according to the supply and demand of the market place; (f) according to the requirements of the common good; (g) so that none falls below a specified minimum; (h) according to their legitimate claims; and (i) so that they have *equal opportunity* to compete without external favoritism and discrimination. As such, an equitable distribution could be practically any mode of allocation as long as it can claim to be just. In an age of advocates, any allocation will indeed be advocated as being legitimate.

Under these circumstances, social distribution will commence and continue for the advantage of the elite because they have the most influence over the political process by which such distributions are mandated. Thus, we find a peculiar situation where the upper class will subsidize the lower class at the expense of the middle class, as alluded to previously.

Majority Rule versus Minority Rights

With the expansion of the service sector in the postindustrial society, the composition of the middle class will become more complex. White-collar workers will make up the bulk of the class, while its lower segment will be further detached from the middle class itself. The lower middle class, including bluecollar workers, will become a class in itself with a precariously maintained incongruence between middleclass expectations and the structural limitations impeding their achievement. This gap between their expectations and achievements will lead to what Davies terms a "revolutionary state of mind" as discussed in Chapter 6. When these lower middle class people are stigmatized, as African-Americans have been, they become a serious source of social unrest, as was sufficiently demonstrated by civil protest movements in the 1960s.

As discussed in the previous chapter, the middle class is the product of industrialization. With the division of labor and professionalization involved in the process of industrial maturity, middleclass people become rationally indifferent to public affairs. Even when they are deprived, they tend to maintain silence. Reality reminds them that there is little they can do to restructure the social order.

By the advent of the resource expansion stage, many people who enjoy middle class status show a series of psychological attributes and behavioral patterns that include rationality, leisure orientation, and a lack of regard toward public institutions. Thus, there is no mystery to the fact that they are relatively indifferent to public issues. They tend to be politically apathetic. On the other hand, the most deprived minorities, especially those with racial and ethnic qualities that have resulted in oppression from the majority class, tend to protest their deprived status at this stage. The extent of their frustration is such that many of them will engage in demonstrations and civil violence. With the help of the mass media, which is another unique aspect of the postindustrial society, minorities effectively can claim their rights through techniques that the establishment cannot afford to ignore. It is beneficial for regime leadership to demonstrate a willingness to help the "underdog," as it can draw widespread sympathy from the public.

It is in this context that we shall look at the origin of "equal opportunity" programs in the United States and the everexpanding welfare state throughout the postindustrial world.

Equal Opportunity

> You do not take a person who for years has been hobbled by chains and liberate him, bring him up to the starting line of a race then say, 'you are free to compete with others' and still justly believe that you have been completely fair. –President Lyndon B. Johnson

The above statement by Lyndon B. Johnson represents the principle of ensuring equal opportunity by taking "compensatory" measures to correct past discrimination. Affirmative action programs in the United States, which intended to restore equal opportunities, grew with the civil rights movement in the 1960s. The civil rights movement of the sixties focused American consciousness on the severe deprivations that minorities suffered as a result of centuries of discrimination and neglect. But no sooner had the programs challenged the establishment than severe counterforces struck back with the argument of "reverse discrimination."

Affirmative action programs in education are more vigorously challenged because their consequences are expected to be more profound in the long run. Regents of the University of California versus Allan Bakke was one of the landmark cases concerning affirmative action programs in education. In this case, Davis Medical School set aside sixteen of one hundred student slots each year for "disadvantaged" applicants. Every person admitted through this special program during the years of 197074 was a minority group member. Bakke was rejected by Davis and twelve other medical schools. Bakke filed suit claiming reverse discrimination because he felt "lessqualified" applicants were admitted. After the ruling on the Bakke case, it was stated that quotas are unconstitutional but that minority status can be considered as one criterion in admissions policies. Many institutions became divided as to what to do with affirmative action programs, leaving them in a virtual state of limbo.

This clearly demonstrates the difficulty in introducing any measure that might challenge the established order of society. People in the upper echelon will allow the deprived to be helped on the grounds of their own idealism, but when that idealism gets promoted to the extent of threatening their own status, they typically react in defense of their interest.

The Welfare State

With the twin phenomena of (l) "losers" coming out in the process of social and economic competition and (2) the losing minority tending to be more vocal and expressive of its discontent, the government is forced to develop policies to quiet the minority. Concurrently, the main body of the middle class, comprised mostly of salaried workers, makes it easier for the government to extract taxes from their paychecks that will be needed to finance skyrocketing government expenditures in areas of welfare and social security.

Throughout industrial societies, provisions have been made for the payment of benefits to seniors, widows, young children, the disabled, the unemployed, and low-income earners. In the United States, Congress passed a bill establishing such provisions for these groups, known as the Social Security Act of 1935. This legislation was a vital component of President Franklin D. Roosevelt's "New Deal." This act established a system of benefits for elderly workers, a welfare state system for unemployment insurance payments, and a program with which the federal government can provide financial assistance to the states. Since its inception, the Social Security program has grown dramatically, and there is no turning point in sight.

There are many other problems with the welfare programs in the United States, and most likely other advanced societies, as well. The major problem lies with the challenge of expanding revenues to cover the explosive welfare spending. Furthermore, the system provides few or no incentives to work for those who earn an income around the minimum wage, since they realize their income is no more than welfare benefit. Being rational human beings, as they are expected to be in the postindustrial society, welfare recipients find little profit in working while under a system such as the American system. Compounding this problem, the expansion of government bureaucracy that is accompanied by the welfare explosion contributes to corruption, inefficiency, and waste.

Alleviating problems with the welfare system can be difficult because the idea of helping the needy has always been associated with the idea of just government, and any effort to undermine it can be condemned for being inhumane. Here lies the dilemma: the political system cannot prolong its snowballing welfare benefits, yet at the same time, no government can afford to lose the basis of mass support by curtailing the welfare system.

The controversial state of the welfare state in the United States is contrasted with the experience of European welfare state, especially in the Nordic countries. In this regard, the European post-industrial systems and Canada embraced the welfare system before the United States. Explaining the difference between the two sides of the Atlantic is intriguing and challenging, yet is beyond the immediate scope of this book.

Celebrity Leadership and the End of Ideology

If the initial regime formation stage is typified by military leadership, the political integration stage characterized by charismatic leadership, and the industrial stage dominated by corporate leadership, then the post-industrial stage brings forth celebrity leadership. In this stage, members of the society tend to be issue-oriented, and are expected to be hedonistically rational and competitive. At the same time, issues are presented to them by professional advocates in such a way that the public becomes confused as to which course of action will be most beneficial. In such confusion, the voter has no alternative but to make his decision based on instinct and affective considerations, in which politicians with personal appeal have the advantage. Furthermore, when issues concerning the allocation of social and economic values are such that not everyone can come out as a winner, a politician who has a superior ability to "show many faces" in order to attract people of conflicting interests will be most successful. Such a politician must be a superb actor. In a mature industrial society such as the U.S., Japan, and some European nations, celebrities of various types -- including sports stars -- sometimes gain elected office.

In an effort to avoid alienating any more people than is absolutely necessary, politicians learn to avoid controversial issues while campaigning. Instead, they focus on such topics as leadership, spirit, and integrity. In general, they run on their images. At some point, there arises a generation of politicians who have not only abandoned ideology in the interests of attracting votes, but who have never internalized any coherent ideology in the first place. These politicians are the end product of the breakdown of social institutions and alienation in the industrial stage. Furthermore, these actors are encouraged not to formulate policy on any ideological basis because constituents are more concerned with results than deontological considerations.

Capricious Mass Media and Politics

In the previous chapter, we discussed the mass media and how it work in conjunction with industries that need its services for market outreach. Mass media has grown in such a way that commercial messages can reach the consumer more easily. We saw the growing circulation of newspapers and the diversification of radio and television programs in the process of industrial expansion.[41] Those media influences fed the spirit of American competition.

Americans identify with politicians, sports figures, and Hollywood celebrities. They also compete in political discussions and in their ability to reflect current trends through clothes, activities, and personal bearing. The media helps in shaping their thoughts, and they readily adapt to media trends. In this

---

41 The growth of the conventional media slowed down as a result of the explosive development and proliferation of *social media* in the current digital era.

stage, the government tries to survive via the process of conflict management. It tries to maintain a high level of support, yet simultaneously must prevent any institution from becoming so powerful that it threatens the government's security. The government has an especially touchy situation in its interaction with the press. It needs the media desperately, yet fears it. All elected representatives depend, in varying degrees, on the support of the media. In addition, they must be certain that they keep the media satisfied enough to avoid negative public portrayals.

As the consumer is already leisure oriented, the more convenient video mediums of television and online media have recently grown uncontested at the expense of newspapers and radio. It is no accident that many prominent newspapers such as the *Boston Globe* are forced to shut down or move their content to a website. Leaning on a comfortable couch in the living room, one can watch colorful programs at a reasonable cost, and for less effort than it takes to enjoy a newspaper. A television viewer in this postindustrial stage looks more to competitive games as a form of entertainment where he can identify himself with a player or team in an effort to seek the psychological glorification that is expected from winning a competition. An average person in this stage of social change has the psychological propensity to participate in competitions, and the desire to emerge as a winner. However, such a desire is most likely to be blocked off due to the increasingly rigidified social structure and class mobility. Thus, this frustrated person seeks to won vicariously through his player or team. To understand the gameloving masses, one only needs to thumb through TV programs in the United States, Japan, and other mature industrial societies. Game players on television will, in turn, find satisfaction for their own egos, since television exposure makes them instant "celebrities." Such celebrated players are valued so highly that they are paid outrageous salaries, salaries that will be paid ultimately by the viewer himself in the form of higher consumer prices. A careful observer will notice that it is the idea of promoting celebrated players that guide TV sports and other game-oriented programs. The business of sports has become an enterprise in every sense of the word.

For this matter, politicians are also actors seeking media exposures. The media not only promotes, but can easily damage politicians as they attempt to manipulate or at least manage public opinion. The success of politicians and politics is so profoundly dependent on the mass media that some authors realistically characterize the media as the fourth branch of government.

The mass media's impact on society is widely recognized as crucial in forming public attitudes and behavior. Through agenda setting, the mass media asserts that audiences learn salient issues from their reports-- which may well represent biases on the part of the journalist. As a result, our knowledge of political affairs may be based on a small sample of the real world. That world shrinks as the news media decides what to cover and which aspects to report. As Lippmann pointed out, our political responses are made to that tiny replica of the real world, the "pseudo-environment," which we have fabricated and assembled almost wholly from mass media materials.

Furthermore, the common viewing, listening, and reading patterns of a large portion of the public tend to set for the entire society some common foci of attention, some common agenda of discussion. The tendency of the media to homogenize the contents of information eventually develops similar "mind sets" including common preferences, values, and behavioral orientations. This, coupled with the commercialization of the media industry, will stimulate the public in such a way that they will become motivated to compete for commonly sought values, and, as a result, social competition will become more intensified. Concurrently, as the horizons of one's world expand, especially through the visual medium of television, the field of competition expands, putting social competition on a national and international scale.

War Technology and Political Terrorism

The concept of terrorism is not new. What is relatively new is the profound destructive potential of technology and the extent of publicity guaranteed by the mass media. The uncontrollable technological innovations that have already attained their autonomous course of development made mass destruction and mass killing possible without the use of significant manpower. For example, much has been written about the availability of nucleardevice design data in publicly available literature, and it appears that there is sufficient material available in unclassified literature to provide a potential bombmaker with enough information to produce such a weapon.

Furthermore, utilizing such a weapon will not inflict the sense of guilt usually expected of a killer whose aggression is directed at specific individuals, since mass killing is ultimately carried out by technologically advanced weapons that separate the killer from the killed. Apel observes,

Neither aggression nor aggression restraints play an essential role in in the act of killing], because the nature and dimensions of modern weapon technology completely shield [the killer] from a human encounter with the socalled enemy. He merely presses the button as ordered; the result of his bombing, however, are so immense that he can no longer experience them on a concrete, emotional level.[42]

With destructive technology enabling a certain moral neutrality toward killing, contemporary politics is marred by political terrorism. Publicity is considered to be the most important motive for terrorism. Bard O'Neill (1978), in a discussion of the Palestinian resistance movement, attributes terrorism to publicity more than anything else. In this sense, we might conclude that the mass media may be the chief unintentional facilitator of political terrorism.

In short, the growth of the mass media as an inevitable outcome of industrial maturity has indeed revolutionized politics and society. With the arrival of the computer age and the certain perpetuation of industrial expansion, we foresee an even greater sophistication and more universal distribution of the mass media which, despite its inherent benefits, will make the world ever more precarious and unpredictable.

Social and Institutional Deterioration

The Affluent Economy and the Poor Society

As one observer put it succinctly, "Future historians will likely characterize the twentyfive years from 1945 to 1970 in American society as a period of foolish affluence fueled by borrowed money."[43] Noted economist John K. Galbraith concluded, "If people are hungry, illclad, unsheltered or diseased, nothing is so important as to remedy their condition. Higher income is the basic remedy; their problem is thus an economic problem." However,

---

42 Fred Dallmayer (1978), p. 83
43 Gary Gappert (1978), p. ix

"with higher income, questions beyond the reach of economics obtrude."[44] Gappert (1978) observes:

> The struggle for subsistence is not the issue for the United States. No. The questions that obtrude beyond the reach of economics are social and personal in nature. The problem of post-affluence is a social problem...The isolation and needs of the urban and rural underclasses provide evidence that the United States now faces the end of the myth that "more will be better." There isn't much more to be had, and some say that there will be less, but there will be enough. That is to say, there will be enough if we redefine what "enough" is.

Just as the nation loses control over its economy, individual members of the society will lose control over their own lifestyles. Their lives are lived in fascination of consumerism and the myth of affluence. The poor consumer is passively overwhelmed by a sense of alienation, loneliness, and above all, helplessness. The traditional institutions of family, school, and religion, which have experienced a process of deterioration, have now become largely incapable of "rehabilitating" the postaffluent loser in this zero-sum game.

It is in this context that the emergent debate over the "quality" of life should be understood. Until recently, indicators such as the Gross National Product, GNP per capita, industrial output, and urbanization were used to measure social and political development. But these measurements have proven to be fallacious as barometers of human development, a concept that is looming large in modern discussions of social change. As alternative metrics, some authors suggest a series of more intimately human factors for measuring the condition of the world's life situations.[45]

A social system is a network of human interactions with an established pattern of relationships among members of the society. In such a system, one maintains his social position by performing a role that is appreciated by other members of the community. It is appreciated because its place in the perpetuation of the

---

44 Gary Gappert (1978), pp. x-xi

45 In an attempt to address this issue, David Morris Morris (1979) introduced *The Physical Quality of Life Index (PQLI)*

selfsubsistence of the community is recognized and perceived to be essential. Industrial and postindustrial social change, however, deprives the community of its selfsubsistence in exchange for the alleged gains in economy and efficiency. No town or city is selfsubsistent anymore. Indeed, no nation is selfsufficient in the wake of the formation of the global system.

The society ceases to be a social system because its members are unaware of their relative social positions or of the pattern of social interaction in which they take part. As discussed in the previous chapter, the urban center has ceased to be a place for common interaction. Social relations in the city are managed by a system of material transactions and through a network of information, rather than by its patterned human interactions. The global system makes its individual members mutually interdependent, and thus, incapable of self-subsistence. Just as in the case of urban life, the global system is managed in its equilibrium through information systems and functional relationships among groups of functional entities, instead of individual members. With the help of sophisticated information storage and processing facilities made available by computer technology, the global system has become ever more structured, and this process is made even more efficient by virtue of its alienation from human attributes. As they say, we are all numbers; if one lacks a number, one is nonexistent!

As we discussed earlier, the family system has responded to industrial change by reducing its structural size from the extended system to the nuclear family unit. When the postindustrial cultural system prevails upon the family, it simply breaks up. The ultrarational personality of the postindustrial man directs the family relationship into a convenient bond maintained by the rule of costbenefit calculations. It is mutual utility that ties a husband and wife together, and the relationship will last so long as such a utility remains. When people fail to see the usefulness of family, they are willing to stay out of the institution of marriage as is amply demonstrated by the critical state of the family in many industrial societies such as the United States and the Scandinavian countries.

When an overwhelming majority of the people reside in urban areas and are engaged in the industrial and service sectors and occupations, and at the same time live in or out of the troubled family, we can safely conclude that they are on the verge of being eliminated from social systems as social systems themselves crumble away.

When there is no pattern of interaction within a society and no mores and norms to help maintain human bonds, it becomes less likely that children will be socialized into patterns of behavior that are supportive of the system. Indeed, children in postindustrial America appear to be removed from the experience of socialization, a process in which they learn the norms and values predominant in the society and become functionally integrated members. With all the promotion of consumer goods throughout the mass media and even in schools, American children seem to be preoccupied with desire for conspicuous consumer goods. If a child fails to go with the tide of consumerism, he is likely to become alienated from his cohorts, a severe social sanction which could be a fatal blow to the tender mind of the child.

In this chapter, I have discussed some aspects of postindustrial development in an effort to demonstrate the fact that the development process does not cease after the attainment of the industrial stage. Indeed, the social and cultural implications of postindustrial change are likely to be detrimental to the maintenance of a social and cultural system, the same system that helped members of the society seek satisfaction for their belonging needs. It is intriguing to observe that just as the third stage of development - the resource expansion stage - destroyed the institutions of the first stage through the perversion of agriculture and the Military Industrial Complex, this fourth stage has adverse impacts on the social institutions of the second stage, hinting at the irony that we tend to neglect what we have and pursue what we don't have. The sad historical reality is that all the mal-symptoms produced by the process of industrial and post-industrial development depicted in this and the previous chapter will worsen as we enter a brand new stage of globalization, a topic for the following chapter.

CHART 1. Stages of Political Change

-This Chart depicts the properties discussed in the stage theory as discussed in Part Two of this book.

	Regime Formation	Political Integration	Resource Expansion	Conflict Management
Human Needs	Survival	Belonging	Leisure	Control
Means	Food Safety Security	"Friends" "Significant Others" Group	Hobbies & Toys Privacy Convenience	Influence Power Prestige
Institutions	Agriculture Police Military	Family Church (Religion) School (Education)	Industrialization Marketing Urbanization	Mass Media Interest Groups Parties
Attitude-Behavior Traits	Pacifism Fate-accepting Compliant-Submissive Authoritarian	Altruism Cooperation Egalitarian Imaginative and Abstract	Consumptive Bargaining and Rational Entertainment Quantitatively Oriented	Competitive Game-loving Legalism Bossism
System Character	Centrism	Ideological	Bureaucratic	Participatory
Leadership Type	Military-Coercive	Intellectual-Philosophical	Technocratic-Cooperative	Actor
Policy Preference	Production of necessities Law and Order Defense	Politicization Power Consolidation	Economic Growth Production of "conspicuous" goods Protection of Industry	"Just" distribution (Who gets What, and How?)

Symptoms	Stubbornness and Rigidity Uniformity Factions and Cliques	"Armchair Philosopher" Politicization of curriculum Purges Politics of Fear	"The bigger, the better" Environmental Decay Morality Confusion Loss of individuality	World of "fantasies" Mutual Distrust Legality replacing Morality
Probable Outcomes	Successive Military Coups	Totalitarian Control	Economic Reliance upon Others	Status quo (at best) Welfare System SLOW AND PAINLESS ROAD TO HUMAN EXTINCTION
Intervening Context	Weather Land Condition Geographical Location Geopolitics	Social-Ethnic Structure Linguistic and Religious Homogeneity Culture and Civilization	Natural Endowment Entrepreneurship Achievement/Ascriptive Orientation	All of the Factors in the Previous Stages
Contextual Characteristics				

Chapter 10

The Birth of a Global Community: A Blessing or a Curse?

Globalization is an extension of development. The postindustrial society cannot be contained within a nation, for industrial expansion defies national boundaries. Industries in the developed societies will find it increasingly difficult to exist within their national boundaries due to, among other things, expensive labor costs, scarce resources, a limited consumer base against the post-industrialists' unlimited appetite for earning, and public pressure from environmentalists which fuels government regulation. These forces will drive businesses to explore foreign markets. It is in this context of the post-industrial economic spillover that we should discuss current topics such as the rapid advent of multinational corporations, technology transfer, immigration of workers, terrorism, cyber warfare, proliferation of weapons of mass destruction, and the formation of the integrated and indivisible global system. This process of globalization coupled with the myriad ills of the post-industrial society will steer the course of history in a new and uncharted direction, a direction that will be explored in the following pages.

This phase of globalization, however, is not prompted by some new system of human needs or wants. Survival, belonging, leisure, and control needs remain the underlying forces that engineer social change and development. Thus, it is correct to say that globalization is a continuation of development as previously discussed in this book.

Withering Away of the State boundaries

A firm drilling an oil well in the Persian Gulf, using American technology, German machines, Chinese labor, and an energy supply from Saudi Arabia, is no longer a company under the influence of a single nation. For the single objective of economizing, industrial firms are becoming multinational and, to that extent, depend on the international economic system. No viable economic unit, whether it is a manufacturing or a service sector entity, can be contained within the boundary of a political system, thus making any one government unable to manage and control it. Here emerged the world of multi-national corporations (MNCs). MNCs have been viewed either as a force of economic development and modernization or a vice that would make the less developed countries helplessly dependent on the post-industrial economies. However, unlike the pre-global era, the globalized economy and the global society at large are mutually becoming so highly interdependent that the global village is now an indivisible structure incorporating both culture and industry. The indivisibility is clearly witnessed in the global financial and market systems, as well as the system of global communication born from advances in information technology. The global financial meltdown seen in the first decade of the 21st Century revealed this indivisibility, suggesting that one country's fiscal state is affected by the fiscal health of other countries. The current European economic crisis definitively shows how intimately the country-specific economic systems are interrelated.

The global economic system is a relatively new concept as it acquired a new meaning in the international economy. In the conventional world, there was no system of order among the nation states. As Raymond Aron observed, the international system "has always been anarchical and oligarchical: anarchical because of the absence of a monopoly of legitimate violence, oligarchical in that, without civil society, rights depend largely on might" (Aron, p. 160). During the Cold War decades, the supremacy of *might*, especially military power, led the bipolar world system to the madness of an arms race that kept the world balanced precariously on the precipice of war and possible annihilation. This was possible through the intimate fear of Mutually Assured Destruction (MAD). In this sense, *might* worked the stability of the world. However, due to the interdependent nature of the global system in the post-Cold War era, the power of *might* has become entirely relative, and is no longer expressed in terms of destructive power alone.

With the increasingly predictable functional system of the international community, one might expect the birth of a new international order. Yet, we can hardly infer from this that this new order will facilitate orderly relationships among diverse states. On the contrary, as states interact with one another from a position of functional utility, they are more likely to expect a greater share of distributions of values and resources that could possibly promote further competition and conflict.

World Order Derailed

Unlike the conventional international order where *might* prevailed, the developing nations in the global age are raising their voices of resentment against the role of developed economy, even in the area of technology transfer. The underdeveloped nations do not hesitate to criticize the fact that sophisticated technology transferred from the industrial world has not achieved what their governments expected of it at the time that they initiated industrialization programs. It did not help create employment, cater to the basic needs of the population, build up the indigenous technological ability, or create the necessary infrastructure for the indigenous technological development of developing nations. As a result, the so-called NorthSouth global system is trending toward confrontation rather than cooperation. The North tends to perceive development as a privilege, while the South is determined to claim development as a right.

In the NorthSouth dispute, what is evident is the notion held by the South that poor countries are forced to remain poor as a result of continuous exploitation by the North, dating to the beginning of colonialism. This suggests that the political independence that new nations have gained simply amounts to a transition from political colonialism to economic colonialism. Nyerere of Tanzania put it unambiguously:

> In one world, as in one nation, when I am rich because you are poor, and I am poor because you are rich, the transfer of wealth from the rich to the poor is a matter of rights, it is not an appropriate matter for charity...

According to this view, the development of the North has been achieved at the expense of the South, and it is now the rich countries that have the moral obligation to return some of the wealth they took away from the poor. It is widely contended that much of the largescale aid provided by the West in the past under the "trickle down" theory of growth has failed to reach the poorest people in less-developed countries (LDCs), thus, it has failed to enhance the conditions in which they live day-to-day. This situation has led some authors in the "dependence" school of thought to claim that foreign aid actually serves the interests of the developed countries, while further incapacitating the LDCs.

Johnson (1972, p. 100) summarizes this contention:

> United States private investment, and programs, foreign
> policy, military assistance, military interventions, and
> international agencies are interwoven and oriented
> toward the promotion and maintenance of influence and
> control in other countries.

The LDCs argue further that the sophisticated technology that
has been made available to the "latecomer" has not achieved what
was expected of it. As Graham put it:

> [Sophisticated technology] did not help in creating
> employment, catering to the basic needs of the
> population or building up the indigenous technological
> ability of the countries concerned. This was
> partly because industrialization took the form of
> importsubstitutions which, in effect, often meant that
> the transfer of technology was geared not to meeting
> the basic needs of the population but rather to the
> satisfaction of a demand for modern sophisticated
> consumer goods by a small but prosperous upper and
> uppermiddle class.

If, as they contend, the LDCs have been exploited for the
prosperity of the developed world, and if the DCs alone have
created dependency on the part of the LDCs, then one might
conclude that the DCs may have the moral responsibility to
help the LDCs overcome developmental difficulties. The DCs,
however, seem to be determined to undermine such accusations
and to maintain that national poverty is selfinflicted, in that the
LDCs lack the cultural and historical prerequisites for economic
development. In addition, political corruption, mismanagement, the
absence of the infrastructure needed for economic development,
and ideological commitment to redistribution as opposed to
reinvestment are frequently cited as the prime sources of fault on
the part of poor countries.

In response to the exploitation charge, Bauer and Yamey (1977)
among others point to the fact that those least developed countries
are the ones that have had little economic contact with the West,

202

and the extreme backwardness of countries such as Chad, Burundi, Lesotho, Rwanda, Afghanistan, Yemen, and Sikkim can hardly be due to exploitation by international economic powers. Indeed, it has been richly documented for the record that the latecomers to the development process, particularly the "newly industrialized countries" (NICs) have benefited from advanced technology, international markets, and foreign capital provided by the already industrialized societies. Thus, in the view of the DCs, the development of the LDCs is in no way within the purview of their moral responsibility. According to this position, poor countries have no right to demand anything but should appreciate with gratitude any humanitarian assistance if and when it comes.

In short, there appears to be no common ground upon which the issue of obligatory relations among nations for international development is understood. Each side seems to have sufficient evidence to rationalize its own contentions but not enough to persuade the other. This lack of consensus has become a new source of international conflict in the postCold War era. Yet, what is evident is the general trend that the rich nations have become richer and the poor have become poorer. The income or wealth gap is also visible in the domestic environment. In the course of active globalization, the middle class in any advanced society will be strained to the point of collapse, leaving behind two divergent and polarized classes. The recent epidemic of "Occupy Wall Street" demonstrations, in which representatives of the "99%" marched against the elite "1%" of society, are indicative of this distributive injustice crisis, which may sap the stability of the political system.

We have been rushed into a world that defies a universally accepted orderly system of relationships. This point will be picked up later in this chapter when we discuss the security paradigm versus peace paradigm.

Mal-development

The concept of *mal-development* is introduced here to provide contrast with underdevelopment. Whereas underdevelopment represents a relatively low level of development in a country as a whole, *mal-development* refers to imbalanced development. When nations of the preindustrial stage come to interact with industrially mature societies, the former can be easily induced to *mal-development* by the premature absorption of foreign institutions and behavior styles. In a society where the predominant public needs remain at the level of physical survival with hunger and starvation as chronic problems, policies aimed solely at industrialization will bear little direct relevance to the masses. Such policies will, however, facilitate social disintegration and economic imbalance, fostering abnormal development of social and political institutions, as well as the behavior styles of the citizenry. As we discussed earlier in this book, electoral institutions and voting behaviors in LDCs often show deviant characteristics, and such a deviance could be attributed to the fact that these institutions have been transplanted by foreign nations into indigenous societies unprepared to receive them. Likewise, when a person in an LDC is uncertain about the more urgent needs such as food and shelter, and yet feels pressured to imitate the conspicuous lifestyle of affluent society, he may exert a parasitic effect on his society and its institutions.

The postindustrial necessity to explore new markets often reaches the remotest corners of the world where the society is unprepared for industrial fruits. Being in contact with foreign commodities and new ways of life is likely to stimulate the people to generate new demand in addition to the more urgent old needs. The presence of diverse demands placed upon the society will make it more difficult for the government to respond effectively, and ultimately make the society more vulnerable to political unrest.

When consumer items produced for leisure are transmitted to a society where the vast majority of its members are still seeking survival and belonging, they are often used for other purposes than convenience and efficiency. In this case, consumer goods such as refrigerators, color television sets, and automobiles become status symbols-- means of displaying a certain lifestyle reserved for a certain social class. Thus, class differences are demonstrated in overt material terms, and as a result, the underprivileged develop an acute sense of class-consciousness. This, too, may eventually lead to social and political unrest.

A balanced development, as opposed to *mal-development*, is one where all areas of the society -- such as human needs, institutions, behavioral dispositions, policy preferences, and leadership characteristics -- make simultaneous and mutually reinforcing progress toward a higher stage. This balanced development is often disrupted by the intrusion of more-advanced foreign countries. In view of this, we might evaluate the role of advanced societies in the development of the LDCs with greater caution.

Distributive Injustice and Relative Deprivation

As the human community is swept by the tide of globalization, the pattern of world's wealth and income distribution has moved away from fairness and equity. This pattern of skewed distribution runs through the global, regional, and domestic arenas.

The recent Occupy Movement, which became a global phenomenon by the end of 2010, must be seen in this context. This movement can be interpreted as a mass revolt against distributive injustice in general, which is seen as the function of the world's prevailing financial and economic structures. These structures constitute a certain kind of structural violence targeted against the overwhelming majority of the world's population.

Income distribution in the United States is so skewed that the average income for the wealthiest top in 2010 was $1.3 million and the lowest 40% earned under $20,000. Although the distribution skew is less extreme in Europe and other developed countries, the polarizing effect is widely seen all over the developed world. What is even more startling is the fact that the same pattern of distributive injustice is no less acute in the LDCs. The segments of population in the LDCs that interact with and benefit from the MNCs become super rich at the expense of the rest of the country, a trend observed in countries in Latin America, the Middle East, Africa, and Asia. In short, the polarization of classes throughout the world may effectively lead to aggregated dissention throughout the globe which could cross fertilize among nations and societies.

No one can say for certain what might constitute a universally agreeable formula of distributive justice, but it can be said that the skewed distribution in favor of a small number of people will become a source of social unrest throughout the global community. With the presence of the Internet, movements of dissention will aggregate and spread more quickly than they have in the past. We have already seen this in the Arab Spring of 2010-2012, which certainly had roots in distributive injustice. In Egypt, Tunisia, Libya, and Syria, a large number of people challenged the power legitimacy of small number of elites. One might find an intriguing connection between these events and the original Marxist theory of revolution: the economic and social ramifications of globalization appear to fall into the track of Marxist expectation on a grand scale.

Fall of the Middle Class

While the middle class was once a formidable force in the industrial society, it has now been economically and socially marginalized by globalization. In the previous chapter, when we discussed the rise of the middle class, we attributed its rise to three new forces that Karl Marx failed to witness: *skills* possessed by the proletariat worker which make him difficult to replace, the empowerment of the worker by *collective bargaining*, and the *consumption power* of the worker. Each of these three boons to the middle class has been, and will continue to be, adversely affected by globalization.

First, the skill factor became insignificant as industrial goods were increasingly produced through mechanization and automation composed primarily of independent modules can be replaced with only basic repair skills. Second, the availability of alternative labor pools in other countries has made collective bargaining ineffective. Industries (both the manufacturing and service sectors) have relocated to new production sites in LDCs where environmental restrictions are largely non-existent and the labor force is inexpensive. At the same time, massive numbers of foreign workers are brought in for no other reason than economic profitability. It is a global phenomenon that no economic entity could avoid addressing. In the presidential campaigns of the United States in 2012, both President Obama and his Democratic Party and Governor Romney of the Republican Party engaged in the rhetoric of returning jobs from foreign countries, especially China, to the United States. In launching his second term, President Obama reiterated his resolve to attract American jobs back to the United States, but one must be skeptical about his ability to counter the law of economic nature.

Third, the middle class pocket was designed and expected to be an important source of consumption without which the post-industrial economy could not survive. The impoverished middle class can no longer afford such consumption, despite all the marketing and banking tricks that can lead the consumer to buy beyond his means. The housing crisis in the United States in the first decade of 21st Century amply demonstrated this phenomenon. The middle class that emerged forcefully in the process of industrialization, our resource expansion stage (Chapter 8), has lost it buying power. The impoverishment of the middle class has been further exacerbated by the fact that they have become the target for government taxation. After all, the middle class, unlike people of wealth and establishment, has no power to avoid increased taxation. In the end, we are witnessing the formation of a bipolar pattern of distribution. In the absence of the middle class, the Marxist theorem materialized in a grand scale. Will there necessarily be a class conflict (class war)? An intriguing question, indeed!

Demographic Challenge: Aging Population, Foreign Workers and Immigrants

One blessing of development is that people live longer by eradicating life- shortening diseases and improving health science and hygienic conditions. Yet, this development has failed to cope with the aging population in advanced societies. In the pre-industrial stage, older people were regarded as the source of wisdom and knowledge, and respected as the reservoir of authority in the extended family structure. But as industrial and post-industrial stages set in, the segment of the population that was unable to keep up with skills and technical knowledge has become increasingly marginalized. Furthermore, when the extended family system eroded with urbanization, family elder care suffered, and the state was forced to expand its welfare programs to cover the growing elderly population.

At the same time, most economically advanced societies experience shrinking birth rates to the extent that their labor pool cannot meet the demand for a productive labor force, opening the door to foreign immigrants. The rate of natural birth is unable to sustain the existing level of population in almost all industrial and post-industrial societies in Europe, North America, Japan, and newly emerging economies of South Korea, Taiwan, and Singapore. Without foreign and immigrant workers, labor demand in these countries is clearly unmet. This is a new and growing problem in the global community; whereas they are needed for the economy, they impose on the host country a tremendous strain in social and political arenas. These workers and their families often require states to expand welfare programs regardless of popular consensus within the host country.

The plight of immigrant workers is a chronic problem throughout the developed world. At the same time, the home country that is losing its most active force is also experiencing a great deal of economic and social strain. This problem is going to be exacerbated further as globalization progresses.

Public Goods Orphaned

What is public and what is private? That is the central question in all of political life! If everything is public, we have totalitarian socialism, and if everything belongs to private individuals, we have a complete liberalism.

Consumption, Consumption, Consumption: A Cure all?

When U.S and European economies were facing recession, their governments set out to increase consumption (and thus, spending) by their citizens. When there were terrorist threats by al-Qaeda and other terrorist groups, Washington initially issued warnings for citizens to stay away from places where a large number of people are clustered such as shopping malls, and at the same time, it encouraged them to shop more and consume more. What a contradictory recipe it was! We established in the previous chapters that market competition is instrumental in mass production, which, in turn, necessitates mass consumption. Without high levels of consumption by the middle class, industry, especially the manufacturing sector, cannot be sustained. We also established the fact that the banking system was developed in a way that allowed consumers to spend far beyond their means. The "precarious consumer," who emerged in the industrial stage (Chapter 8), and the "conspicuous consumer" discussed in the post-industrial stage (Chapter 9) both have the predisposition for competitive consumption at the global scale. The international financial system encourages consumptive behavior upon which the financial system itself is dependent. Nothing in the economic or political system can curtail people's rising appetite for consumption, except for the consumer's willpower. This willpower is not likely to emerge as long as the market lures consumers with sophisticated strategies and the consumers themselves are helplessly addicted to consumption. All institutions and influential people advocate for unbound consumption. The government does it, commercial advertisements do it, financial institutions encourage it, and the consumers have long been arrested by the obsession to consume.

The global community has indeed entered the era of consumption, which is deeply inculcated with consumption culture and consumption behavior. The greatest force in engineering social change during the consumption era is the might of commercial advertisements. The market economy promotes the development of marketing strategies to the extent that institutions of higher education have adopted the disciplinary specialization of marketing in business schools throughout the world. The art and science of marketing strategy has been endlessly refined toward "hypnotizing" the consumer to become enticed to the product. To make the matter worse, the intensely competitive nature of the global economic system forces the producer to offer increasingly more attractive consumer goods. We can see in the electronics industry, particularly with cellular phones, computer hardware and software, television sets, and the creation of virtual reality through electronic games.

Mass media emerged originally for the purpose of information dissemination and exchange, but soon became completely dependent on advertisement revenues. When these revenues are not sustained, media outlets are forced to go out of business, as evidenced by the incursion of online "social media" into the revenue streams of traditional print media. The parasitic effects of consumption culture are multi-faceted, including cultural stagnation as excessive consumerism and materialism draw away from commitment to community and neighbors.

Moneytalkcracy

In the consumption society, a new cultural disposition sets in, a culture in which people of all walks of life worship money. The desire to make and accumulate money is pervasive not only in the market economy but also in any economy at all levels of development. Indeed, money has become a global religion that supersedes any mass belief system such as democracy and capitalism. When money talks, people listen! This makes "moneytalkcracy" universally valid in all societies regardless of their ideological identities that every political system is affected by this "ideology" where people listen to money uniformly, so much so that the term "moneytalkcracy" is regarded appropriate as a super ideology!

Breakdown of the Community

A community is a social and cultural space where people maintain their patterned relationship through communication.

The course of development in the industrial, postindustrial, and global stages that brought urbanization, suburbanization, and globalization has proven to be irreversible, and this process has permanently destroyed the agrarian community. Urban centers, as seen in the industrialization stage, have sprung up as commercial centers where human relationships are largely dictated by contractual terms, as opposed to human commitments. In this environment, people are not inclined to find a sense of mutual belonging through interpersonal communication. Rural neighbors, even if they live geographically far apart from one another, still interact and maintain a sense of mutual belonging. By contrast, urban dwellers, even when they live in the same apartment complex, often function as strangers, and are disinclined to establish any pattern of relationship among their fellow occupants. They may meet at nearby shopping centers, but no meaningful communication is expected at the market place. Therefore, a large number of people living in close proximity might not necessarily constitute a social community.

The breakdown of community contributes to criminal behavior by those individuals who lost a sense of belonging and community. When community is broken down, social institutions, especially the primary institution of family will suffer as discussed in the following section. I will advance the premise that the revival of community is impossible without communication in Chapter 14.

The Decline of Capitalism

The development paradigm as explained in the previous chapters was able to explain industrialization and the accompanying growth of the market economy. The market economy here follows the core principles of capitalism: private ownership, the rule of supply/demand, and rational decision-making behavior of both the consumer and the producer. Indeed, capitalism was instrumental in economic growth in all kinds of political systems irrespective of ideology. Capitalism, with its competitive landscape, has been the only relevant economic system in the global market.

As competition among multinational corporations became endlessly fierce, big conglomerates became vulnerable to acquisitions and mergers among themselves, having a massive effect on both populations and politics at the international level. This phenomenon generated what Robert Rich called "super-capitalism," which practically makes fair competition impossible.

The global economy is now operated by monopolies of all types, and the ideals behind the Anti-Trust Act are largely obsolete notion in global practice. Coupled by this is the prevalence of military economies that defy the capitalist principle of open competition. Led by the United States, Russia, Great Britain, France, and China, the global arms market has shown a steady increase in the last decade. All of these states have developed some version of a military-industrial complex. Even lesser economies that import weapons and military technology such as India, South Korea, and Israel have succumbed to the force of military-industrial-political complex, siphoning money away from the general health of capitalist economy.

Military economies are managed outside a working system of accountability. The government primarily conducts with public funds, and open bidding within the arms industry is either limited or virtually nonexistent. In fact, this industry is quite secretive, and many public demands for openness are blocked under the pretext of national security. Private contractors for the military play a large role in shaping the mission and require considerable expenditures, all from public funds and with little or no accountability.

Corporate mergers and the military economy are the twin culprits for distributive injustice in the global society, and they are expected to grow as economies, societies, and conflicts continue to globalize.

Deterioration of Institutions

The over-extension of development, coupled with the degeneration of the primary social institution, creates a situation in which many other institutions are largely unable to perform the functions for which they were created in the first place. A cursory survey of the institutions that have been created in the process of historical evolution as documented in this book suggests that those institutions have weakened or become dysfunctional in the process of post-industrial and global development.

Agriculture:

The commercialization of agriculture has crippled farm communities and farmers themselves who can no longer survive without government subsidies. Even with subsidies, or perhaps because of them, indigenous farmers have been removed from their land only to see the intrusion of the commercialists whose only interest is the maximization of production and profit margin. The plight of farmers in America and other advanced countries aptly demonstrates this phenomenon. To maximize economic utility, commercial farmers convert multi-purpose farmland into cash-crop operations, exacerbating food shortages around the world. Fueled by the desire to earn greater profit, commercial farmers often genetically engineer crops and livestock, introducing a new set of health hazards into the food supply. Foreign food aid is largely made of food produced this way. As discussed in the previous chapters, the erosion of traditional farming will inevitably strain traditional agricultural communities to the point of collapse.

The Military:

Commercialization of the military, as discussed earlier, reinforces the expansion of the military-industrial complex (MIC). In the globalization process, the reach of the MIC extends across national boundaries as domestic producers and international consumers of weapons develop mutual interdependence.

In underdeveloped countries, the weapons trade is often controlled by corrupt politicians and governments, thus for these countries, what is likely to be formed is the Military-Political Complex (MPC) used to perpetuate the current regime, even in light of capricious policies. This is particularly the case when the politicians are installed by the military through coups. The militarization of politics can lead to brutal dictatorships as we have seen in a number of countries in Africa and the Middle East, most recently in Egypt and Libya. As we have seen in the American military involvement in Iraq and Afghanistan, the privatization of the military has made military operations not only more expensive but, in many ways, less efficient.

Under the sway of a military-industrial complex, the military tends to stray from its intended role on defense of the nation from external aggression. The interests of the military-industrial complex encourage conflict around the world for the precise motive of economic and political benefit.

When wars are fought without the necessity of national defense, soldiers may have difficulty in rationalizing the acts they commit and life-threatening circumstances they endure in combat. This often leads to emotional disturbances in returning soldiers, increasing the occurrence of suicide and criminal violence among veteran populations struggling to adjust to post-war civilian life. Such was the case among American soldiers returning from Iraq and Afghanistan in the early decades of the 21st Century, themselves victims of two wars fought under questionable pretense

Education:

When a society becomes globalized, education is given less attention or priority. As a result, public educational institutions supported by governments suffer for lack of funding. On the other hand, private schools proliferate in areas where education is marketed for money to those who can afford it. In the United States, for instance, it is no longer too farfetched to hear someone state publically that the government should abolish the Department of Education all together. Schoolteachers in this global era are least appreciated and poorly compensated, contributing to the degeneration of education in both quality and quantity.

The commercialization of the academia becomes even more rampant among the institutions of higher education. Professors at colleges and universities in the United Sates, for example, have commoditized themselves by habitually chasing higher paying jobs. Both administrators and teaching faculty are evaluated by their ability to raise funds and donations, rather than their ability to teach and inspire students. Here, the ultimate loser is the student, who is left with no recourse to rectify the situation. The commercialization of academia has also profoundly affected school curricula in a manner in which education becomes little more than an instrument for moneymaking. The noble goal of character development and establishment of intellectual self-identity has been subsumed by monetary concerns in the advanced global community.

Religion:

During the stage of social development in which people seek and expand their sense of belonging and self-identity, religious institutions are given a primary emphasis. However, when society evolves through the industrial, post-industrial, and global stages, they have become more of a market place where money buys privileges and even "buys" the ticket to heaven. Indeed, religious institutions have become quite lucrative in their "earnings" through the indoctrination of the masses who desperately seek to fulfill a belonging need that is deprived in both developed and undeveloped worlds.

In this global era, some religions collaborate with political powers to form theocracies of various kinds. These theocratic beliefs are often emboldened by actual or perceived threats from the outside world. Such was the case in the Middle East, where the presence of the Western powers, especially the United States, provided an incentive to the Jihadist campaign by Muslim extremists.

Politicization of religion is prevalent throughout the world in the globalized community, and once political systems become infused with religious dogma, their actions become more deterministic and less open to compromise. In this situation, negotiating settlement of differences or conflicts becomes more difficult. One distinct development in the religious lives of advanced societies is the proliferation of sectarian religious groups. A sectarian faith organization typically has a "savior" figure as the spiritual leader, a concretely drawn roadmap to "heaven" in the form of scripture of sorts, and a tightly knit interpersonal system in which members seek, and often find, a credible sense of mutual belonging. As the family institution struggles to provide that same sense of belonging in the commercialized world, sectarian religions can be an effective source of the fulfillment of the belonging need. These sectarian groups usually do not sustain beyond the life span of their leaders. Some, however, are more solidly institutionalized, as seen in the Unification Church of Rev. Sun Myung Moon.

In short, the process of post-industrial development and globalization has systematically undermined the institutions that were invented for the purpose of need satisfaction in the earlier stages of development, regime formation, and political integration, to the extent that they have become unable to deliver their originally assigned functions.

Health of the Planet

The Trauma of the Ecosystem

During the early stages of political development, man lived in close harmony with the physical environment. In the days before industry, man could not disturb the environment permanently due to the small population and localized nature of agricultural production. Some disturbance was seen in the burning of fields and forests for crop and pasture, but it was not total devastation by any means. The ecosystem survived, and so did man. When food gathering turned to larger scale food planting, it was a step toward regime formation, but it was also a small step away from the ecological harmony that he had enjoyed for centuries.

The building of walled cities for the storage and protection of surplus grain is a good example of how man began to manipulate his household at the expense of the environment. This in itself was not bad, but when cities became nations and populations increased dramatically, man became more exploitative. The history of man from the early river valley civilizations to the modern super powers has been an avalanche of political integration at the expense of the environment. The nature of the nation requires that it be built on something, and the people erroneously believe that the land can support them indefinitely.

As the cities and nation states outgrew their boundaries, the need for new frontiers was great. Man found new frontiers and was, for a while, satisfied. In the nineteenth century, however, it was discovered that there was no more frontier land for man to conquer. Frederick Jackson Turner not only shocked historians at the turn of the century, but also inadvertently aroused the environmentalists. He reminded us that we had reached the boundaries of our ecosystem, and that we would now have to look back at our environment and see what we had missed in the years of pillage. It is interesting to note that while man spent his first 15,000 years surviving and the last 5,000 trying to belong in human communities, only within the last century and a half has our lust for leisure and control put all of our accomplishments in jeopardy.

Man was fairly safe with his ecosystem up until the Industrial Revolution, when man's efforts toward resource expansion became too strong to be effectively controlled. The increased need for greater leisure, efficiency, and social status drove man into an industrial boom, which, in turn, led societies to dig more deeply into the natural world to fuel economic growth.

The answer to much of the competitive resource expansion came with the marriage of science and technology. Science had opened the door for technology to expand. The urbanization that followed on the heels of invention of heavy industry was formidable. There developed from this an even more dangerous feeling that, with time, technology and science could solve any problem man has created. This human self-confidence has proven to be an absolute fallacy. The idea of controlling the excesses of industry in the environment is alien to man. Even the great economist Adam Smith, who advanced the optimistic notion that the "invisible hand" would eventually do what is good for most people, failed to foresee that mankind's industrial drive would eventually lead it roughshod over the environment. Theology encouraged environmental exploitation, as well, with the JudeoChristian doctrine of man as master over nature justifying efforts to subdue the environment. Easy-going economics and misguided notions of religious dominion combined to facilitate gross materialism, and left the environment with little consideration in man's vision of his future.

As the life environment becomes unhealthy, people look for a better clime by deserting cities and moving to the suburbs. The phenomenon of suburbanization in postindustrial society is indeed interesting in the sense that people are "pushed" away from the city just as they were "pushed" away from the rural areas in the process of industrialization. Suburbanization, as a common phenomenon of postindustrial societies, leaves behind the urban ghetto and all the problems associated with it. As few are equipped with the desire and resources to deal with urban problems in social, economic, and political arenas, the responsibility falls to the government, forcing a rapid expansion of welfare programs.

In an effort to avoid government interference, pollutant industries, some with radioactive waste, search for a haven abroad. As affluent countries enact stricter environmental regulations, their businesses find themselves becoming less profitable. They look to less-developed countries as factory sites, and find an attractive haven in poor countries. As Enloe observes (1975, p. 131):

> The dilemma of underdevelopment is choosing
> between two unwanted and uncompromising
> conditions. A government that wants economic growth
> may feel that it must accept foreign intervention and

potential environmental hazards. The very opportunity for attracting overseas capital may come from an affluent nation protecting its own environment.

Countries that are considered successful developing systems, such as Brazil, Singapore, Nigeria, South Korea, and Malaysia, have achieved their economic growth at the expense of environmental degradation. They are the countries that have opted for economic industrialization over environmental quality, and have readily offered their lands to foreign investors who need "pollution havens." This process has accelerated in the context of the globalization process.

The underdeveloped countries are selling their "havens" not only to foreign investors but to tourists, as well. People of industrialized societies find their own territories eaten up by industrial and commercial exploitations but they are the ones who possess more time and funds for leisure. They look around the world for "unspoiled" areas where air and land are still pollutionfree and life is reminiscent of their own "good old days," and go on foreign tours.

Competitive exploitation of the environment has penetrated into a number of areas such as water supply, deforestation, and global warming. These problems threaten the very foundation of human existence. Whether these problems are manmade or not is a moot question because anyone with commonsense realizes that our lifestyle has everything to do with these problems. What can be done? The scope of these environmental problems, let alone their complicated solutions, is mind-boggling. Among many questions, we must ask: who will pay for the cost?

The pressing issues of environmental quality and ecosystem preservation are public in nature. A public issue is one that benefits or hurts everyone regardless of one's contribution to its creation or solution. In this regard, the heart of the issue lies in the fact that a rational individual will be unwilling to make sacrifices for the "public" benefit since this is exactly what he is not supposed to do as a "rational" man. Here we should be reminded of the fact that citizens of the mature industrial society have already acquired a rational personality and calculating attitudes in the process of industrial development. In the case of air pollution, for example, clean air is a commodity that does not distinguish those who have contributed to its creation or preservation from those who have not, as long as it benefits all people who breathe. It would be perfectly rational for any individual to avoid paying the cost of clean air if he expects someone who needs clean air more desperately to pay for it, as the benefit will reach him anyway.

In an effort to fight energy shortages in recent years in the United States, drivers have been sufficiently informed of the bleak energy future and asked to drive less and seek alternative forms of transportation. The public, however, did not respond effectively until gasoline prices went up. This price response behavior indicates that rational individuals will only behave "rationally" and cannot be persuaded by the noble idea of public regard or altruism. As long as citizens of the industrial society remain rational, social problems of a public nature will need the merciful hand of the government, no matter how wasteful and inefficient its operations may be. The expansion of the welfare state is not a public choice but the inevitable result of industrial development.

Depletion of Non-renewable Energy:

Once propelled, the momentum of development is almost unstoppable. There is no known boundary within which the human drive toward industrial and economic supremacy can be contained. Another alarming problem is the sustained availability of our energy sources. If renewable energy fails to provide human energy needs locally and globally in a hurry, the future of humanity is going to be bleak, indeed. If we should continue to prolong the status quo, which is heavily dependent on fossil fuels, the earth's reserves will surely be exhausted in decades-- not centuries. The easy way out is by expanding nuclear energy, but no mater how you look at, the safety issue is not going to be fundamentally resolved. Then, it has to be from natural sources such as solar, wind, ocean wave, and geothermal energy. Nordic countries such as Norway, Denmark, Sweden, and Finland are far ahead of everyone else, and credible advancement is made in Germany. We need far greater strides by governments and people in the most populous and heavy consumers of energy including the United States, China, and India, as well as the developing world in Asia, Africa, and South America.

In short, the intense competition for the control of more resources has led to the depletion of energy sources, as well as the deterioration of the environment. If this course of development continues unchecked, the human species will be left with no destiny but selfinflicted extinction.

Human Survival at Risk, All Over Again

It is a great irony that the journey of development started out with the common needs and desires to live, and live better through advancing through the stages of development but in the end, we may have ended up with life environments that threaten the very survival of mankind. This journey has also deprived the dwellers of the global village of sense of belonging and identity. Are we in this global village better off than we were in less developed stages of the preindustrial world? There is no denying that development has elevated life situations in a number of areas, notably by expanding the average life expectancy and general levels of material comfort. Yet, in many places, the quality of physical existence, psychological identity, and social dignity has deteriorated in the face of economic expansion and globalization.

Physical safety and security, for which the human race invented the military and police institutions, also cannot be said to have improved over the last five decades.

Population Growth and Food

While industrial development tends to curtail traditional agricultural productivity, science and technology, which also accompany industrialization, contribute to a prolonged life expectancy and a reduction in infant mortality. This causes a population increase, especially in the so-called nonproductive age groups such as the elderly and children.[4] This phenomenon, as discussed earlier, encourages the expansion of welfare policies and the growth of the governmental sector. Globally speaking, the transfer of science and technology contributes to the population explosion in such a way that the kinds government policies needed for effective population management will only lag behind. The population imbalance between the poor countries and the affluent nations will intensify, leading to massive food production problems in less developed countries. The United Nations Food and Agricultural Organization projects that import requirements will only increase on the coming decades. Whatever surplus food the world may be able to raise to meet these requirements will be produced primarily in the United States and Canada. It will be well beyond the financial ability of the developing countries to purchase this vast quantity of food, even if the needy countries can develop the necessary infrastructure for distribution to the people.

Beyond these practical considerations, there are a number of unavoidable values-based issues. Among these is the issue of the moral obligation of the haves to feed the needy. If some developing countries are unable to pay for food imports, can developed countries withhold food shipments when people die of hunger and malnutrition? In these days of discussions on human rights, a predominant view seems to be that humans have the inherent right to life; thus, basic needs such as food are within the purview of natural human rights. This humanist sentiment, however, may not be acceptable to the producers of the developed countries.

Global inequities in food distribution are indeed scandalous. The most industrialized countries feed more cereal to their livestock than is consumed by the populations of many developing countries combined. What are the ethical dimensions of this inequality? Does such an unequal distribution of food constitute a human injustice in and of itself, thus requiring corrective measures?

There are also policy issues regarding food, particularly in its relationship to labor. New agricultural equipment such as the ricethreshing machines often replaces laborers in the underdeveloped world, posing a dilemma: which is more important, jobs for farmers or greater production efficiency? Furthermore, in places like the Philippines, Okinawa, and South Korea, U.S. bases occupy large acreages of prime productive land. Which is more important, the use of land for food production or for strategic interests? If U.S. grain reserves are to help feed the world's hungry, should American farmers receive special subsidies for growing wheat?

The issue of food aid is further complicated by the fact that these problems are not limited to the underdeveloped countries. As we discussed in this and previous chapters, industrial and postindustrial development deteriorates the agricultural sector and alienates the farmer from the mainstream of the commercial society. At the same time, the increasing polarization of the rich and the poor leads to an expansion of the segment of the population that suffers from malnutrition.

Industrial development and the transfer of science and technology have contributed to the exponential growth of world population, leaving a stack of seemingly insurmountable dilemmas concerning food production and distribution. Thus, feeding the hungry has become a focal issue in a world where increasing numbers of people are entering the threshold to industrial and postindustrial stages. Humans huddled together to cultivate crops

220

when survival was the ultimate goal for primitive man. But, as ironic as it may sound, the long journey of "development" has left us with the same task of feeding humans. What have we truly accomplished when getting food has once again become a focal concern?

Medical and Health Care: Science and Distribution System

The advancement of medical and hygiene science clearly helps people live longer in the economically developed societies. Yet, the prolonged life itself does not tell the whole story about the quality of life. The elderly people are not only socially marginalized but are also maintaining their bodies through heavy dependence on medication, which in itself is responsible for a myriad of health problems. Medical treatment in Western advanced societies, especially the United States, is largely symptom-oriented, alleviating symptoms as opposed to targeting the causes. As symptoms are felt in the form of pain, covering up the pain is accepted as a treatment. But no medicine intake is free of adverse side effects, and the side effects often lead to other health issues requiring further medication. This vicious cycle continues until the patient is unable to handle the complications caused by combined effects of multiple medications.

The life expectancy of Americans fall behind most industrialized societies, and this trend of treatment could be at least partially to blame. The profit-seeking pharmaceutical industry is widely criticized for its insensitive attitude and care for public health, especially in the United States. Responding to this conventional health care approach, a growing number of individuals and groups are exploring alternative health science from a fundamentally different knowledge of the nature of the human body. This view holds the body as an equilibrated system of "force" ("*gi*" in Chinese), which is the underlying premise for acupuncture in Asia. It has also been incorporated into "*biontology*" in Europe, a view that sees the human body as an integrated system of light. According to this perspective, the universe is a huge system to which the human body must be connected as a part of the earth and the universe itself. When parts or segments of human body are not mutually connected, the disconnection must be rectified by the needle or the light in order for the body to restore its equilibrium. Great strides have been made in Europe as well as Asia, but the medical and pharmaceutical industries have resisted the alternative health care idea.

The "gi" science is also advancing the view that the Electronic Magnetic Field (EMF) has become a new source of health disorders, especially in neuropsychological health. In the global world today, people are exposed to an ever-growing electronic magnetic environment due to on-line communication networking, wireless communication devices, and smart-phones. The cyber space to which practically everyone on the planet is exposed has a great, but largely unknown, impact on the human body.

Then, we have the same old problem of distributive injustice and unfairness within the healthcare system. When we have highly developed health science that is not readily accessible to the people who need its service, we have a dysfunctional system, constituting a case of "structural violence." Such is the case in many places around the world.

Loss of Identity and Dignity

Identity of a person is the meaningful address of the person. It is the symbolic name of any individual. Then, what is the property of identity and what does it do to the person? Identity consists of values, beliefs, norms, and often life-guiding principles held by the person. It is not defined in terms of material possession or social position. Thus, one is not born with identity; it is attained through socialization and education in a specific context of life environment.

If identity is voided, the person loses the symbolic name within the society, meaning that the person does not exist as a symbolic entity. When this happens, the person undergoes a profound experience of self-denial and worthlessness as a living creature. This will lead to nonconformist or abnormal behavior that includes suicide or reaching for the help of alcohol and drugs as a means of escape. If a "comfort zone" is not attained, people with identity crises are likely to hibernate for a while before outwardly behaving unpredictably, randomly, and often destructively. The hibernation manifests as a period of depression during which destructive behavior can be inner-directed (suicide) or outer-directed (homicide). High suicides rates are increasingly commonplace, especially in economically advanced countries. The explosive increase of mass murder on school campuses in the United States may, in some ways, be attributable to the mental and emotional disturbance that pervades post-industrial society. It is obvious that the erosion of the family system and the transition of modern education to keep up with technological and commercial advancement have contributed to identity crisis on the part of the children. It is also obvious that instability in identity causes emotional attributes and behavioral patterns that might explain the increase in destructive action against the society.

Sense of identity develops in the process of socialization and interactions. As discussed in earlier chapters, social institutions that facilitate the need of belonging such as the family and religious groups are crucial to enriching identities. If those institutions are unable to satisfy the belonging need, an identity crisis is likely to develop. When human relationships are guided primarily by contractual and legal obligations as the case might be in the post-industrial and global stages, rather than affection and sense of mutual belonging, the state of one's identity is likely to be insecure. When a sense of identity is lacking, one suffers from the loss of self-esteem and human dignity.

In the final analysis, we come back to ask ourselves the question: is globalization a blessing or a curse? The answer must be a qualified one; it all depends on who is being asked. It is a blessing for expanding the framework of reference for human existence; it is a blessing for prolonging physical life, thus, increasing life expectancy; it is a blessing for making life expedient in doing things in less time and with less effort. Yes, it would be a blessing for profit-obsessed businesses; it is definitely a blessing for the military industry; it is a definite blessing for tourism and tourists. Yet, as we discussed in this chapter, there are a host of profound "victims" of postindustrial and global development. Among them, the quality, not quantity, of life as it relates to sense of security and safety for human physical survival, health vulnerability, environmental health and ecology (both visible and invisible), distributive justice, middle class viability, social unrests and conflicts, human self-esteem, human dignity, community, and peace. The adverse consequences are factual and they may eventually threaten the very sustenance of the human race and the course of history. In the chapters that follow in Part Three, I intend to offer some constructive ideas to reverse the adversarial course of development.

A final remark is in order before leaving this chapter on the nature and impact of globalization. A most common question: is globalization Americanization? It should be clear by this point in the book that globalization is to be understood on the same continuum of the process of development. America is and has been following the path of development as depicted in Part Two of this book. Thus, America represents an empirical example of development. The theory (paradigm of development) was constructed as an "ideal type" (Max Weber's conception) just as any theory should be, and the pattern of American development is simply a demonstrated empirical and historical case. In this sense, I might reiterate that the human needs-based paradigm introduced in this book differs from most modernization theories that have been correctly criticized as "Western biased."

Chapter 11

Human Development

Where is the human species itself in the literature of social and political development? There are many sources in literature that use institutions as a yardstick of development, thus we find the common contention that a more advanced society consists of institutions that are more specialized and standardized. Many scholars, particularly since Max Weber, have used culture as the central criterion of development. Some cultures are regarded to be more developed than others. Still others think that certain value systems or behavioral traits are more developed than others as shown by Talcott Parson's juxtaposition of the "pattern variables," where affectivity (not affective neutrality), self-orientation (not collective orientation), universalism (not particularism), ascription (not achievement), and specificity (not diffusivity) are regarded as indicative of modern or developed patterns in social interactions. The "pattern variables" have been emulated by many psychological reductionists in the Cold-War contemporary development studies as portrayed earlier in Chapter 2. Some even assume that certain political ideologies are more advanced than others, even to the extent that people like Francis Fukuyama argued that liberal democracy was the most perfect political ideology. Even though the human needs/wants-based theory of development advanced in this book is about human situations, the theory still only deals with the human condition, rather than humans themselves. It is illogical to discuss development of societies or polities without addressing human beings themselves. Society, after all, is made of the people, managed by the people, and exists for the people. Therefore, I make a desperate plea that any credible study of development (social or political) begin with an analysis of the development of humans themselves.

In order for us to talk about human development, we must first know the complete properties of a person. The most common view holds that a person consists of the body and the mind. Some expand this dichotomous anatomy of man to include the spirit, thus, an individual is composed of body, mind, and spirit (BMS). But the most expansive perspective should include four distinct properties: body, mind, spirit, and soul. These four components are inherent in any human being. We define each of these four parts in the anatomy of person by its unique function:

Body *feels* (sensory);

Mind *thinks* (reasons);

Spirit *values* (evaluates);

Soul *frees* (emancipates).

Body performs sensory functions; Mind performs the function of reasoning that includes logical and scientific thinking; Spirit performs the function of evaluating; and Soul performs the function of emancipating mankind from the bondage of time and space restrictions. Human development should refer to the process in which these four properties of a human being are made sounder and healthier. Unlike the four human needs we established for the empirical paradigm of development (survival, belonging, leisure, and control), these four components are mutually reinforcing. A healthy body is conducive to promoting the health of other three components, and the same may be said about the other components in regards to their relationship with one another.

The Body

Of all the properties of Man, the body is the most common and universally recognizable property. Human development must begin with the survival and health of the body itself. Bodily survival requires a set of necessities including food, clothing, shelter, health care, safety, and security. Thus, to ensure physical survival for members of the community, one must first and foremost have a supply of food. With technological advancements that have made global agricultural productivity sufficient to feed the world's population, we seem to have sufficient food. However, as we enter into the global era, the food supply for the neediest of humans has become a great concern. While the globe itself still has the capability to produce ample amounts of food, the distributive system is utterly inadequate to achieve the goal of feeding all the people of the world. This is coupled by mismanagement of the land leading to ecological degeneration and a resulting decrease in agricultural productivity. The food shortage problem is further exacerbated by the population growth on the planet; the most growth is in those areas and regions that are already most desperately impoverished. Here, we must come up with a global monitoring system of food production and needs, and devise and implement a distributive mechanism to benefit the optimal number of people. The United Nation's World Food Program is the right idea, but it should be greatly expanded with enhanced authority and funding.

It is almost a cliché to say that the healthcare system in the United States is broken. In the United States, the most economically advanced and politically influential country in the global community, there is a huge disconnect between the available healthcare services and goods, on one hand, and ailing people who desperately need them, on the other. There are enough people and theories that rationalize this discrepancy, but the bottom line is that people are suffering needlessly. The problem is even deeper than the delivery system itself; the real problem is a medical and pharmaceutical industry that is helplessly arrested by economic and monetary interests. A commonly recognized problem in Western medicine is that it deals with mostly the symptom and its approach is mostly piecemeal and incremental. What is needed is the holistic approach that will complement the incremental treatment. We must pay far more attention to preventive medicine, not just the treatment of symptoms. A holistic approach of any kind should begin with a holistic view of human body, a view that incorporates two philosophical perspectives: (1) the human body is a total and complete system in which every element in the system is indispensable to the system; (2) the human body is to be seen as a part of the universe, and it will survive best when it lives in consonance with the natural universe. As discussed in the previous chapter (Chapter 10), advanced Western medical science and its methods of healthcare should be complemented by holistic comprehension of the human body and its methods of dealing with bodily illness. One significant and often neglected area is in the preventive or proactive approach to health problems.

In this global era, more countries and governments are forced to address the challenge of maintaining law and order which has become unprecedentedly complicated due to urbanization and suburbanization. With the influx of foreign migrant workers, which is necessitated by economic needs, the community experiences difficulty not only in the physical management of services and goods but, more profoundly, the alteration of norms and mores that have tied the community together for millennia. Thus, the challenge of law and order on the part of the state has increased in difficultly as communities strain to incorporate new cultural elements.

In Europe, most immigrant workers are from former Eastern Europe and Africa. In Japan and South Korea, the workers are attracted from Southeast Asia and China. One common problem to all of these countries, especially Japan, is that the workers are not only assigned to low-paying jobs but they are also socially and culturally marginalized to the extent that the workers seldom feel themselves welcomed to the host country. With no reason to show loyalty to their host country, immigrant worker populations may contribute to social unrest. Japan is a striking example. The country was made of very homogeneous people who share a common culture that includes a strong sense of morality and loyalty to the community. For millennia, there were practically no social crimes such as robbery and pickpocketing. But today, Japan is suffering from petty crimes that the Japanese are attributing to the growing numbers of foreign immigrants workers. They say that these workers have no loyalty to the community, little concern for how they are perceived by others, there for the singular purpose of making money with no intention or desire to maintain long-term residence in Japan. A similar situation is observed in Western European countries with foreign migrants from Africa and former Eastern European countries. Any credible examination of the immigrant worker issue must involve at least three dimensions: the immigrants themselves, their impact on the home country, and the ramifications for the host country. But for now, it is suffice that the immigrant workers are struggling in the host countries to the extent that their livelihood is hardly secure, and, in some cases, criminal activity and social unrest may result.

The security challenge has already become insurmountable to manage. With terrorism and the implosion of regimes and political systems as a result of domestic uprisings, we face a serious threat to human survival from non-conventional warfare. Arab uprisings and insurgencies in the initial decades of the 21st Century have brought many civilian casualties as a result of suicide bombings and other methods of civil violence meant to kill large numbers of people. The violence is not limited to foreign wars or developing nations--it has become a growing concern in advanced countries such as the United States, Britain, and Japan. The Oklahoma City bombing and the recent mass murder of school children in Newtown, Connecticut., are vivid reminders that real threats to human life can originate from diverse and unpredictable sources.

For the survival and health of the body, not only do we need to supply the basic needs, but we must also establish an orderly society with the function of the police institution. Further, to deter external threats, one must develop security measures that neutralize external hostility. As the separation between domestic security and external hostility has become blurred, one must work with a more integrated perspective. There is a consensus that terrorism should never be allowed in a civil world. The fact of life is, however, that we do have terrorism, much of which currently originates from the militant teachings of Islamic extremists. Their belief is guided by what they interpret to be God's divine teaching that those enemies who target members of your faith should be destroyed in kind. This particular form of terrorism does not stem solely from a political disagreement or structural violence by distributive injustice. It is, to some extent, a result of Western militarism and insensitivity to faith-based cultural values that have been upheld as the foundation of social justice for many centuries in these regions. History reminds us that peoples of different religious persuasions must actively seek a way of living together side by side in peace, or conflict will result. If civilizations with religions in their cores were to clash in today's world that is completely saturated with weapons that could annihilate humanity, as Samuel Huntington envisioned in his *Clash of Civilizations,* then we have no other business more urgent than addressing the issue of terrorism in a most comprehensive and effective way. This will take no less that a revolutionary change in the conscience of humanity so that the pursuit of security for and by nations and states must be replaced by the pursuit of peace on earth, a topic reserved for Chapter 13.

For bodily survival and health, we are facing a new challenge that our pre-industrial societies never envisioned, and that is the planetary environment, as discussed in the previous chapter. Our ability to accomplish sustainable energy sources and manage sustainable environment is vital to survival of humanity. As long as life is a basic human right, thus, it is an entitlement and falls under collective or societal responsibility, the environmental problem must be at the forefront of all governments and international organizations.

Individual survival is threatened by the deterioration of social ecology. Social ecology refers to the notion that society is supposed to constantly reinvent itself to maintain its internal equilibrium and coordinate with the external world in a way that it can maintain sustainable development. Due to compartmentalization of the social system and role specialization of functions, this cycle of reinvention and coordination has been severely challenged. The outcome of a dis-equilibrated social system and uncoordinated society is abnormality in patterns of human behavior and relationships, as well as institutional dysfunction. The deleterious consequences of disturbed social ecology are numerous, leading to destructive forms of behavior that endanger people's lives.

Healthcare of the body begins with preventive measures -- including regular exercises and healthy dietary living habits -- and all social organizations, especially education, must take this challenge as a high priority. Lifestyles in advanced post-industrial societies are structured in a way that preventive healthcare is virtually neglected. Most service sector occupations do not require any significant degree of physical movements or exercises. This, along with unhealthy diets, contributes to obesity, which is a chronic problem in many advanced societies.

The Mind:

It is a great irony that the scientific and technological innovations made possible by the function of the human mind have, in many cases, served to cripple the human mind itself. Automated gadgets and means of electronically processing data and information have made the human mind lazy and timid. Beyond this, the real problem is seen in the derailed function of education. We should realize and act on the presumption that the purpose of education is to increase the ability to think. To think is to connect different objects in a systemic way. The trend of education has shifted away from reasoning and thinking in almost all developed societies. Memorization for the purpose of accomplishing good scores on standardized tests has become the goal of today's education system.

The challenge for the global community and its constituent states and organizations is to instate the enhancement of the human ability to reason and think as the central goal of education, as opposed to storing information with or without understanding.

The Spirit:

Human faculty cannot be complete without the function of valuing. All the adjectives we use -- good, high, great, noble, significant, and a host of other words -- are conceptualized by of our ability to assign value. These are all subjectively derived from the perceiver's personal experiences, chosen beliefs, and education. But in today's global life, our ability to make value judgments is seriously curtailed. The culprit here is the cult of science. This cult denounces the worth of values, norms, feelings, and anything else that is subjective. The cult of science has indeed become the mythical pinnacle of human existence, striving in the name of uniformity and objectivity. In the process of the scientific transformation of human faculty, aesthetic and artistic life experiences have been downgraded, even ridiculed. We need not dwell on the dismal failure of our education in this area. However, one spectacular failure I must recount is the misguided trend in American education at universities and college. Educators and researchers are forced to punch out cookie-cutter research papers published in "refereed" journals for the recognition of their scholarship and advancement of their positions and compensation packages. In all of social science, there are one or another patterned prototype research procedures and methods: (1) form a hypothesis; (2) collect data for the variables and concepts contained in the hypothesis; (3) run or process the data to test your hypothesis in quantitative terms. Any serious philosophy of science will tell you that the definition of hypothesis is a relational statement in which two or more variables (concepts) are claimed to be related in a way that the relationship is deductively plausible and empirically uncertain or unknown. Testing a hypothesis is aimed at finding out if the relationship is empirically valid or not. Here, deductive plausibility is established only by already proven theories or conventional wisdom, rather than just a claim for a relationship that is "assumed" by the researcher himself.

One of the most fashionable assumptions in social and political research is that man is rational: he pursues the maximum interest or gain at a minimum cost or loss, ruling out the possibility that some people can behave altruistically or for other personal reasons. Altruism in this case is regarded as being atypical or exceptional to the norm. Pursued interests are defined mostly in economic and tangible material terms. Further, a relationship being asserted in the hypothesis has no grounding in theories or conventionally established wisdom but it tends to be a random and unexplainable relationship. No matter how rigorously the empirical testing is conducted and no matter how strongly the variables are mutually related, the lack of deductive plausibility is still unaddressed. This means that the tested hypothesis can at best be an empirical generalization; lacking deductive plausibility, the proven hypothesis can never be a theory or a law. As a result, the research will be of little value in explaining or understanding any systems of behavior or anything else. For our ultimate challenge of problem solving, this kind of research is useless at best and often harmful because researchers fool themselves as though they have produced causal explanations.

Another glaring "wrong" is found in the abuse of the tenure system for teaching professors at educational institutions. The tenure privilege is reserved for professors (along with federal judges in the legal system) for the exclusive reason to protect them from political repercussions for their "professing" ideological or political statements in teaching students that might be inconsistent with or offensive to the political establishment or officially sanctioned ideologies.

As expected, the tenure system evolved in response to the political wind of McCarthyism, adapting in the wake of the Cold War politics. In short, the tenure system was created so that students will be open to a variety of views, norms, and perspectives that would be necessary for them to articulate their own perspectives as future citizens and leaders.

One overarching goal of education is to help students develop their intellectual and value systems with which they might articulate their identities as members of society. Professors are expected to help them by "professing" their own identities. A university is a place that accommodates a universe of diverse identities presented within the academic community, at times even mutually contested and in conflict. The students should be inspired by rich and diverse sets of value systems that nurture their minds, spirits, and souls in a way that they will be able to develop their own identities through discussions, debates, and in-depth deliberations. Identity or character formation for youthful intellectuals is a sacred goal for institutions of higher education. Tragically, commercialization and vocationalization of academia in this post-industrial and global world have helplessly contaminated scholarship in such a way that few seem to have an interest or desire to "profess" their views. Worse yet, not too many professors are doing their job of "professing." Instead, professors are transmitting information in a given field in exchange for job security. After having taught all my adult life, I have come to the opinion that some American educators at higher educational institutions today are undeserving of the tenure privilege because they seldom express their normative stances on dominant public issues. They are either indifferent to them or incapable of articulating value positions on controversial public issues of the time. When we had the Vietnam War in 1960s and 1970s, professors joined with the students who expressed their opinions on the war. The campuses around the country were vibrant political forums, thus, professors had to be protected by the tenure system. But since the end of the Vietnam War in mid-1970s, the tide of globalization and marketization has penetrated into all corners of the world, with the greatest impact on the most advanced societies. In the turbulent years since U.S. intervention in Iraq in 2003, massive American military forces have been sent to the Middle

East in Iraq and Afghanistan, resulting in tens of thousand U.S. military casualties and all forms of tragic consequences in terms of human lives and material destruction. Throughout this, American campuses have been mysteriously silent. Most academics in America today may think that tenure is a reward or prize for their achievement in quantity of publications. This tendency is especially acute in research institutions throughout the United States and also in other countries where American scholarship has a heavy influence.

Another serious problem with American academia is that the academic administrators' primary responsibility lies with fundraising, rather than providing leadership in scholarship and the academic community. Assessment of job performance in this manner is not limited to the administrators, however. Research scholars are hard pressed to generate research funds that include overhead charges for the institution. The researchers' performance is heavily weighed for evaluation and treatment of them. In this case, teaching takes a backseat.

In view of the dark cloud hanging over academic community, a series of corrective measures must be explored. Some drastic ideas and recommendations will be offered in the concluding chapter of this book.

It is a reality that the emphasis on the arts in education has steadily evaporated in America as the priority has shifted to science, math, and vocational skill development. Despite this, America trails far behind most of the advanced European countries and some Asian countries in the less-developed world. In fact, education in the arts serves to reinforce, not undercut, the other fields, suggesting that holistic approach is more effective for all fields of education. We must acknowledge as universal truth that arts education enriches education in general and facilitates socialization processes at all levels. Then, students will realize that the arts are a source of fulfillment and deeper inner satisfaction which can enrich and elevate the quality of human existence in a unique way that material abundance cannot.

We must also acknowledge the importance of value education, including ethics and morality. No less central to desirable education is the orientation of students toward a set of principles and a sense of justice and injustice. This requires the learning of history and historical figures and the principles and values that guided them. Today's young students are embarrassingly devoid of role models, and they hardly develop attitudes and behaviors founded on principles. As we discussed in Chapters 9 and 10, today's young people (and not-so-young alike) are disposed to entertainment and the pursuit of competition. These traits are not only reinforced by their educational experiences, but evident in the manner in which they evaluated and rewarded. All standardized tests and school grading systems are designed to delineate winners and losers, as opposed to helping students to realize personal potential or search for inner gratification.

The Soul:

Finally, there is the sphere of human soul. There is a domain in human existence that is metaphysical and subliminal. In this sphere, the soul works to help us in overcoming anxieties and inner pains originating from constraints of time and worldly events. We seek ultimate freedom from these fundamental bonds by transcending them through the power of soul. For many, this requires the intervention of religious faith. When human development fails to reach this sphere, the full quality of life is yet unfulfilled.

An intriguing truth is that with physical aging, the other three properties (body, mind, and spirit) may become weakened and even deteriorate but the soul will not vanish with the passing of time. As the essential teaching of many religions and a universally admired value, love can be regarded as the work of the soul. Love, the thing itself, does not change through the passing of time, nor is its meaning altered from place to place. A mother holding her infant baby would have had exactly the same feeling of love back in ancient times as a mother living today. The feeling of love is constant across the globe regardless of social, political, and cultural differences. When something does not change and hold its validity throughout time and space, we refer to this as the truth. Love as truth frees humanity from the constraints and anxieties of limitations in time and space. We have the inherent desire to be freed in this ultimate sense. This is one powerful and common reason behind the creation of religion. All religions have by their definitions offered a vision of an eternal life (i.e., emancipation from the limit of this worldly life). As the way to such absolute freedom, Buddhism teaches us to induce "inner transformation" or "empty one's self," which will move us to reach the transcendental sphere of emancipation. The fact that we have the inherent desire to free ourselves from the limitations of space is convincingly demonstrated by the fact that a prison is a physical arrangement to confine the criminal to a limited space, and no normal person desires to live in such space.

The soul supersedes the body, the mind, and the spirit. It transcends them but interacts with them in a way that all other human properties will become enriched, and a balanced system of relationships among them (equilibrium) will be facilitated. The soul makes us wiser, not smarter, in making decisions. The work of wisdom is farsighted and elevates the level of happiness; it never results in regret. By contrast, a smart decision refers to a decision produced by rational calculation for short-term benefits but seldom ensures lasting gratification. Wisdom, as the work of the soul, is not expected to result from science (the work of the mind) or value systems (the work of the spirit). Wisdom comes only from the life itself (life experience). Then, it is obvious that experience is the food and the nursing ground for the soul. Life experience expands the realm of human existence beyond *here* and *now*. Educational experience should help us expand our special frame of reference and religious experience should help us expand the realm of time beyond today. Therefore, it is an essential task of education to expose students to diverse cultures and life situations in the world through purposefully designed curricula including foreign languages and expanded existential experiences through programs facilitating international exchange. Even a cursory examination of education and student life environment suggests that education in contemporary societies, especially the advanced countries, is far from being adequate; indeed, it has deteriorated in the post-industrial and globalization stages of development. Cognitive exposure to history and historical events and historic thinkers and achievers is practically dead in school education. As an educator, I have been amazed by the fact that many students do not read and their knowledge of history or the world is shockingly shallow. Even college-level students are helplessly arrested within their enclaves of limited information and knowledge. Practical knowledge that might be useful in defining their own environment or political life is utterly lacking: when I ask my college students to meaningfully evaluate the theory of historical evolution by Karl Marx, many of them are embarrassingly ignorant.

Human Development and Happiness:

Imagine a person who has established all four domains of human development on solid healthy grounds. We can declare that we have a happy person. What more can one possible want?

The beauty about this is that these domains are never mutually incompatible. Furthermore, different individuals may pursue their respective paths of human development without interfering with one another because one's development is never pursued at the detriment of another's pursuit of the same human development. This is radically different from the zero-sum winning desire portrayed in the empirical paradigm of development in the previous chapters.

Human happiness is more than physical health and safety; it is more than being smart and possessing a superb intellect; it is more than developing artistic or philosophical identities; it is even more than experiencing the ultimate kind of freedom. Human happiness requires all of these in an integrated system, which may best be represented by the concept of "equilibrium" or homeostasis. The four properties of mankind are by nature coordinated in a way that they are not only mutually reinforcing but also mutually indispensible. Thus, the development of all four attributes of mankind should be cultivated simultaneously in coordination among them.

In this chapter, we established that the existing definitions and theories of development have left out human beings themselves, as most of them have focused their attention to structures, cultures, economic sizes, and even ideologies. We also established that human development must be at the core of development studies, as called for in Chapter of this book. We also made it clear that the proper approach to the study of human beings should be holistic and homeostatic. Each of the four attributes must be included in equilibrium for education and other forms of socialization processes to function optimally. Some concrete ideas will be specified in the concluding chapter of this book.

I suggested that when a person achieves all of the four "attributes," he or she would feel a degree of satisfaction. But man, as a social animal, lives in the context of other people who are significant to him. "Significant others" do matter in one's state of happiness. Relationships, not just personal attributes, create human dignity. In the following chapter, we will turn to this question: what makes human dignity and how is it created?

Chapter 12

Human Rights for Human Dignity

Once the desirable course of development is established in that all the desirable "attributes" of Man are attained, the next question should be how to establish a desirable form of inter-personal relationship. As discussed earlier, Man is the core and the building block of the society and the world. The immediate outer-layer of Man is his relationship with others. Inter-personal connections ought to be established by the guiding principle that *human dignity* result from the process of building inter-connections. Dignity is a social and inter-relational concept. A person's dignity must come from relationships within society. Like human development, human dignity is a universal aspiration common to all individuals and members of the society, yet it is seldom recognized as a relevant and important concept in the literature of development and modernization. Yet, it is undeniable that every member of a society wants to be treated by all others with dignity.

It is the central thesis of this chapter that human dignity resides where *human rights* are observed and revered. This thesis will become obviously truthful when we examine the inherent conceptual principles or rules of human rights, which I would call the "Cardinal Rules."

Human Rights: Three Cardinal Rules

The very concept of human rights has a set of three principles inherent in the concept itself. They are *universality, inalienability,* and *entitlement.*

1. *Universality* of human rights means that these rights are not relative to political systems, socio-cultural characteristics, or economic conditions. Rights are not subject to being defined subjectively. There may be disagreements about the specific components of the rights as seen by the contending views and priorities evidenced in *The Universal Declaration of Human Rights, The International Covenant on Civil and Political Rights, and The International Covenant on Economic, Social, and Cultural Rights by*

the United Nations, but the assertion that rights should be applied to all people universally is the unshakable principle upon which the concept is founded.

Once one departs from the principle of universality and condones the notion that rights are relative and subjective, one now has justifications for all kinds of human rights violations. Human rights violations have been typically justified by the claim that rights are subjective and relative. In view of this, the rights themselves must be identified and defined as universal.

2. *Inalienability* of human rights means that rights are not earned but given as a birth right. Thus, no one or justification can undermine these basic rights. Here lies the limit of government power, as well as its obligation. The United Nations Universal Declaration of Human Rights and other documents cited above clearly specify this nature of human rights. Inalienability means that the rights are permanent throughout the entire life of a person.

3. *Entitlement* means that if one member of a society is entitled to human rights, the society as a whole has the obligation to see that the rights are not denied to anyone. The crucial notion here is that the deprivation of one person's rights is and should be the concern of everyone in the society. The whole society, country, or world is obligated to ensure these rights for every member of the community regardless of race, nationality, economic status, or cultural/ideological orientation. In this sense, human rights are "public goods" which implies that the public sector of the government is mandated and obligated to ensure the attainment and maintenance of these rights for all members of the society.

In comprehending the nature of human rights, the above three "cardinal rules" must be observed. By accepting these rules, we will be able to chart the course of human rights implementation with greater policy relevancy.

The Components of Human Rights

Human rights are always plural as there are different components or properties within the concept. Although the original *Declaration of Human Rights* was signed by a number of member states, subsequent *"Covenants"* generated from the United Nations highlighted specifically economic, social, and cultural rights, but suggested that there is no obvious system of priorities among those rights. That is, while the Western advanced countries emphasize the political and civil rights, underdeveloped countries tend to focus on economic and social rights. This book offers a different perspective, one in which human rights consist of four distinct components: life, identity, choice, and love. In the rest of this chapter, an elaboration on each of these four will be made.

1. The Life Right

The Universal Declaration of Human Rights states in Article 3 that, "everyone has the right to life..." This right requires all the basic needs and means for the survival of the body (discussed in Chapter 12) including safe food, clean water, decent shelter, and security from domestic and foreign sources of threat. The right to life is universal, inalienable, and everyone is "entitled" to it, as affirmed in Article 2.

In this discussion, we need to shed some light on the role of the government in the preservation of these rights. It is crucially important to accept the premise that the people of a political system create a government and obligate it first and foremost to protect the life of each and every member of the population. This is the norm for all types of political systems in modern times. To allow the government to perform the obligatory function of protecting and preserving the life of every member of the community, people empower it and provide it with resources. As is the case of national security, for which the government is obligated to ensure survival for the people through the institution of the military and a host of other policies, the needs for food, safe water, and health service are also within the purview of the public agency of government. This does not necessarily mean that the government should be socialist or some extreme form of welfare state. This does, however, mean that the government must be overseeing and performing functions that will guarantee the provision of basic needs for the largest number of the people. No matter what ideologies or institutional arrangements are activated, the goal here has to realize the entitlement of the people to life. If one prefers liberal democracy based on private ownership, one has to devise a policy plan, not just removing the government from the private sphere. The private sector is fundamentally different from the public sector in that the former is designed to pursue private interest and has no responsibility to provide the basic needs for the community. In the United States, where the "giving culture" is vibrant relative to most other countries, there are so many nonprofit charity organizations that solicit money from the general public who are already overburdened by taxation for the purpose of helping needy people -- even including war veterans. These solicitations often succeed in invoking a sense of guilt in the minds of ordinary and decent people, while the government is incapable of doing its job. No ideology or political institution can be excused for allowing people to be denied this most fundamental right because one has to live first in order to enjoy other rights. Therefore, of all roles of government, none precedes this. Globally, there are sufficient sources of food and abundant food production in some parts of the world, notably the United States and Canada, yet there are billions of people who suffer from shortages of food. This is a question of distributive justice, not production.

Then, there is the health issue. Health is a public good, as clearly seen in the case of contagious disease. But more fundamentally, health is the life right. Therefore, healthcare cannot and should not be left with the profit-seeking private sector. Most European countries, especially the Nordic states, are admirably dealing with public health as a public issue, and the government is assuming the massive responsibility of providing healthcare to all, even immigrant workers and traveling foreign tourists. And still, they maintain the political institution of a liberal democracy. Even most of the less-developed and newly-developed countries of the world, including all of the Asian Tigers (South Korea, Taiwan, Singapore, and Hong Kong), are extending government service to healthcare for the general public. But the story of the United States is embarrassingly inadequate because of the cooptation of politicians -- especially the legislators who have partnered with the healthcare industry (medical, pharmaceutical, and insurance). It is due to the gross failure of the government that there is flawed connectedness between the abundant supply of healthcare providers (physicians, hospital beds, dentists, hygiene professionals, etc.) on the one hand, and the helplessly large number of ailing people on the other.

Now, we move to the area of law and order within a country and national security from foreign hostility. One must be mindful of the definition of "public" goods and services, which is distinctly different from the private in that they are the goods and services that benefit every member of the community regardless of the amount of their contribution to the goods and services. "Private" goods and services, on the other hand, are generated by the private sector and distributed in accordance with the amount of contribution to the production of those goods and services. Given this, it cannot be clearer that law and order and national security ought to remain in the public domain. As we discussed in Chapter 10, because of the changing demographic structures of most countries in this globalization era and the daunting diverse sources of security threats felt in many advanced countries, the task of maintaining an orderly society and global community has become a much more complex and complicated matter. To deal with this, the public sector of the government must put together its ingenuity in devising actionable policies. Under the untimely pretext that "small" government equals virtuous government, we should never curtail the responsibility of the public sector. The Classical Liberalist doctrine of "the least government as the best government" is a myth. In fact, even in a participatory democracy like the United States, the question is not the size of the government but whether or not the government performs effectively its legitimate and rightful functions. A government function becomes legitimate when the people authorize their government to perform certain functions expressed through elections; a government's function becomes rightful when it fulfills its obligation to protect and preserve the rights of the people, particularly the right to life. In principle, military service should be mandatory. The operational phase of the military should also adhere to the principle of "public" service.

The Military-Industrial Complex that President Eisenhower warned of in his 1961 farewell address from the White House after two terms of presidency has grown to a point that the government, especially the legislative body, is almost completely entangled with it. Eisenhower coined the term to discuss the dangers of the formidable union between armed forces leadership, members of congress, and defense contractors. What a prophetic observation! Here is an excerpt: "In the councils of government, we must guard against the acquisition of unwarranted influence, whether sought or unsought, by the military-industrial complex. The potential for the disastrous rise of misplaced power exists, and will persist."

The government as the manager for the institution of the military has allowed itself to be coopted by the defense industry. The military industry includes an array of private sector contractors in a wide range of areas such as R & D for new weapons, manufacturing software programs, communication infrastructure, and the design and manufacture of weapons themselves. The only client for the military industrialists is the government, and there is typically no accountability or supervision over the implementation of these deals. Here, the government is authorized to use public tax money. Delegating or contracting out the production of public goods and services to the private sector is inherently wrong, and such practice often leads to misuse of public resources or outright corruption. One can easily see the evidence by examining the management of the wars in Iraq and Afghanistan. Non-combat civilian personnel actually outnumbered the soldiers in Afghanistan in some phases of the operation. The military should return to its primary function of defending the homeland from external threat. The same may be said with regard to the police institution.

Natural disasters caused by global warming are more frequent and widespread throughout the world, causing a real concern for the safety of human life. Along with environmental deterioration, the safety of nuclear power plants, as well as the management of nuclear bombs themselves, has also become a realistic threat to human life. Here, too, we should come up with actionable programs to combat and prevent these new sources of life-threatening developments in the contemporary world.

2. The Identity Right

The attainment and sustenance of a healthy and safe physical life is undoubtedly of vital importance for human existence, but it is hardly sufficient for human happiness. While the life right is a right to live physically as a biological being, the identity right is to maintain life with symbolic attributes with which the person identifies himself/herself as a social being. Social identity is established by virtue of one's having norms, values, and beliefs that collectively separates the person from other individuals in the society. Therefore, social identity is not a function of personal name, occupational name, nationality, race, age, or sex. Identity is the the crystallization of values and norms such as those of the liberal democrat, anarchist, socialist, nihilist, existentialist, nonviolent activist, and racist. These manifest normative value positions. They constitute personal characters that are exhibited in the context of relationships with others. Such identity can be the source of self-worth and self-esteem. When an identity is absent in a person, he/she will experience an "identity crisis" that is detrimental to psychological and emotional health, causing unpredictable and destructive behaviors. The killings on school campuses in the United States observed in recent years could at least partially be explained by profound identity crises on the part of the killers. Reviewing the processes of socialization of children in schools and the greater society will lead us to the conclusion that modern schools in the advanced and developing countries are failing in helping students and children to develop their identities constructively. As briefly discussed in Chapter 11, education in post-industrial and global societies is eschewing value education in favor of science, math, and vocational training. Identity development must become a priority of education and educators, for value education carries far-reaching implications.

Just as important as social identity is political identity. Whereas social identity is formed by acquiring norms and values for establishing meaningful relationships to other members of the society, political identity is created as one develops a stable sense of proper relationship with the government concerning governance. When the political identity is acquired, one becomes a legitimate member of the polity. Most political ideologues at all levels of intelligence are people with political identities. Then, we might conclude that a person's identity becomes complete when both social identity and political identity (these two may be represented by the concept of *socio-political identity*) symbolically represent the person. A person with the full spectrum of identities can be expected to be opinionated member of the community.

Sociopolitical identity of individuals paves the way for dialogue and communication among members of the society. As will be discussed in Chapters 13 and 14, the ability to accept diverse identities presented in the community will steer the course of social change in the direction of peace building.

3. The Right to Choice

The choice right refers to the right to make choices. This right clearly gives Man a life with dignity. The right to choose separates the slave from his master. In reality, however, the right to choice is hampered by the choice-makers inability or unwillingness to exercise this right due to the "structural violence" that surrounds him. Choice making requires a set of requisite conditions, including: (a) the presence of alternative choices; (b) reliable and sufficient information about the alternatives; (c) preference ordering on the part of the choice maker; (d) political freedom to commence the act of actual choice making, and (e) psychological and attitudinal predisposition or motivation to make the choice. These conditions are the same as the conditions for "rational" choice-making behavior, but I assume that all choice decisions are in fact "rational" even though preference orderings may not be the same to different individuals. The first requirement of the presence and availability of alternatives is basic to any choice making behavior, but what is important here is the idea that not only do the people have the right to choice making, but they have the right and entitlement to create and expand the available pool of alternatives. Alternatives are not just given and static. Rather, they are to be created, refined, and expanded to allow the dynamic reservoir of alternative choices. The second condition of reliable information on the choices for the decision maker to compare and contrast the available (and to be available) alternatives is of paramount importance. Here rests the proper role of education and other agents of socialization and communication. If information is guided by predetermined ideological or political agendas and filtered by parties with vested interest in manipulating the nature and contents of information, then the authenticity and reliability of information will be compromised, and the choice-making will be flawed. In this case, the furtherance of human right may never be served by the choices made. All the autocratic and dictatorial systems in recent history have been in violation of the choice right, undermining human dignity. The celebrated ideology of liberal or participatory democracy, on the other hand, has championed with the ideal of the choice right by advocating all the above conditions of choice making as seen in the promotion of a free election. Free election means voluntary and uninhibited choice making.

In reality, however, democracy has often failed in areas where it was transplanted by foreign powers to replace an authoritarian regime. This suggests that one must work at realizing the requisite conditions for choice-making before expecting democracy to flourish in any country. The third condition, for the choice maker to have a consistent ordering of preferences, is also problematic in that it is not a simple or easy matter to determine the preference ordering of a decision maker. While many behave "rationally," others may be altruistically motivated, and still others may consider self-interest to be collective interest for a group, the community, or the country. The fourth requisite condition referring to the presence of political and legal freedom and protection by the government is conceptually and theoretically simple and straight-forward. But democracies around the world including the United States have struggled with irregularities and even illegalities that have been committed by the government, particularly by the "illiberal" democracies. The "illiberal" conducts have included intimidating voters, legally making the voters illegitimate, and propagating misinformation and disinformation designed to steer the voter behavior in a certain direction favorable of the leadership. Despite these problems and shameful experiences, the United States and the Western democracies have put forth the agenda for democratization of the world. Ten years after American invasion of Iraq in 2003, Washington declared that U.S withdrew all its troops and the war ended officially in 2013. For the ten years, the Bush Administration recorded several "achievements" including: (a) Saddam Hussein did not have chemical and biological weapons, nor did he have programs or facilities for manufacturing nuclear weapons; (b) the pretext that Iraq was going to attack the United States with weapons of mass destruction and possibly with nuclear bombs which was used to justify the U.S. invasion turned out to a naked lie; (c) Saddam was eliminated and a new government was installed but it was far removed from a democratic government, and true participatory democracy is not in sight; (d) the invasion and occupation resulted in heavy casualties, including nearly 4,500 American soldiers killed and roughly 50,000 wounded. There are no official counts on Iraqi civilian casualties, perhaps in the hundreds of thousands (possibly in the millions). The recession-stricken U.S. economy suffered from the mounting cost of well over $3 trillion, and the financial impact will continue for decades to come. All these began with the blind myth for democratization of the world, and Saddam Hussein as part of the "axis of evil" must not be allowed to exist. The belief on the part of Washington that choice-making is a universal human right was sound and correct, but there was no roadmap to democracy in the particular context of a specific country. Democracy should be created through democratic means, not through military invasion.

4. The Love Right

Finally, the right to love is the most noble of the human rights. The experience of love represents a sphere of human existence that is rooted in the domain of the soul that was discussed in the previous chapter. As love is a form of human right, every person is entitled to this right. I do not intend to even propose an authoritative definition of love, but we should have a minimum agreement on the conception of what love is before we claim a right to love. Unlike most other concepts, love is not subjective. In fact, a concept is a subjective, not objective, articulation. When a term or word is given a definition, it necessarily becomes subjective for the definition of the word definition is "subjective meaning-giving." In other words, an objective term cannot and should not be defined because the moment it is defined, it ceases to be objective. In this sense, love is indeed objective because it defies a definition. Even the Christian good book, the Bible, does not define what love is; rather the book enumerates what love is not. Indeed, love is the only concept in the epistemic universe that is objective. What is objective is constant, not subject to change from a social or cultural context to another. Love as the function of the soul emancipates Man from all sorts of confinements and constraints, time or space. Love is not created by cognitive or intellectual endeavor. Love is only to be felt by anyone, anywhere, and anytime when human relationships are genuine and beneficial.

Where and how, then, does love show up? Love normally is found in an intimate human relationship such as between spouses, lovers, and within a family. Thus, forceful separation of loved ones from each other is a violation of the love right. During periods of political turmoil such as a war, family members become vulnerable to family separation, in many instances, unable to be reunited for a prolonged time. A dramatic example is found in the 20th century history of Korea. During the period of an active war in Korea (1950-1953), over one million people found themselves separated from their family members across the divide that has to this date never been reunited. The division of the country since the Korean War has lasted over 60 years and counting. A majority of the dispersed family members have died of old age but there still are so many separated families. In the family-centered Confucian culture of Korea, the children of the first generation are in a desperate desire to find their relatives. All these people have been deprived of the right to love for such a long time. To varying degrees, war-torn areas of the world are experiencing the same kind of human right violations. Refugees from areas of armed conflicts often experience family separation, and this case too should be dealt with the human rights perspective.

The issue of marriage should be brought to the forefront from the perspective of the love right. As alluded to earlier, our human needs paradigm concluded that the family as a social institution is, in its genesis, a human invention that is designed to promote a sense of mutual belonging or to facilitate social identity for family members. Therefore, where there is love, there should be the accommodation to revere it, and the formation of a family should fall within the purview of the institution. This can have a direct implication for the controversial "same-sex marriage." The government cannot and should not "produce" love but, as the public agent, it must take the love right issue as its legitimate and obligatory function, rather than dumping it over the private sector.

Love can evolve within itself without changing the conception or definition itself. Initially, love is conceived with some rationale. That is to say, one loves another person for some conscious or unconscious reasons such as personal attractiveness (good looking, personal character), financial status, education, social status, religion, and social pressure (in the case of arranged marriage). This is the "reason-based" love or the *Because-Love*. Whatever the reason, the significance as the engineering force behind the love will evaporate in time. Thus, the duration of such love can be shortened ending up with a divorce. The rampant phenomenon of divorce in all types of society of the world today testifies this. In fact, the *Because-Love* may not be seen even as a variation of love, it is a pretended love or pseudo love. Then, there is a love that lacks or defies a reason, which might be called the *"Blind-Love"* which can be truly romantic or continuation of a "love" relationship habitually or forcefully due to social pressures, often with a degree of numbness. But this form of love is not completely devoid of the determinants of love, as love should be with affection, caring, willingness to sacrifice, and devotion to one another. How many spouses have endured their relationships as a family for the sake of their children's wellbeing? There is nothing wrong in this, as they endure a phase in the passing of time, their love could mature. Hasty divorce can be detrimental to the children. In fact, this Blind-Love could be the force behind most "successful" marriages or enduing relationships or in actual society. Then, there is the most admirable or mature form of love, and it is just about the opposite to the *Because-Love*; that is, there might be no reason to love or there may be sufficient reasons not to love but love is felt despite all the negativities. This form of love, I would refer to as *"Despite Love."* In the Christian persuasion, the love that Jesus Christ showed in his own life was exactly of this kind of love. In other religious belief systems such as Buddhism and Islam, one will find similar conceptions of love (or however love is termed). The *Despite Love* requires empathy in that the lover puts himself or herself in the "shoes" of another, and feels the pains and joys of the person being loved. When this happens, the love-giver will experience inner transformation through peace and selflessness, and reach the sphere of transcendental *freedom* that was portrayed as the function of the Soul in the previous chapter.

Strategies for the Realization of Human Rights

Our discussion on human rights in this chapter began with the premise that the acquisition of the rights will make human existence dignified. Thus, with human development established, individuals seek human dignity through interaction with other members of the society. Dignity will be served as the life right is securely obtained, the identity right stably established, the choice right realized, and the love right fulfilled. Then, the question becomes how the rights might be pursued. Here, we might consider what different components of the political community might assume responsibilities and functions to promote the rights.

1) The State or Government

One must never forget that the people have created the state or government for the purpose of pursuing their human development and human dignity. This theorem for the genesis and legitimation of the state is not limited to liberal democracies. All forms of political system in the modern era agree with this theorem.

What might be in disagreement is the boundary of legitimate power and functions of the government. Different political ideologies have advocated different positions on this question. While a totalitarian dictatorship advocates the necessity of total control of the people by the state, liberal, or polyarchal democracies tend to minimize the sphere of state power. But, we maintained earlier that what matters is not the size of the government, but its nature and functions. More specifically, then, we are prepared to delineate the boundaries and legitimate role of the government. Based on the discussion in this chapter, we can conclude that (a) the state is ultimately responsible for ensuring the right of the people to life by ensuring through the use of its authoritative power that people are adequately provided with the supply of basic needs and services. It may use a diverse set of policy strategies and tactics but ultimately the peoples life right must be optimally guaranteed; (b) as power is defined in terms of the "authoritative allocation of values," the state must be responsible for creating and maintaining a just (equitable) distribution of resources and opportunities; (c) as long as healthcare remains a basic requisite for life, the state must ensure universal healthcare for *all* members of the society; (d) as the environmental quality affects directly the life right of all the people and the private sector is not designed for the public good of the planetary health, the state must be charged with the task of protecting and preserving the planet; (e) the government has always been and will continue to be responsible for domestic and external security. It should be in a complete charge of providing the necessary service, rather than delegating or contracting it out the private sector; (f) lastly, the state must also regulate, coordinate all the private sector entities including individuals in a way that they will function to serve all components of the human rights.

2) The Civil Society

As people pursue their identity right, civil society is likely to be formed. A civil society is a community of non-governmental organizations that have their own interests to pursue. Some of the interests could be against the will of the ruling leadership or they can be for the incumbent government. Therefore, the civic groups are expected to be diverse in their ideological and political dispositions. Through these groups, people articulate and aggregate their interests to form political pressure groups. In the process, citizens establish their value positions and political identities. Unionization is an important process for interest group activities. In a participatory democracy, we expect the proliferation of these groups in all domains of the society including economic interest groups, cultural organizations, and professional and occupational associations.

3) Socialization Agents

Socialization takes place throughout one's life. It is a process and experience in which a person, initially a purely biological being, undergoes the transition to a social and political being by acquiring and internalizing the norms and values that are prevalent in the society and the polity. In this process, the person establishes his or her own social and/or political identity. Thus, the socialization agents of the family, school, and religious groups are important in forging the symbolic identities of their respective members. Organizations in a civil society are the homes for the seekers of the life right, identity right, and the choice right. When life gets tough with low wages and income, collective bargaining becomes a tool for the laborers to improve poor life conditions; when people pursue the choice right, they attempt to enlarge the pool of available alternatives. Often an organization itself helps its members to make rational choices by providing them relevant information and guidelines for decision making.

a) The Family

The family institution is the identity provider into which a child is born. The norms and belief systems of the family in any given society and polity will provide the child with a cultural context in which socialization takes place. The child will find a physical identity in the form of a shared surname (family name). Each family has a "culture" that affects the character and behavioral attributes of its children. Early socialization goes a long way, and the impact of the family has a lasting effect on the formation of one's identity.

b) Education

School has a vital role in developing students' norms and beliefs about the society and the state. In public or publicly funded schools, political socialization of the students looms large as the political system expects the educational institutions to inculcate them with the ideology and belief systems that are consistent with and supportive of the ideology and political culture of the state. Through civic education, children are specifically socialized to become functioning members of the political system. Education is essential in fulfilling the conditions for choice making, and by extension, participatory democracy. As most empirical analyses confirm, the level of education of the people and all sectors of human rights (life and economy, social capital, and political democracy) are positively associated. In fact, if we were to identify the most important single factor that propagates adherence to human rights, it would likely be education.

c) Religion

The ultimate authority for socialization of the people resides with religious organizations. The teaching of any religion will contain a comprehensive system of norms, values, and beliefs, and members of the religion are expected to identify themselves with it. The Bible for Christian civilization, Koran for Islam, Buddha's Teaching for Buddhism, and numerous other religious persuasions, even including sectarian faith groups. Personal identity in a religious civilization is built in consonance with its teachings. Faith in a religion is a powerful source of personal identity and most influential force behind the attitudes and behaviors that include the choice of loyalty, personal traits guiding relationships of all kinds. A faith can be doctrinaire and shut itself off from all other value systems, causing a hostile attitude toward certain groups or states, even prompting wars. As we will discuss in the following chapter, in a world without inter-faith dialogue and mutual acceptance, peace is not likely to be maintained.

d) The State

The state is a powerful agent of political socialization. Even a cursory examination of the Cold War politics shows that it was the state, especially the totalitarian communist states, that "indoctrinated" the people. With the authority to rule, coercive capability, and the ability to penetrate into all segments of the population, the state can be almost omnipotent in manipulating and molding the minds of the people. The state uses public education, for which it often dictates the curriculum, writes textbooks, and manipulates other policies. Furthermore, with its intelligence arms, the state can intimidate, provoke fear for punishment, and reward "good" behavior on the part of the people. This trait of the state is universally observed throughout the world, not just limited to autocracies and dictatorships. Thus, it is absolutely essential for the state to be held accountable for its use and abuse of this power. Currently, there is no international or supra-state authority to oversee the power of the state, a topic we will pick up in Chapter 14.

Distributive Justice and the State

The right for every person to live on equal terms within a community is directly related to the question of *distributive justice.* This right is often paraphrased as the "social right" or "economic right" but the concept of the life right is more direct and clearer. The role of government for all forms of political system lies in the management of *distributive justice.* What is a "just" distribution? Is it distribution by need (Karl Marx)? Is it distribution by one's ability in the state of the survival of the fittest (anarchy)? Is it distribution by market forces (capitalism)? Is it distribution by the principle of equality for all (socialism)? We have seen repeated trial errors for each of the above modes of distribution but none worked for justice. Just distribution, as envisioned in this book, is a distribution in which all four kinds of human rights (life, identity, choice, and love) are promoted, protected, and preserved. The role and obligation of the state, as the public sector, is far-reaching and essential for the optimal realization of the human rights:

1) The Life Right and Socialism

No ideology should den*y any* citizen to survive physically. Regardless of specific policies or ideological stances, *all* citizens must have the guarantee of the life right! The provision of minimum requirements for sustaining life including food, shelter, healthcare, social safety, and national (state) security must ultimately fall in the legitimate function and obligation of the government as the public sector. If socialism is the vehicle of such guarantee, it should be legitimately accepted. This obligation should never be left with the private sector. It is wrong and demeaning for charity organizations to raise resources from the citizenry and "hand out" the collections to the needy. There is nothing more demeaning than to be dependent on the charity of fellow citizens and private organizations. One would rather be on government benefits for which the recipient may have made a contribution or feel some sense of rightful entitlement. If a socialist or state-controlled mechanism is objectionable for any reason, one could use a mixed ideological system to fulfill this obligation, but the accountability should remain with the government. This does not mean that the state's power is or should be limitless. On the contrary, the state role should be strictly limited to guaranteeing the survival or life right of all the citizens. Nonetheless, for the other forms of human rights (identity, choice, and love), we must delineate the boundary of state power.

2) The Identity Right and Polyarchy

Except for cases where the state provides a sense of identity through an official ideology and coercive mechanisms as the case might be in the Nazi state and the Communist totalitarian systems, people seek their identities in associating with "significant" others. Therefore, the state should tolerate and even encourage the formation of a pluralist political community where groups and associations will contend for comparative superiority and populism. The "danger" here could be the massive emergence of social and political groups and organizations that can hardly be regulated or managed for sustained social stability and civility, leading to a state of anarchism. However, the role of the state should be limited to managing and regulating their interactive activities, rather than cracking them down with the pretext of restoring law and order. Even with the risk of social unrest and instability, pluralist political system is desired for the development of a civil society where diverse groups and organizations are accommodated and coordinated. In this process, the identity right for the citizenry will optimally be achieved.

3) The Choice Right and Participatory Democracy

Then, we have the third of our human rights, the choice right. The Western, primarily American, interpretation of the concept of human rights heavily favors the choice right because the essence of liberal democracy lies in this right. Everything about the celebrated institution of election has to do with choice-making. In order for the citizens to fulfill this component of the human right, no system is better suited than participatory democracy. Participation in any process of decision-making involves making choices from available alternatives. A participatory culture should be in place for democracy to work. Such culture requires the orientation of the people to find a sense of dignity and self-esteem in making choices. To make a choice is to exercise power and express self-worth. In addition to culture, there must be structural and political conditions such as the presence of alternative choices and political mechanism and freedom to commence the choice-making action. In economically advanced and politically liberal systems, one could expect that the presence of a culture, structural conditions, and political freedom for citizens' political participation. Less developed systems would experience difficulties and irregularities in realizing such forms of government.

4) The Love Right and State Pacifism

The final component of human rights, the love right, is one the state cannot create but it can protect once the people have attained it. The state can build a structural environment in which people's pursuit of love may become viable and the expression of love not be discouraged. To this end, the government can protect the institution of the family as the primary group for the identity right, rather than attempting to define family. This point is pertinent to the current debate in the United States over same-sex marriage. If the state controls the most primary group of the family, its power is grossly abused. The role of the state, therefore, should be one of non-interference in this situation. A political environment must be conducive to open and free association, and loving interactions among individuals must be created and preserved. For this, the state must create an environment of peace for the community, a topic for the next chapter.

This chapter advanced the view that human dignity will be achieved through meaningful social relationships in which the entire spectrum of human rights is observed. In the previous chapter, we called for human development, not economic or institutional modernization as the core agenda for development. Human development helps individual members of the community to acquire a set of "attributes" but those attributes in themselves do not speak to the concept of human dignity. Now that, we have a desirable course for human development at the micro (individual) level and the middle (relational) level for human dignity, we must address the macro (community) level for a complete coverage of development as it ought to be. The macrolevel phenomenon being advocated here is the norm of *peace*, the topic of the next chapter.

A Case for Composite System of Ideology

The complete range of human rights requires various social and political contexts and policies that no one ideological system can encompass: the life right that needs the provision of basic needs such as food, shelter, healthcare, and environmental health. Furthermore, it needs safe and secure community. All these are public goods and services that the public sector of the government should ultimately be obligated to provide. The public (people) extends loyalty and patriotism to the state, and also subsidizes the government not only with material resources through paying taxes but also with personal sacrifices by serving the armed forces. The legitimate role of the government should begin with serving the people by assuring people's life right be attained and sustained. This means that the state should be held responsible for not only national security and community safety, but also the provision of people's basic needs. Of the political ideologies that have been experimented with throughout history, socialism (or the welfare state doctrine) appears to be most appropriately oriented towards this end. But in this era of globalization, we must install a supra-national entity of governance, particularly for public health and planetary health. The eruption of a contagious disease in any part of the world is a global concern. Institutions such as the World Health Organization (WHO), as well as the World Food Organization (WFO) are on the right track, but they are not supported sufficiently by all the sovereign states of the world. We also need global efforts at improving the health of the planet, and this, too, requires heightened efforts and tangible support by the global community.

The identity right, however, is not going to be optimally served by socialism or the welfare state. People reach out to each other to establish more "significant others" by creating and joining groups and organizations. As pointed earlier, the government finds the proliferation of social and political groups to be uncomfortable, and the instinctive reaction of the state is to crack them down as many centrist governments have done throughout the world. Yet, for the identity right of the people, it is essential that civic groups and organizations be allowed for a civil society to emerge. Thus, the ideology should be a form of polyarchy that is designed to promote political diversity. The government in this case should create and protect a legal and political environment conducive to a vibrant civil society. As a desirable form of ideology, polyarchy might be most suitable. Then, our third component of human rights, the choice right, requires participatory democracy. Participation in political processes is nothing other than choice-making! It is understandable that the United States that is founded on the premise of government by the people advocates the election system throughout the world as its key foreign policy objective, but Washington must realize that there are specific requisite conditions for instilling a participatory system. Washington must also realize that human rights include more than the choice right. The American military campaigns in Iraq, Afghanistan, Iraq, and Korea, among others in the initial decades of the twenty first century were aimed at spreading participatory democracy in spite of cultural readiness to receive such a system of government. Washington must realize that a participatory democracy does not emerge from the barrel of a gun. Eventually, though, for the advancement of the choice right, participatory democracy is a desirable form of ideology.

Then, there is the love right. This is a right for which the government should simply step aside. Love is the most private attribute, and the public sector of the government has little to do with it except for the fact that people's activities of love have often been hampered by military conflicts and wars that almost always involve the state. Here, (classical) liberal democracy, predicated on the principle of "a minimum government is the best government" seems to be the most desirable.

The above discussion rationalizes a composite form of ideology. In fact, most political systems of the world are utilizing different forms of ideology to deal with their problems. It is time for the intellectuals of today in various political systems to create a composite ideological system and ruling structure that suits their own system. More importantly, it is time for the world community to respect system-specific ideological structures and embrace a diverse world community. The time has passed when contending ideologies vie for supremacy. We have seen ideological cultural, religious, and even civilizational clashes in history. However, we still fail to live in peace without instances of international conflict. We must be mindful that political ideologies are mere human inventions constructed as an instrumental means to achieve the political goals inherent in the state system. We have come to a point in history, following generations of trial and error, where the world must evolve into a community that embraces diversity if we, as one human race, are to be sustained. The topic of peace, then, will follow in the next chapter.

Chapter 13

Peace, Not Security, for Community

In the previous two chapters, we established that human development should be the focus of developmental studies, and that social or interpersonal relationships must be guided by the pursuit of human dignity founded on the realization of the human rights. Then, we can be assured of healthy, spirited, and dignified life. Yet, the macro system of societies is beyond the level of the changes that can be more easily implemented in a single society. Here, I would suggest that a "community" must be built at the global level. A community is to be understood in structural terms as a collection of parts in which the parts are mutually interdependent and indispensable. We already have a world of interdependence and mutual reliance in terms of the economy, information, and market system. However, a global community should also have a cultural aura that ties its constituent parts in a way that each of the parts will be better off by becoming integrated into the whole. We demonstrated in earlier chapters that the world has become a global "village" that is integrated for economic needs and financial expediency, but the community itself is hardly orderly or even stable. We are reminded again and again that the greatest challenge for mankind is to find a way of living together without killing each other. It is proven that global security cannot be tenable as long as we seek security through the age-old concept of hierarchical world order enforced by coercive power. This power is usually manifested in the form of military might, but it can be economy, information, ideology, culture, and even science and technology. By employing one or a combination of these means, a nation seeks a position of domination over other nations.

This world order was possible for most of the world history but it is not working anymore for this global system in the 21st Century. Given the massive destructive power available to even small armed forces and militant groups, wars must be stopped. In reality, the security paradigm has lived its life, and it can no longer ensure safety and security for the global population at-large. Looking back, for 2000 years, mankind has sought an orderly world through security regimes. A security regime is an international system of relationships in which a variation of colonialism is perpetuated into an unequal and unjust political order. Such a regime is created as a result of military conflicts whereby winners and losers are

257

assigned their proper positions in the world order. The winner has dominated the loser, and the latter assumes a submissive position to the former. As typified by colonial times, the world order in this case is a vertical one, rather than horizontal, in which the loser is exploited and manipulated by the winner. The cultural aura of the winner includes not only guardianship and paternalism, but also a sense of racial, ideological, and human superiority. In the interdependent global community, inequality and cultural imperialism will not be tolerated by world public opinion. The world public today is enlightened with the norm of equity as the core norm of justice. Yet, the policy framers who represent the old world order are stuck obsessively to the security system where they find themselves in the position of domination. But the rest of the world, where the "losers" are typically found, refuses to accept the old world order. A world system predicated upon a security paradigm may provide a sense of predictability, accountability, and regulated patterns of relationships. With the end of the Cold War world order coupled by the unchecked progression of globalization, human history has shown the diminishing prevalence of the security paradigm.

It is a reality of the post-Cold War world that physical might alone can no longer guarantee security. Two grand historical forces have made this fundamental transformation possible. First, since the world first witnessed the destructive power of the atomic bomb that ended WWII, governments and non-government entities with the ambition of either becoming a dominant power or avoiding a surrogate position have competed to develop weapons of mass destruction (WMD), including the nuclear bomb itself. Some have succeeded in equipping themselves with WMDs, and many more are on the verge of acquiring these deadly capacities. Yet, the inherently secretive nature of these weapons makes it difficult for us to manage or curtail their explosive proliferation. Some non-Western states, including the so called "rogue" states and terrorist groups, are often empowered by the acquisition of WMD, and we seem to have no viable means of stopping them, short of outright war. Second, the massive force of globalization, which is often seen as a spillover of American and Western capitalist economies, creates a homogeneous culture whereby local and indigenous cultural attributes are threatened. Many outside traditional Judeo-Christian civilization view globalization as a grand imperialist strategy by the dominant post-industrial forces. This provides them with the incentive to mobilize their forces against the forces of globalization ("Americanization"). The resurgence of ethnic and religious groups around the world can be seen as the expression of their desperate desire to restore and maintain their identities.

To many of these people, values and cultural identities are more important than material and bodily assets.

In regards to the current "war on terrorism" sparked by 9/11, we must not rely on military means to restore our security and the security of the world. The sooner we realize the destined failure of the security regime, the better. We have no choice, nor do we seem to have time to waste as more soldiers and civilians are killed and wounded each passing day in military confrontations of all kinds, ranging from full-blown wars to tribal skirmishes. The security paradigm is couched in a series of its facilitating and reinforcing forces in our belief systems and our social and political dynamics, paving the way to the following fundamental premises of the security paradigm.

The Creed of the Security Paradigm:

1. World order must be vertical, where the relationship among states is managed by the *hierarchy of power*;
2. The world is a system of *dominations* (and subjugations);
3. The creation or management of orderly relations among states or sub-state entities is pursued through *violent* means, not peaceful means;
4. Social and human relationships are defined in terms of a *zero-sum* relationship where someone's winning satisfaction is overshadowed by someone else's losing agony; Here, the strong will eat up the weak;
5. The world is viewed from a *dichotomous* perspective where there is only the winner or the loser with no middle ground between them;
6. Submission to the strong by the weak is possible because of the *fear* of losing even more, including life itself; the loser or potential loser feels helpless but to surrender and give in to the wishes of the strong;
7. Security system requires *secrecy* and information withholding or crafting misinformation or disinformation.
8. *The state is the initiator*: The security system as a norm is created and maintained by the public sector of the government, rather than non-government citizens or groups.

The above premises have made the foundation of the colonial and imperialist world order. The persistence of this imperialist world-order in the post-Colonial era or in our global era has created instability and dilemmas in the security paradigm, with the emergence of the new realization that the world has changed. Along with it, what has emerged is a new world culture or a new belief system with new normative dispositions among the inhabitants of the global community. In other words, the world has awakened to the new reality.

New Reality (The Shift of Historical Context): The Advent of Terrorism

1. Power, especially military power, can no longer guarantee security for the strong and dominant. Today's global community has created a new vulnerability from organized terrorism and unconventional small states that defy the domination-based world order. Moreover, some "terrorists" are not deterred by the fear of being harmed or destroyed, as the case of suicide bombers might suggest.

2. The strong and dominant can no longer physically subdue the weak and small in today's world for a good many reasons, but particularly because of the awakening of the citizenry to the global information system. This awakening has been made possible by the open infrastructure of communication in both the conventional mass media and the surge of unconventional electronic networking ("social media"). People also become informed of other societies through tourism and the rise of convenient transportation systems. The deprived people of the world have been able to extend their frame of reference to develop "alliances" for their cause and action and aggregate dissentions across the world. The Arab uprising campaigns and movements would have been unthinkable without the new system of communication.

3. The loser or potential loser does not feel his cause is helpless and does not submit himself to the oppressor because of his faith in the cause and even in the subliminal world as a martyr. How else can one explain the behavior of a mother strapping explosives on the body of her son who is about to commit an act of suicide bombing?

4. Non-violence has attained a powerful moral value within protest movements, a legacy of Mahatma Gandhi and Martin Luther King, Aung San Suu Kyi, Daisaku Ikeda, as well as a number of pacifist religious and civic leaders and pacifist organizations. Pacifists have attained a greater moral authority, and they are invariably associated with superior intellectuals and profound thinkers.

5. The world political culture has turned its attention towards the common and deprived people. The election of Pope Francis in 2013, as well as the reelection of Obama in 2012, serves as evidence of this. While the common people are suffering from material deprivation and political marginalization, they are the reservoir of moral authority.

6. Mutual adversaries in conflict tend to have strong commitments to values and principles that are mutually incompatible. Thus, negotiated settlement of differences is often insurmountably difficult.

7. Global mass media play a decisive role in articulating and publicizing the nature and structure of conflicts, and reveal the policy positions of the contending parties. This makes behind the scene negotiations even more difficult as they must stick to their publicized policy positions; otherwise they run the risk of "losing face" both to their domestic audiences and the international community.

From 9/11 to North Korea and ISIS

The shift of historical context discussed above has clearly been highlighted by a series of major historical events since the dawn of the twenty first century, from 9/11 in 2001 to the never-ending crisis surrounding North Korea's nuclear weapons. Both cases involve the United States. What does 9/11 signify? It signifies the opening of a new era in which military might alone will be unable to deter hostile behavior from small groups or individuals, meaning that the security paradigm is losing its validity. It also signifies that attitudes and beliefs of people of the world toward a particular state do matter as a force in security for that state. It signifies that we have seen the dawning of a new wave of political terrorism that must be dealt with by the global community in the 21st Century and beyond.

Political terrorism is not an ideology but a phenomenon with distinct characteristics: (1) frustration with "structural violence" surrounding the life environment of segments of world population from which terrorists emerge. This structural violence includes impoverished economic conditions and the accompanying sense of relative deprivation; (2) there is a common notion of who is to blame and a definitive target for terrorist aggression; (3) the terrorists hold a believe they have a mission to emancipate their people from the forces that marginalize their existence; (4) the terrorist attaches his sense of self-worth to his status as a martyr. With the instrument of the "social media," terrorist interests can be readily aggregated throughout the world facilitating the spread of terrorist sentiments and ideas beyond political boundaries. The availability and accessibility of weapons of all kinds by terrorists and would-be-terrorists poses a formidable challenge, especially considering the political leverage on the part of weapons producers and the military-industrial complex. The arms manufacturer lobby was powerful enough to prevent even the most basic gun control measures from passing the Senate in the wake of Sandy Hook Elementary School shootings in Newtown, Connecticut on December 14, where 28 people were killed, including 20 children between the ages of 5-10. Terrorists will not be discouraged due to difficulty in obtaining weapons. Further, weapons availability does not come even close to explaining political terrorism. The causes and motives for terrorism are complicated and multi-facetted that require a comprehensive and interdisciplinary study. Even if we had such a study and ascertained probable contributing factors to terrorism, there has to be the political will on the part of all governments and civil societies. The current state in this regard is discouraging and the prospects for improvement are cloudy at best.

Since 9/11, the United States of America has committed acts that many around the world consider to be state-sponsored terrorism. Under the pretext of preventing Saddam Hussein from acquiring weapons of mass destruction (WMD), especially the nuclear bomb, the United States invaded Iraq and destroyed the ruling structure including Saddam himself. But after ten years of occupation, the United States failed to substantiate the allegations that the Iraqi regime possessed WMDs. Still, the Bush Administration persisted in its rationalization that the "evil" system of Iraq should be replaced by a democratic system, shifting the goal of the invasion from regime change to nation building. Similarly, the campaign in Afghanistan to remove the terrorist-friendly Taliban regime has suffered from "mission creep," becoming more and more about nation-building and the installation of traditional western democracy. In the process, the costs in human lives and physical destruction have continued to pile up: Iraq resulted in the deaths of thousands of American soldiers, and tens-of-thousands of wounded men and women came home with scars in the form of their own physical and mental injuries. For these soldiers and their families, the pain will not be alleviated for decades to come. Casualties among Iraqi and Afghanistan civilians have been much higher than those suffered by U.S. and NATO forces, with Iraqi civilian casualties as high as 100,000 by some estimates. These military campaigns have produced absolutely nothing that could begin to justify this kind of cost in lives, coin, and destruction. The stark reality is that military domination is not the route to security and stability anymore. This reality is even more clearly evidenced by the case of North Korea.

North Korea is a little country occupying the northern part of the Korean peninsula in the heart of the Confucian civilization, with a population of 22 million. It is poverty-stricken, with severe food shortages. Yet, it is a political system with military preparedness that challenges its much more affluent advanced neighbor, South Korea. North Korea is a *de facto* nuclear state with a long-range missile system. How can we explain the anomaly that a starving country has made itself a formidable military power? More importantly, North Korea has shown an established pattern of policy orientations and policy behaviors that many believe are in defiance of the "prevailing norms" and practices of international politics. The prevailing norms here are the norms that guided the world politics for millennia in the past, and that is, that the practices drawn from the aforementioned security paradigm. How should one comprehend the seemingly irrational policy behaviors of that political system?

The founder, Kim Il Sung (spelled in North Korea as Kim Il Song), was an energetic leader of a guerrilla group in northeast China during the Japanese Colonial Rule of his youth (1911-1945), where he earned a positive reputation among his followers in and out of the peninsula. When he assumed the leadership as the head of the Korean Workers Party (the Communist Party of Korea), he had already gained a charismatic status. He is known as the creator of the state with a distinct ideological character of *Juche* (Self-Reliance) that was in sharp contrast with Syngman Rhree's regime in the South. When he died abruptly in 1994, his son, Kim Jong Il, emerged as the successor. Kim Jong Il faced immediately the challenge of famine after flooding wiped out much of the nation's arable land. His regime also faced what they perceived to be an enormous security challenge as the Soviet security umbrella disappeared at the end of the Cold War. The twin task of growing the security state and the economy was much too difficult, and Kim Jong Il opted to prioritize national security by developing nuclear capability. The nuclear program was conceived and initiated much earlier by Kim Il Sung who had been overwhelmed by the power of the nuclear bombs used in Hiroshima and Nagasaki in WWII, but it was not until the rein of Kim Jong Il that the nuclear program was pursued with a high priority. This was due to several facts such as: (1) the demise of the Soviet Union along with its nuclear umbrella; (2) nuclear science and technology had already been developed indigenously during the Kim Il Sung era; (3) the nuclear option would have been most economical in securing self-defense. Kim Jong Il launched the massive campaign for the Military First (*Songun*) Politics, in which nuclear self-defense became the core of national politics. Kim Jong Il's regime managed to test missiles of various ranges and also tested nuclear devices in 2006 and 2009, followed by the third test in February 2013 (after his sudden death on December 17, 2011).

Soon after the death of Kim Jong Il, Kim Jong Un was installed as the new leader at the age of 29. Pyongyang demonstrated its ability to send a multi-stage, long-range rocket into the space in on December 12, 2012. Following this, the young Kim demonstrated his resolve to further nuclearize by testing more powerful and more combat ready bombs along with missiles of diverse ranges from underground, mobile launching pads, and submarines. Both Washington and Seoul became so alarmed that they propelled joint military exercises along the inter-Korea border. The highly controversial THAAD (TERMINAL HIGH ALTITUDE AREA DEFENSE) installation in South Korea designed to neutralize North Korean nuclear missiles can continue to be an explosive political dynamite in the region. The Kim Jong Un regime appears to be confident that it finally has achieved the self-defense capability which his father and grandfather were instrumental in developing but they themselves did not have during their reins. The young Kim, from the very beginning of his leadership, proclaimed that on the foundation of national self-defense, his own mission is to make the country economically prosperous. To this end, Kim Jong Un realized that the numerous and accumulated sanctions since the first nuclear test in December 2006 by the United Nations and the United States must be eliminated. He believed that the 65-year old Armistice Agreement on the peninsula is meaningless and detrimental to stability in the region, and he wants a peace treaty with Washington. He publicly declared that he will not return to the "limbo" (Not War, Nor Peace) which, in his mind, is ultimately responsible for the economic hardships experienced by his people.

Despite many critics and harsh words toward him, the stark reality is that Kim Jong Un regime is going to continue its defiance against what it views as U.S./U.N. domination in the peninsula and the region. At this stalemate and crisis in March-April of 2013, the United States was cornered in the unenviable position of having to choose between the unacceptable and the unwanted. It is unacceptable for Washington to militarily strike North Korea in a massive war in the Korean peninsula for political, strategic, moral reasons, and it would be much too humiliating to give into North Korean demands (some say "extortion") for a peace treaty, particularly since human rights conditions in North Korea are deplorable, at best. The bottom line for our discussion is that the United States is no longer able to arm-twist small states in this global community. In the North Korean episode, it is clearly seen that the traditional Security Paradigm is not enough to ensure stability and cooperation.

ISIS: A Legitimate Advancement of Terrorism

Despite the Obama government successful elimination of Bin Laden by means of assassination on May 2 in 2011, the Al Qaeda forces became more diversified throughout the world. ISIS (Islamic State in Iraq and Syria) is a different breed of terrorism. Unlike all previous terrorist groups, it emerged in defined territories and economic base for generating tax revenues. This state-like organization has attracted sympathizers throughout the Islamic world with solidified anti-American and anti-Western sentiment and terrorist agenda. Other than military maneuverings, the United States and the West are simply unable to find an effective way of dealing with this disruptive organization. As in the case of North Korea, the ISIS issue cannot be resolved by conventional military means. There is no military solution for these security dilemmas.

If Not Security, Then, What?

We have concluded in this book that the security paradigm by which the global system has order is bankrupt, and it does not work even for creating and maintaining security itself. Indeed, in the course of political history, we have always maintained the world order by the security paradigm. At times, there were anarchistic political disorderly situation. When an existing order was to be replaced, there has always been chaos and destruction with no authority structure established. But anarchy has never been and will continue to be an unacceptable political order. At this historical juncture, we must view history in a grand stride and must offer an alternative paradigm for a world order. The paradigm that is required is one in which diverse nations and interests become mutually beneficial, thus creating a system of win-win relationships. Such a system reflects a legitimate peace regime under which peace, and not security, becomes the overarching objective. Indeed, peace and security are two distinct concepts. Peace is not a state devoid of conflict. In fact, security and peace are mutually independent. We shall turn to this notion of a positive piece in Chapter 14.

Chapter 14

Positive Peace

Once we succeeded in achieving individual well-being through obtaining basic needs and health (physical and mental) and acquired dignified social and interpersonal relations, then the greater community should strive for peace. Peace is not just the absence of violence, killing, and conflicts. Peace is harmony, and harmony is the creation of oneness out of diversity. The concept of harmony as a positive peace was advocated by Han S. Park on a TEDTALK program (*YouTube, A New Paradigm for Peace Han Park)*

Diversity is the requisite condition for harmony. A perfect analogy can be observed in orchestra music. The property of an orchestra includes a number of different musical instruments (even human voices can be added as instruments), the maestro, and the music scores that are made available by composers. The conductor studies the music to learn and interpret the music; the instrumentalists get familiarize themselves with the music, especially their own parts, and practice; and the composer who authored the scores. Each musician (instrumentalist) practice to the perfection; the conductor coordinates all parts to create the integrated and harmonious whole; the orchestra as a whole follows the lead of the conductor to adjust their parts to the creation of the music as envisioned by the composer and interpreted by the maestro. Then, the audience is drawn into "the creation of oneness out of diversity" that is harmony. Here, one must realize that each individual member "disappears" into the harmony as an integral part of the orchestrated harmony. The conductor, who is in a position to coordinate all the parts, will be responsible for the final product. In a real community, members of the society, as well as its diverse occupational groups and organizations, are analogous to the musicians who play various diverse instruments: the composer is the policy framers, including scholars, think-tanks, and policy advisors, and the maestro's responsibilities and functions are to be assumed by the government. Thus, a "peace regime" should include all the constituent parts and elements of orchestral music.

The harmonious relationship is not a command or centralized system. Rather, it is a system of coordination of diverse parts with a mutually complementing (equilibrate) status. In a peace regime, differences are accepted and respected, domination is replaced by coordination and cooperation, accommodation is favored over assimilation, and ultimately, dialogue is used as the only instrument for its creation. A peace regime requires a culture of diversity and relativism. A culture of diversity does not mean that there is no consensus in human aspirations and it does not mean that the overarching goals of human development and human dignity are relative and subject to diverse interpretation. The culture of diversity means that the same goal may be served by different strategies and tactics: the goal of survival may be served by diverse kinds of food and the way food is consumed or by diverse kinds of clothes, but the goal of physical survival remains the same.

In fact, a culture is formed as a way of rationalizing or justifying certain manifestations in behavioral and attitudinal traits that have evolved in the process of pursuing the goal of development. By the same token, social institutions and structures that may be diverse are also created for the purpose of serving the objective of human aspirations for achieving common goals of human development. Therefore cultural and institutional diversity should not and could not be a sufficient ground for violent conflicts. One might ask: can we and should we accommodate terrorist behavior in the name of harmony and accommodation? Certainly not. Terrorism should not be allowed any harbor in a civilized world. In the name of diversity and accommodation, an orchestra cannot just accept any sound-producing object. The employed musical instruments must be those required by the music itself. Terrorists are harmony-breakers and disturbances, and should never be allowed in a peace regime. We must realize that even terrorists can be induced to becoming valuable members of the society by proper socialization and education. It is crucial for us to understand that efforts to eliminate terrorism should never resort to the instruments of a security regime, i.e., physical coercion through military or economic sanction. In the post-Cold War era, neither has worked effectively in the pursuit of that goal. Treating those with different orientations that may contradict or be incompatible with our own as being sub-human, controllable only by military threat or economic punishment, is a fruitless endeavor. Those people defiant of our coercive attempts at reform are precisely those that turn to unconventional means of expressing their will through terrorist acts or nuclear threats. We are losing the war against terrorism not because of our inability to "punish" the insurgents militarily or economically, but because we are using outmoded, counterproductive strategies borrowed from the security paradigm.

If the United States is to build peace, Washington should not discriminate against anyone in engaging for a dialogue. As the most powerful state in the world, the United States should not "outsource" diplomacy to other countries. It is short-sighted to avoid direct talks with North Korea by commissioning China and others to deal with our own diplomatic issues. It is ill-advised to expect the European Union to handle the nuclear issue of Iran for the United States. A tragic legacy of the security paradigm is that the dominant power must continuously have an enemy to fuel military expansion. With the Soviets gone, the United States was left with no one to challenge its superpower status, and then 9/11 criminals disturbed the American self-esteem and sense of security. Sadly, the Bush Administration used the events of 9/11 to push towards full-scale war, thus, through no small measure of irony, providing the terrorists the "legitimacy" they so craved. Provoking a sense of security threat and engaging oneself with external conflicts can, as history testifies, justify dictatorships and undermine democratic norms and processes. With the "war against terrorism," we may indeed be witnessing this inevitable consequence, embodied in our acceptance of the Patriot Act and the recent compromises to our right to privacy through spurious wiretapping. The United States cannot win this war, and the grim prospect is that it will drift on into the uncharted future, imposing death and injury on young members of the military, draining resources, and alienating the country in world's public opinion. If America continues to carry out its security aspirations through coercive means, she will face a certain fall. I am reminded of the chilling words of Osama Bin Laden, "We cannot destroy America but we will make it bleed to death." Defeating Al-Qaida and other terrorists means engineering a campaign for peace-building, creating a civilized world in which the outlaws will find no comfort or means to legitimize their actions -- otherwise, we play into their hands by waging the unwinnable war. We are at a crossroads in history that challenges us to deliver a new world order to future generations. Meeting this challenge begins with realizing and accepting the shortcomings of the security regime, and valuing the wisdom of the peace paradigm.

Peace does not and should not have a system of normative and philosophical values or beliefs within itself. Peace, therefore, is not a doctrine or an ideology. It is a culture, a particular culture that is advocating the accommodation of diverse orientations, ideas, values, behavioral traits, and lifestyles of nonviolence. The only value-neutral value of peace is *empathy*, simply the willingness to perceive the world from others' perspectives by putting ourselves into the shoes of one another. Thus, peace may be defined as a *harmonious* system of diversities in all domains of human existence. When one becomes empathetic to others, one may not agree with the others but will "understand" the others. Understanding does not require agreement. On the contrary, when there is agreement, understanding is not needed or desirable. Harmony is the creation of "oneness" on a higher plane out of diversity. This does not mean that diversity and differences are to be made homogeneous. This means that harmony or peace is possible only when diversity is accepted and preserved.

If we examine the security-based U.S. policies throughout history, it will be shockingly clear that the security paradigm has run its course and become counterproductive.

Peace Through Mediation

President George W. Bush declared in his State of the Union address on January 29, 2002, that certain states such as Iran, Iraq, and North Korea are helping terrorism and seeking weapons of mass destruction, thus constituting the Axis of Evil. It is remarkable to note that those "rogue" states lack the moral qualification to gain the right to talk with the United States, thus, for them, there will be no diplomacy or negotiated settlement of differences. The stark reality of world politic landscape today is that many countries and political entities regard their enemies to be terrorists and are unable to utilize diplomacy. Instead, the fate of the "rogue" states is destruction and death – prompting American invasion and senseless destructions and killings. The situations and cases where dialogue and negotiated settlement are prohibited, we must have a third party mediator who will mediate the conflict that seems to be no way out if we are limited to negotiated settlement. The role of mediation can be assumed by a third country, a neutral organization, or even an individual who is committed to peace. The mediator must be well-versed in the nature of their differences and trusted by all adversarial parties involved in the conflict. Finding such a mediator is not easy in most cases, but once the parties are committed to bringing in a mediator, it can be done.

The Creed of the Peace Paradigm

Much was covered in the preceding pages, but the creed of the Security Paradigm discussed earlier in this chapter can be juxtaposed by a set of imperatives that constitute the core norms and values of the peace paradigm as shown below:

1. The world should be a system of coordinated *equilibrium (not domination-subjugation)*;

2. In a given political system, *Diversity* in cultural disposition, social structure, demographic composition, and policy strategies (and tactics) to achieve common goals is necessary and should be promoted;

3. The world should be viewed as a system of *diversity* (not uniformity or dichotomy);

4. The creation or management of orderly relations among states or sub-state entities should be pursued through *nonviolent* or peaceful means;

5. Social and human relationships are to be defined in terms of a *win-win relationship;*

6. A culture of *trust* (not fear) is required for peace in relationships at all levels;

7. A culture of *non-discrimination* is imperative for peace, especially in race, ethnicity, national origin, or religion;

8. Peace requires *transparency* (not secrecy) in communication;

9. *Non-sate actors and groups* (not the government) need to be the initiators of peace.

10. World order must be horizontal, where the relationship among states is managed by an *equitable distribution of power (not monopoly of power)*.

America at a Crossroads: Is America Hopeless or Can She Be the Hope?

The reader of this book may realize that the pattern of development pursued by the United States has been portrayed and critically assessed by advancing several thematic observations:

1. The empirical theory of development that was based on the premise of human needs/wants as the locus of social and political evolution was, in fact, precisely the track on which America has journeyed. The theories and all the conceptions surrounding the phenomenon of development the way it has been (Chapters 5-9) were mostly the product of American scholarship. That pattern of development was

declared to be misguided and even inaccurate as it failed to account for the development of the existential conditions of human life.

2. The United States that emerged as the only superpower through the decades of the second half of the 20th Century and early 21st Century has championed a world order that relies on all the premises of the Security Paradigm.

3. The structural and cultural changes of the world during the "Pax-Americana" have created a great many challenges for the United States and the security paradigm.

4. The security paradigm under American guardianship has failed to produce and maintain safe, secure life environments around the world.

5. Despite economic affluence for the country as a whole, distributive injustice has created a serious source of popular dissent within the system, and it has also created "structural violence" in the global community resulting in pervasive anti-American sentiment and terrorism in many parts of the world.

6. It is all too clear that the course of development engineered and spearheaded by the United States is bound to cause human self-extinction and global calamity.

7. Because of its "accomplishments," America itself may be unable to continue its prosperous journey much longer.

The above assessment suggests that the United States appears to be on the wrong track. She is on the wrong track because she is arrested by the interests of the security paradigm where her own "success" becomes a. Unless she frees herself from this predicament, the United States' ability to maintain her leadership position in all areas of accomplishments is likely to dissipate gradually and surely. But one must realize that the United States can become an effective leader in humanity's campaign for peace-building if she finds her true assets and works to engineer the course of peace between nations. The true American assets are not in the military, economy, technology, or even the ideology of democracy. Her true assets are two-fold: demographic diversity and social accommodation.

Diversity: Demographic and Cultural:

From the very inception of the polity, demographic diversity has been in the DNA of American population. Mainstream America started out along white, European Christian lines. When faced the indigenous Indians, the early settlers fought off and destroyed their community by coercive means and forced them to isolated reservations; when the early settlers were in need of farm laborers, they forcefully shipped colored people from Africa to use them as farm and house slaves. After the Civil War, the slavery system was officially disallowed and the need for laborers on sugar cane farms and for the construction of railroad system went unfulfilled. Thus, they "imported" laborers from Asia, mostly China, Japan, and Korea. More recently, when cheaper laborers were needed to address labor shortages in production and service areas, especially those "3-D" occupational areas (Dangerous, Dirty, and Demeaning), they brought in Latinos from South America. The Latinos have been more readily accepted by the mainstream America due in large part to the fact they share religious affiliation as Christians (Catholics), a fact that most Asian and African immigrants did not share. The explosive growth in foreign workers and immigrants riding the tide of globalization has permanently changed the demographic structure of the United States. The trend will continue.

In the end, America will become progressively more diverse in its demographic structure. The immigrant groups when they reach a certain threshold of numbers tend to establish their ethnic and cultural activities by forming networks of interaction including the formation of ethnic towns in large cities.

Most of the immigrants maintain their languages and life styles. In ethnic towns, such as Chinatown in New York City, cultural activities are preserved and displayed regularly. They have their own collective efforts to promote their cultural and political interest. Often, they secure assistance and cooperation from their home countries. Some of the immigrants are successfully integrated into the mainstream America in a number of occupational areas but others are committed to retaining their ethnic and cultural identities. Either case would work for the good of America by enriching social and cultural diversity.

Assimilation and Accommodation

Sociologically, assimilation and accommodation are two distinct and contrasting concept but when they are applied to demographic integration, both processes are utilized selectively in concrete historical realities: the People's Republic of China, in dealing with the large number of minority nationalities, used the assimilation model during the Great Leap Forward campaign in the late 1950s and the Great Proletariat Cultural Revolution (mid-1960s through mid-1970s), but the strategy of accommodating diverse nationalities for maintaining political stability has been more effective throughout its history. The United States, on the other hand, began with the principle of the "melting pot," where cultural differences are assimilated into the greater American community. The "melting pot" was an ideal that lasted until America became the center of globalization, when that ideal was confronted by an increasing immigrant population with diverse ethnic and cultural attributes, especially those from neighboring Latin American countries. By the opening of the 21st Century, many Americans, especially younger people, found themselves in the midst of a population with diverse ethnic, racial, and cultural backgrounds. Thus, the norm of accommodating diversity became the prevailing value of the community and the country. In fact, as a nation of immigrants, America has not only "accepted" immigrants from any country of the world but also accommodated foreign immigrants. The way they are "accommodated" is an exceptional attribute of America -- not just by the government but more importantly by non-government organizations and individuals.

In no country in the world can we find refugee policies as extensive and consistent as the United States. The U.S. government enacted the initial refugee legislation in 1948 to accommodate more than 650,000 displaced Europeans. Later, during the Cold War years, refugees from Communist regimes predominantly from Poland, Hungary, Yugoslavia, and Cuba, and China. With the fall of Vietnam in April 1975, the United States faced the massive challenge of accepting and accommodating a large number of incoming Indochinese, which led to the adoption of the Refugee Act in 1980. Since 1975, the United States has resettled more than 3 million refugees, over 75 percent of who have been Indochinese or citizens of the former Soviet Union. Since the enactment of the Refugee Act of 1980, annual admissions have been steady at hundreds of thousand people. For the resettlement of the refugees, the government in Washington has been working in collaboration with local and state governments, as well as a myriad of non-government organizations. The American attribute for accommodation of immigrants is evidenced in a number of other areas. At schools (public and private), foreign children are given special attention and care with specially-tailored programs to help them to settle in. Even providing the driver's test in multiple languages in many states and localities throughout the country is a simple but significant nod to this American attribute. A culture of giving, sharing, and extending a helping hand when needed, an offspring of the traditional Judeo-Christian value system, is widely shared by most Americans. But the same cannot be said for most other countries, not even those European democracies with predominantly Christian populations. This admirable attribute has also been demonstrated by the fact that Americans have become progressively color blind in coping with racial barriers, dramatically demonstrated by the election of Barak Obama as the President of the United States in 2008 and his reelection in 2012, not to speak of the advent of growing number of minority political leaders in both Democratic and Republican parties.

These two attributes of American society are exactly the kind of attributes that are needed in the global community if we are to build peace. What is truly great about America is not what she possesses, but who the Americans are! It is the same America that has led the course of global development for much of the 20th Century through military and market power that is also best positioned to lead the transformative movement toward a world guided by the pursuit of peace. If America wakes up and accept this challenge, the goal of peace for the global community will be expedited. If not, the world will still have to move toward that end, only with greater difficulties along the way. The world and mankind do not seem to have any other alternative.

Chapter 15

Development and Communication

Through the preceding thirteen chapters, we have established that the leading theoretical and conceptual expositions in the scholarship of development studies espoused during the Cold War decades are deplorably inadequate and biased. We have also offered a more accurate means of describing and explaining the actual course of development through the agrarian, industrial, and post-industrial stages, paving the way to globalization as an extension of development. This was achieved by offering an alternative theory of development based on the structure of human needs and human wants, where development was defined as the process of needs/wants satisfaction. Then, this book explored a series of ideas intended to discern the nature and structure of a desirable and meaningful course of development at all levels of social complexity. Such a desirable course of development was defined as one in which *human development* is addressed at the individual level, *human dignity is gained through the attainment of human rights*, and *peace* is built and maintained at all community levels. How, then, can we get there? What is the roadmap for us to follow as we engineer the course of development? In a nutshell, we can get there through realizing the art and science of *communication*. Communication or dialogue is so crucial, and is proposed here as the "magic bullet" that might cure all ills at all levels and all sectors of the society and eventually the global community itself. Thus, I would suggest a "normative" definition of *development as the process in which the individual, the society, and the global community develop the ability and capability to communicate.*

Development through Communication

Definition: What is Communication?

What is communication and what are the requisite conditions for communication? Communicative action is a meaningful or purposeful act designed for the exchange of values, norms, and beliefs that comprise the identity of the communicator. Communication occurs when value positions or opinions are exchanged through human interaction. As values and opinions are the ingredients of self-identity, communication is all about the exchange of identities. Thus, the purpose of communication is not acquiring knowledge or information to make one smarter. Rather, communication is intended to enhance the level of mutual understanding by the communicators. The definition of understanding is the acceptance of differences with or without agreement. Habermas (1984, p.75), a towering figure in linguistic epistemology and the author of a seminal work in two volumes, *Communicative Actions,* advanced the view that "communicative rationality is the processes by which different validity claims are brought to a satisfactory resolution" to conflict. A conflict is likely to occur due to a lack of understanding that is mostly generated by the breakdown of communication.

The Correlates of Communication:

The requisite conditions for communication include first and foremost the establishment of self-identity (an integral part of human rights as established in Chapter 12), the willingness and disposition to listen to others, open-mindedness, empathy (that is prepared to consider or even accept others' views), the ability to communicate using languages, symbolic means such as gestures, and more importantly, through the arts of various forms. In addition to the individual psychological requisites, there are a series of social and political conditions for communicative action. Socially, an open society where class mobility is unhampered by a rigid class or caste system is desirable. Demographic social mobility is also helpful as it will help people expose to diverse life situations and possibly empathy, a vital element for peace. In the area of culture, diversity is important for communicative action, as well as the ability to accommodate differences is vital to participation in communicative interaction. For active communication, the presence of communication tools and channels is imperative. First and foremost, one has to be able to use the language effectively; multilingual capability is yet better.

The availability and accessibility of media, traditional as well as "social media," are necessary conditions, for which education and socialization loom large. Finally, political freedom to engage in public and interpersonal debates on public issues is vital to communication, suggesting that a mature civil society should be conducive to communication.

1) Psychological Correlates:

    a. Open Mind

    b. Empathy

2) Social Correlates:

    a. Class Mobility

    b. Social Mobility

3) Cultural Correlates:

    a. Achievement Orientation

    b. Accommodation Culture

4) Instrumental Correlates:

    a. Education and Experiential Exposures

    b. Language(s)

    c. Media (Traditional and "social media")

    d. The Arts

5) Political Correlates:

    a. Legal Protection for Communicative Activities

    b. The Civil Society

In the end, when people relate to one another through communication, they will find themselves living in a community at peace, be it in interpersonal relationships (spousal, friends, all significant others), social systems and institutions, or the global village.

The role and impact of communication would be such that all elements of the of history in a desirable direction. How can communication do this?society are going to be inter-connected to comprise a comprehensive system called "community." Therefore, a desirable definition of development itself might be communicative capability at the systemic level. In fact, this definition is proposed, as a normative concept, to replace the human needs/wants-based definition of development. It is posited here that the pursuit of human needs/wants satisfaction invited the detrimental conditions signaling toward the end of civilization. The normative definition utilizing the communicative capability could steer the direction

Development through Communication

If there is one concept that fundamentally affects all three layers of the polity, it is communication. For human development at the individual layer, communication facilitates both cognitive capacity and aesthetic and artistic maturity. It will even enrich the metaphysical soul of the person. Thus, the holistic development of Man will directly benefit from communication in which all four spheres of human existence (body, mind, spirit, and soul) are will be decisively affected. But in reality, as Habermas himself observed, communication is adversely affected by modernity. In modern educational curriculum and the actual working of education, meaningful communication is overlooked as education favors science and vocational training, at the detriment of the development of the spirit and the soul as conceptualized in Chapter 11. This negligence of spiritual and transcendental education may have a significant implication for the explosive criminal and terrorist activities on campuses in the United States that could be attributed to psychological disorder and emotional disturbance on the part of juveniles. Communication to stimulate human development must begin with the family during the early phase of a child's early socialization and development.

At the level of groups and organization, communication enriches all aspects of human rights as established in Chapter 12: life, identity, choice, and love. Communication is crucial for all four of them. For the optimal attainment of life's basic needs, communication makes people informed of the availability and accessibility of the needs in a way that people can strategize the pursuit of those needs. For the identity right, communication helps us establish and strengthen identity; after all, it is the identity that is to be shared through communication. Thus, identity right and communication are inseparable. Through communication, we interact with our "significant others" and through communication, we create new significant people or systems of ideas with which we seek to identify ourselves. The choice right is pursued through communication that will improve the decision-making process. One must realize that love is a perfect form of communication, one that is truly designed for mutual understanding. In the end, it is communication through which we pursue both human development and human dignity. Then, for the challenge of building peace in the global community, as espoused in Chapter 13, where does communication come in? Everything about peace building, in fact, has to do with communication and dialogue. The creation and maintenance of peace and harmony requires intense and transparent communication. Indeed, communication is what sets peace apart from security (Chapter 13).

Communication and Community

As we lamented in Chapter 9, the process of development eventuating the birth of a global village has all but extinguished the community as it was once known to us. Most sociologists define the community as a collective unit of society where members of the society are mutually dependent, collectively self-sufficient, and interconnected through systems of communication. These two concepts, community and communication, should share a common semantic origin. If we wish to strive toward a common global community where multiple layers of sub-communities are viable, we must begin by building the requisite conditions for communication espoused above. Without necessarily reverting back to the romantic "small" towns consistent with E.F. Schumacher's community portrayed in his *Small Is Beautiful* (1999), we could work on the requisites for communication to improve the quality of out collective existence. We realize that the world has been swept by the massive tide of "the bigger, the better" syndrome that has systematically destroyed folk societies and traditional communities in every corner of the world. Today's lifestyle for citizens of modernized societies makes individual human beings totally powerless in dealing with their own needs, such as electric power, food supply, epidemic diseases, environmental health, and safety or security. Riding the tide of modernization and globalization will only exacerbate this problem. Yet, no one can advocate for the revival of old, little communities in the twenty first century; rather, regardless of the size of the community, we must revitalize the engine of community building, and that is communication. Now, it should be abundantly clear that communication is the "magic bullet" for holistic development. The final weighted question is how to craft a concrete roadmap to such development.

Chapter 16

The New Global Order:
From Unipolar to Multipolar System

This Chapter is designed to advance three themes: First, the Post-Cold War era ushered in an age of Americanism which has risen but has since declined; Second, the fatal demise of existing Cold War ideologies opened up room for the emergence of a new ideology; Third, the resurgence of nationalism is leading the global ideological system toward a Multipolar system. Proposed here is the advancement of human rights as the core components of a new ideology superseding the old Cold War ideologies. While the concepts of human rights were discussed earlier in this book in the context of development (Chapter 12), here we reframe the perspective as a basis for a new overarching human rights ideology that can shape a new world order.

The Age of Ideology: The Rise and Fall of The American Unipolar System

The Cold War era has effectively ended as the Soviet Union and its satellite states were transformed away from the various forms of socialist communism in the late 20th Century. With the ending of the Cold War politics, two epoch making changes have resulted: (1) the bipolar system of competing ideologies has virtually dissipated and are made meaningless in determining the typical policy behavior of most countries of the world; (2) the economy of military industry has been boosted throughout the world; thus, the military industrial complex has become a formidable phenomenon in most countries.

How have the ideologies of capitalist democracy and socialist communism lost their practical significance as the world's dominant guiding principles? During the Cold War decades and the post-Cold War years, the market economy prevailed throughout the world. Indeed, it was the market economy that eroded and eventually overpowered the socialist planned economy. The market economy changed the whole life environment by encouraging a set of values and behavioral orientations. Most of all, the market dynamics boost quantitative values in place of traditional qualitative values. Since market dynamics revolve around the quantitative yardstick of money, everything in the market place is seen as a quantity (price), even including human services and intellectual values. All forms of human behavior, and human beings themselves, become price tagged (quantified). Thus, as man behaves "rationally," he is expected to pursue a maximum interest at a minimum cost. The rational actor does not wish to share with others and would be least concerned about the health of public goods and common interest. As a result, public goods have deteriorated in both quantity and quality. Such concerns of public goods as the environment, production of basic necessities including food, clean air and water, as well as safety and security in the political environment are uniformly insufficient or inadequate to sustain the inhabitants of this planet. As the competing ideologies of capitalist democracy and socialist communism are unable to overcome the problem caused by the market economy, the age of ideologies in human history has ended, beginning with the demise of Soviet and European socialist systems and now followed by American capitalist democracy. No alternative ideology appears to be emerging. However, recognizing the reality that both socialist communism and capitalist democracy have forced the market economy to overwhelm cultural development (norms, values, and belief systems) of the entire human community, the stage is set for a new ideology to find its footing in this complicated ideological vacuum.

A new useful and desirable ideology should once again bring humanity to the main stage. Instead of material and economic indicators such as income, wealth, and trade volume, we should focus on human conditions. A direct indicator of human condition is human rights.

As the Cold War ended with the apparent victory of liberal democracy engineered by the United States, America assumed leadership of the world, thus ushering in an era of Americanism across the globe. This Americanism is none other than globalism itself. There was no other state challenging American hegemony. With absolute superiority in military might and economic power, American globalism flourished quickly, eventually leading to the myth of "America First" – most recently advanced by Donald Trump. Since the demise of the Soviet Union in 1989 – 1991 the United States was able to flex its muscle freely over the world, irrespective of ideological systems, cultural orientations, and levels of development.

American capitalism intruded everywhere with three forefronts of colonialism: religion, market, and weapons! Evangelists are usually the first group of people that enter chosen countries with the intention of indoctrinating the cultural legacy of Christianity. This was the case in colonialization policy strategies employed by the British empire in India and other Third World countries. Great Britain used the same strategy to enter America as the Pilgrims were essentially evangelical Christians. These evangelists had a set of three mission-oriented perspectives: (1) A dichotomist worldview that humanity consists of the chosen people and the abandoned (dispensable) people; The former will go to Heaven and the latter to Hell; (2) The chosen people are also racists (white-male supremacists); (3) Militarists who believe that all human conflicts can and should be resolved by militant and military means. At this juncture of our discussion, we should be reminded of the American "original sin" with a set of twin blades: racism and militarism.

The slavery system in the southern part of America in the 19th Century was prompted by the need for cheap farming labor. Farm owners throughout the South bought and sold African laborers, who were treated as private property on the open market. In this inhumane process, family members were separated, with most never to be reunited with their parents and siblings. The slaves were often given new names, thus losing their ethnic identities. They never had any freedom of choice for their beliefs and behaviors. The slavery system may have been long abolished, yet, their descendants have struggled for centuries to gain the right to choose or even exist in the political realm. Even today, the fight for voting rights reflects the ongoing struggle to free the black minorities from discrimination. The slavery system was a reservoir for racism where white supremacists regarded minorities as subhuman. By the same token, the Anglo-Saxon tradition of white supremacy endured – a decisive consideration for the deployment of atomic bombs in Japan rather than Nazi occupied Europe during World War II.

The other element of original sin – American Militarism – originated from the indiscriminate massacre of indigenous natives for their land. Using European modern weaponry, the genocide of Native Americans was the impetus for the American Militarism that prevails to this day. Lethal weaponry remains the foundation of every conflict, domestic or foreign.

There has been a serious and unending debate on the issue of gun control in America. The helplessly expanding mass murders, especially by young white criminals, have become a standard in our reality today. Yet gun control alone cannot solve the epidemic. America has built a war-loving culture, continuously fueled by Militarism and justified by misguided Christian values. But the ongoing fall of America is not only attributed to a changing world system, but even more directly a result of internal contradictions generated by distributive injustice and the disappearance of the Middle Class.

The United States has become a nation of two halves. Economically and socially, inequality has reached an ultra-polarization of wealth and income to a point where bi-polar class consciousness has set in; politically, intra-class mobility is virtually non-existent; culturally, classes have developed mutual antagonism and violent hostility. This "structural violence" has created a landscape ripe for actual hostility fueled by the American reverence of lethal weapons.

An "original sin" once publicly entrusted cannot be easily washed away. In America, the twin original sins will not be easily overcome and will lead to massive class conflict ultimately triggering the demise of the American system as an experimental democracy. The era of "America First" is coming to an end, and soon.

We have argued that Socialist Communism as the Soviet experimental system was uprooted for its inability to address the rising material expectations of the people. We also argued the subsequent system of Americanism has failed to address its own challenges stemming from both foreign and domestic sources. Accordingly, a viable vision for the post-American era must be equipped with an ideology that supersedes both socialist communism and capitalist democracy, yet that can be acceptable and compatible with them. We must put forth an ideological system for the post-global era that is universally applicable to a variety of systems in the world. For this ambitious challenge, we now propose an ideology of and for human rights.

The Ideology of Human Rights

The introduction of the concept of human rights was made for the realization of world peace during the creation of the United Nations in 1948. The Universal Declaration was adopted by the General Assembly of the United Nations on 10 December 1948. Motivated by the experiences of the preceding world wars, the Universal Declaration was a product of general agreement on a comprehensive statement of inalienable human rights. According

286

to the agreement, there are three inherent characteristics of human rights: (1) universality; (2) inalienability; (3) entitlement. Universality means that every member of a community, without conditions or restrictions, enjoys the rights; Inalienability means that no one such as the state or employer can take away the rights; and Entitlement means that securing the rights for anyone is the obligation of the community (state) as a whole.

What are, then, the specific human rights that are agreeable by all conceivable kinds of political systems and cultures and satisfy all three inherent characteristics? There are a wide range of concrete rights. The United Nations Human Rights Convention at one point claimed that there are as many as thirty operational definitions of human rights. Considering a wide range of political systems and ideologies, we conclude that there are a set of five (5) practical and convincing types of human rights:

1. The Life Right:

First, one has to maintain physical life itself before all else – basic physical existence is minimally required in the first place. Physical survival necessitates basic needs such as: Food including drinking water, shelter, clean air to breath, health care including the elimination of diseases, social safety within a nonviolent environment, security from external existential threat, and health of the planet to sustain these obvious needs.

2. The Love Right:

Second, every living person will admit that living itself is not sufficient, but rather, living "well", which is a complex psycho-sociological concept. Living well requires the presence of "significant others" that the community can offer. Significant others include a wide range of people such as family members and relatives, friends, and colleagues. These significant others are generated from social, cultural, and political institutions and groups that could be primary or secondary, and formal as well as informal. The capacity to seek and maintain significant others is referred to as the Love Right.

3. The Freedom Right:

Once people are comfortable with physical survival, and live happily in association with other people that they are in loving relationships, the right to be free from constraints of behavior and choice is imperative. We distinguish constraints or restrictions in the workplace or from government mandates as "negative" freedoms, while freedoms to act and choose are "positive" freedoms.

The positive nature of freedom is none other than "choice making" freedom or Choice Right. The Choice Right requires a set of social, cultural, and economic conditions. When freedom is conceptualized as Choice-Making, there will be a few requisite conditions: First, choices or alternatives obviously requires the presence of choices. Thus, a diverse social and political system is necessary. A diverse civil society will be helpful with various ideological organizations, multiple political parties, diverse religious groups, and economic interest groups. If the existing alternative choices are all unacceptable, then, members of the community should be allowed to create new alternatives. The civil society is ordinarily facilitated by the market dynamics and the sound middle class. Another requisite condition for positive freedom is the presence of informed people who can gather relevant and reliable information on the available choices and the ability to compare them. Thus, education becomes a requisite condition for freedom. In order for any decision maker to make a rational and coherent decision, the decision maker must have the faculty and wisdom to make a meaningful decision.

4. The Equality Right:

For dignified life, there must be equality. Yet, freedom in a stratified society or caste system cannot be enjoyed if one has to live with others who are regarded as being superior and in a position to undermine his or her dignity. Equality comes from either equal opportunities or equal distribution. The necessities in human life are subjected to equal distribution but human wants (desires) must be distributed by a number of different strategic means that are considered just and fair in the particular society. For instance, the basic needs for survival are rooted in expectations of food, shelter, health services, social safety, national security, and environmental homeostasis. However, these human desires should be distributed fairly through a variety of strategic means such as the capitalist market mechanism and government rationing. The central question in distributive justice is the notion of public or private ownership. This issue will be discussed later in this Chapter.

Peace is often disturbed by inequality in the community. Unequal distribution is responsible for what is called "structural violence" as a source of socio-political instability and unrest.

5. The State Right (or the Right to Statehood or Nationhood):

Human rights literature tends to fail to recognize the crucial human right that the members of the global community are entitled to a nation state that is independent and sovereign. Those peoples who do have their ethnic and national origins but were denied having their own political independence under a variety of colonialist restrictions feel the significance of their sovereign nationhood, as seen in the histories of Israel, Korea, and many others. When one has to live in a state under the control of a foreign government, other human rights become practically meaningless. Two Asian US allies that are economically advanced but whose political sovereignty has been transferred to the United States – Japan and South Korea – have seen their human rights compromised, as their security right is not with their own states.

The five Human Rights constitute a complete list of human privileges that are universal and comprehensive. When and if a person in any system has achieved all the conditions for existential survival (Life), endowed with significant other people (Love), freedom to be free from governmental and non-governmental restrictions (Freedom), managing dignified life in association with others (Equality), and comforted under the umbrella of sovereign and independent government (State), such a person lives a utopian life! This ideal life is what the ideology of human rights purports to create in the post-American stage. This ambitious goal will be pursued through diverse ideological strategies and different policy (tactical) means such as capitalism, socialism, liberal democracy, proletariat dictatorship, people's democracy, welfare system. and participatory democracy, just to name the obvious ones.

The significance here is that we can work for and with a unified ideological goal (Meeting the Human Rights), yet also be open to diverse strategies and approaches for the post global era!

One Ideology with a Multi-Polar System

An ideology may represent a system of norms, values, and beliefs held by the believers of that ideology, but it is essentially an instrument or strategic means to justify power politics. An ideology, as we have seen in recent history, has been employed by certain systems to legitimize the pursuit, acquisition, and administration of power for a certain group of ideologues, as exemplified by democrats, communists, and others. An ideology is not an end itself. Rather, it is an institutional or strategic means designed to serve a certain system of values, including human rights. Both socialism and capitalism can work together, hand in hand, for the five human rights. Essentially, there is no reason for ideological values to collide and compete, as long as they are in service to the same goal of enhancing human rights! The five human rights are never mutually incompatible or contradictory to each other, as suggested in typically fabricated dichotomies like socialism versus capitalism, or public ownership versus private ownership. In fact, equality-oriented socialism and freedom-oriented capitalism can find mutual positive-sum relationships. Ideologies are not in mutual conflict. Rather, it is the interest of people who side with their ideologies that is deliberately made incompatible with each other. Therefore, once we transcend the ideological incongruence, the ideologies themselves can be harmonized. This is happening in real politics in the transformation of European capitalism and Chinese and Russian socialism.

What is really happening today is the traumatic transformation of the world order away from the America-centered unilateral system to a Multilateral system. Contrary to the apparent resurgence of a bi-polar system due to the conflict in Ukraine started in March 2022 where Russian forces were in confrontation with America-backed Ukraine forces, the Cold War world order will not recur. Instead, a new global order that we never expected is becoming a reality, leading the way to a multipolar world order. This new world order will have the following characteristics:

1. No more tension between advanced capitalism and developmental socialism;
2. The domestic political dynamics in all parts of the world are becoming rapidly similar along the line of capitalist economic relationships where the market is the functional hub of all interactions;
3. Security alliances and military collaborations in the international arena are increasingly superficial;
4. Sophistication of weapons technology is such that small and even impoverished countries can threaten once dominant nations;
5. The proliferation of weapons of mass destruction (WMD) is unstoppable;
6. World economy is so tightly interconnected that any country's economy cannot be independent;

7. The conventional political ideologies of Communism and Democracy may have lost their historical context but various forms of Nationalism are on the verge of dominating world political map;

8. Nations will always be equipped with race, ethnic identity, cultural, and civilizational attributes that determine the course of politics;

9. Religious beliefs and ritual organizations do influence the course of history and foreign policy; American Christianity and Chinese Confucianism are particularly noteworthy;

The Story of China

The resurgence of nationalism and the ethnic and cultural attributes coming with it will dominate the global community.

These attributes are of the quality, and not quantity, of human existence. Human faculty and characteristics are not measurable and comparable as quantitative amounts. They are qualities. It is time to bring back human characteristics to the mainstream of human existence (Refer to Chapter 11 of this book). Time is overdue for freeing humanity from the global trappings of quantifying everything about human life and life environment. The proposal advanced in this chapterwhere the selected human rights will be the ultimate goal of the new global ideology is a genuine effort to call humanity's attention to human beings themselves.

Of all countries in the world, nearly no country has been as consistently misunderstood as China. The Maoist revolution leading to the inauguration of the People's Republic was a genuine nationalist revolution, as opposed to a Communist one! The invention of the term "people" was a departure from Lenin-Stalinist "proletariat" in a way that the "people" were in the minds of Mao and his associates, inclusive of all Chinese, including all the 56 minority nationality communities. As a nation, China is uniquely formidable, exhibiting a number of significant national characteristics:

1. The largest population in the world (1.45 billion and 19% of world population);

2. Large land with ample arable capacity;

3. Minority nationalities (56) that are strategically located along the territorial border regions such as Xinjiang Autonomous Region and Inner Mongolian Autonomous Region;

4. Homogeneous population of Han Chinese (93 %);
5. One unified Language;
6. Confucianism as the virtual religion;
7. Sweeping Economic Giant;
8. Most advanced Military Might;
9. UN Security Council Permanent Member with Veto power.

The national characteristics have affected the course of social, cultural, and political changes in such a way that Chinese nationalism will come out in the post-American era as an overwhelming force in the world, particularly in the post-Ukraine world politics. As an economic and military force, China is certainly a "waking dragon"; but it will be in the cultural and civilizational arenas that China will prevail!

Culturally, China has mostly sided with the diplomacy of the "pen" rather than the physical might of the "sword", believing moral superiority to dominate physical advantage. In dealing with minority nationalities, the government prefers using persuasion over coercion. China regardless of leadership wants to be seen as a country with ideas and values that can claim cultural superiority and moral authority.

China has a long and successful history in dealing with large ethnic nationalities, including the Xinjiang and Inner Mongolia provinces, each with populations of 25 million. To accommodate the diversity of religion, culture, and language in such regions, the ruling elite has traditionally granted "autonomous" status to these areas. Despite some difficulties with Beijing authority, these regions have generally benefited from principles of tolerance, rather than assimilation, for maintaining national peace and harmony. There are many Autonomous Regions, Prefectures, and Townships that have been managed similarly. People living in the Autonomous areas are allowed to have their own schools and ethnic cultural activities. Furthermore, they are allowed to use their own languages and dialects as their official languages along with Chinese. Special considerations are given to the minority nationalities. When China employed the policy of "One Family, One Child," they were allowed to raise as many children as they wish. The Politics of Accommodation that China has successfully developed could be extended to the international arena.

In the context of Ukraine, in dealing with international affairs and the American expansionist paradigm, China is unlikely to match American military involvement with its own military commitment. Even with the controversial issue of Taiwan, China will not use its military operation toward absorbing the island. Beijing will not change its principle of "One State with Two Systems" and be prepared to wait as long as it takes. When the people of Taiwan want to come back to the mainland, they will find their homes there. On the other hand, if the people wish to live in the capitalist system for as long as they want, that too is perfectly acceptable.

The current Chinese system accepts that every nation has its own issues with the five Human Rights. It further believes that every state should be sovereign and independent. Further, a sovereign state should be allowed to pursue its own strategies and policy measures in the unique context of national characteristics, without foreign intervention. In this sense, China has earned its leadership in the global campaign to promote diverse forms of nationalism ranging from America, Russia, India, Indonesia, South Korea, North Korea, and all others. This principle is hardly imperialistic, and the world should hold China as an example for creating a new global order centered around the five human rights!

The Knife-Fork versus the Chopsticks

In many ways, the differences between China and other national systems can be portrayed as the contrast between the chopstick and knife-fork cultures. Developed in China over 5000 years ago, the widespread use of chopsticks was born from observations from Confucius himself, who noted the barbarism reflected in the cutting and stabbing of food when using knife and fork utensils. While the use of knives and forks reflected an inherent violence, destruction, and domination of food, the use of chopsticks embodied the principles of cooperation, coordination, and harmony to achieve a common goal. The so-called "chopstick culture" evident throughout a number of Asian territories is an apt metaphor for China's approach to global order and development, particularly in the post-Americanism era.

Furthermore, China is unlikely to rely on its military and economic influence to build hegemony or imperialistic power. Rather, China will pursue its national interests while also encouraging members of the global community to develop their own nationalistic systems, multipolar as a whole, and devoid of strictly military alliances.

A Note on the DPRK

There have been a wide-range of manifested types of nationalism witnessed in the recent history of the world: America, Russia, China, European Union (EU), Iran, India, and the list goes on. But no political system is as unique and demonstrably significant as the Democratic People's Republic of Korea (North Korea). Misinformation and disinformation engineered by the United States and South Korea give us the impression that North Korea is a human rights void. But an insightful observation of that system opens up a completely different factual picture of the paternal autocratic system. The DPRK has been a divided nation since the end of the Second World War, and it is technically still at a war that started in 1950. According to Western media, North Korea is a country unacceptable in the global community of countries in all conceivable aspects: economically, most people are poor and starving; politically, a ruthless authoritarian dictatorship with no rule of law or judicial system, where people are mobilized for the perpetuation of existing leadership; socially, people of all ages are coerced to comply with government indoctrination programs; culturally, all the people are under heavy brainwashing programs;, and for ordinary people overall, it is nothing short of a living hell! Yet, most socialist systems are in admiration of the effective socialist republic of North Korea. The Western perception of North Korea cannot be readily altered because no one knows much about the closed system due to the paucity of reliable information. Furthermore, what little information that does appear to emerge from the system, such as political defectors, is heavily distorted with Western and South Korean biases. However, if one examines the Democratic People's Republic of Korea through the lens of the five human rights introduced earlier in this Chapter, North Korea does not fare too poorly. Although this specific topic is beyond the scope of this book, the important point here is that we may evaluate truly diverse forms of political systems more fairly and factually by adopting a human rights perspective, rather than the narrow views of liberal democracy or autocratic socialism.

Chapter 17

Social Engineering for Development: an Actionable Roadmap

In the previous chapters, we discerned what ought to be done to direct the course of development of human history in a different direction, a direction that averts the extinction of mankind and end of history. In this final chapter, I will outline specific steps for a synoptic or holistic approach towards problem solving across the diverse cluster areas of human existence. These steps are actionable recommendations for proper social and political engineering. No roadmap can be justifiably complete, especially one for the massive task of making actionable recommendations for individuals, groups and organizations, and the public sector of the government. The actions recommended below are very incomplete, intended to serve as examples for how such a thing might be accomplished. Although the examples are meant to be relevant to all societies of the world, they are more directly relevant to some than others.

Cluster One: Early Socialization: Family and Primary School

1. Do have dialogue at dinner table: share stories and experiences of what happened on the day or any subject at all;
2. Do respect children's opinions and preferences as much as possible: pick up a subject relevant to the community or the country, and solicit everyone's opinion;
3. Do talk about what makes human life most fulfilling and gratifying: discuss the topic of human development;
4. Do talk about "role models" both in today's world and historical figures;
5. Do introduce to children to a topic of public interest of the day or the week from items of headline news;
6. Do schedule a group physical exercise session at the beginning of a school day;

7. Do require one art course for all school children;

8. Do encourage art training such as music by parents for children;

9. Do expose students experientially, cognitively, and affectively to the diverse world. To expand the realm of children's world reference, teach about history and societies from comparative perspectives;

10. Do train students to induce self-improvement over time and free them from zero-sum gaming environment (never evaluate students' performance by comparing them with one another, certainly not quantitatively);

11. Do teach communicative capabilities. Communication takes more than language; it requires first and foremost the admission of inadequacies of self and the acknowledgement of others' unique values! Communication calls for our open-mindedness, willingness to change ourselves, willingness to put ourselves in other people's situations (empathy).

12. Do teach at least one foreign language;

13. Do expand extra-curricular programs and activities for students to develop further their unique attributes and to form personal identities;

14. Do not reward children on a contractual basis; do not bargain with them. What they need should be provided unconditionally.

15. Do help children interact with nature, wonders of the planet, and the universe.

Cluster Two: Further Socialization: Universities and Higher Educational Institutions

16. Do further promote human development by facilitating logical thinking, expanding the real of the life world, forming credible opinions regarding public issues;

17. To enhance the communicative capability in a way that students can become an effective opinion leader in all social contexts, a creative thinker in exploring alternatives (to make choices from) in designing blueprints for social actions for themselves and others;

18. Make it mandatory to take courses strategically chosen to broaden the scope of one's life experience such as, to name just a few, world history, arts history, archeology, philosophy, world religions, comparative literature, and world politics;

19. It might be a good idea to require all students to go abroad for a specific period of time to places that are strategically chosen for their interest areas;

20. Teach and train students to become effective problem solvers in their chosen areas of expertise;

21. Allocate or increase budgets for functional institutions that facilitate interaction between families and schools (such as the PTA);

22. Teachers should be required to visit with families of their students for conferences;

23. Professors should show diversity in their scholarship, value positions, and ideological leanings, especially once they have attained the tenure;

Cluster Three: Groups and Society

24. Expand communicative dialogues, not just commercial or transactional conversations;

25. Respect and acknowledge the important of the elderly population as they are the source of experience and wisdom. Consider providing a tax break and/or government subsidies for families that house and provide care for the elderly;

26. Religious organizations should only take care of the spiritual (soulful) dimension of human existence. They should not engage in economic and political activities;

27. The agricultural sector must be the concern of the public sector in such a way that it needs to be protected by the government through subsidies and other means;

28. The military should be prohibited from engaging in political or economic activities, directly or indirectly. This institution's sole purpose must remain strictly within the bounds of protecting the people from external aggression. The military-industrial-political triangular ties must be broken up, rather than reinforced;

29. The battlefield or war zone should be a place where only military personnel should be allowed to perform security-related work for the country; military contractors should never replace military personnel in uniform;

30. Only the military and law-enforcement organizations and individuals thereof should have the right to possess and use military-grade weapons. These types of weapons must go with political authority. Authority here is defined as legitimate power, and legitimacy is created only by the consent of the governed;

31. Political ideology can only be an instrument for expanding the people's identity rights. An ideology, being a strategic means for the enhancement of human rights, may change as the condition of human rights evolves. Therefore, ideological debate must be part of educational experience, and should be encouraged at educational institutions and also by the public at large. School curriculum or extra-curricular programs should include foci on comparing diverse ideologies;

32. The market system should never be designed to destroy the middle class. That class should be promoted and protected through government's extractive and redistributive policies. From this point of view, small business activities and interests must be strengthened;

33. Mass media's role should include public education, not just "reporting" with supposed "objectivity." Public media is the most powerful force in shaping opinions. As such, it must bear some moral responsibility for its impact. For this, one might consider the creation of a public board to oversee the ethical consequences of the media. This board may be given a great deal of authority in guiding the contents of broadcasting. The video, audio, and print media should be included.

Cluster Four: The Public Sector: the Government

34. To ensure the life right for all, basic food items and clothes that are seen as necessities may be at least partly subsidized by the government. Children's clothes should be exempt from taxation. However, goods that are considered "conspicuous" should be taxed heavily;

35. Public schools should entirely be funded by the public at large the government;

36. All public organizations, ranging from local governments to international governing organizations must bear the responsibility of monitoring the production and distribution of food, and of ensuring maximum level of physical survival of all.

37. The above should be applied to other forms of basic needs including healthcare; health care and services should be made available not only for treatment but for prevention, as well.

Cluster Five: The Environment

38. A massive incentive system should be developed at various organizations, which in turn should be promoted by the government with its own incentive structures.

39. Recycling bins with artistic and aesthetically attractive appearances might be placed throughout town (as seen in some European cities). To promote environmental awareness and to improve aesthetic senses of the students, open competition for artwork on the recycling bins might be a great idea;

40. Governments or voluntary civic organizations might develop a system whereby recyclable wastes may be purchased;

41. Fees should be collected in proportion to pollution generated. The revenues must be for environmental rehabilitation;

42. Each person on this planet who earns money must be levied an environmental tax, for which a system of global management is desired;

43. A World Organization for the Environment (WOE) may be created, and subsidized by tax revenues from governments, industries, and individuals in accordance with a carefully crafted system of management. This organization should be responsible for the management of the planet;

Cluster Six: Peace Building

44. The paradigm of security must be replaced by the paradigm of peace. This fact should be the subject of education in and out of schools Peace "alliances" (or peace regimes), not security alliances, must be created;

45. To maximize the exchange of views held by mutually adversarial entities, the forum of Tract II must be encouraged. A Track-II dialogue must be based on the principles of confidentiality (closed door, un-officiality, informality, and unaccountability.

46. Along with Track-II, a number of diplomatic tracks for peace-building should be explored and utilized such as the sports track, the track of the arts (especially, music), joint research on subjects of common interests, and many forms of entertainment;

47. Quiet diplomacy (or underwater diplomacy) should explored and utilized more extensively;

48. Mediation by a third party should be utilized for resolving certain conflicts;

Cluster Seven: Global Grand Challenges

49. Global monitoring systems should be established or revitalized such as the World Food Organization WFO, UN Environment Organization (UNEO), and the World Health Organization (WHO) for the purpose of monitoring the global structure of distributions of values and services. Their findings should be publicly disseminated. Global terrorism must be examined as a symptom of deeper problems. At the global level, an institute on terrorism might be created for the purpose of effectively alleviating terrorism;

50. Global structural violence should also be monitored and measured for each country to know where it stands and what it needs to address and improve the situation, especially for the purposes of equitable distribution.

The above numbered items are suggestions for creating a society and world based on the normative paradigm of development espoused in Part Three of this book (Chapters 11-14). They are meant to be illustrations and examples, not a complete list measures for social engineering. But it is hoped that the ideas clearly represent an alternative paradigm of development.

I should mention that this book is designed to offer with justification an architectural structure that would require substantiation by experts in a great many number of fields and subfields of many academic disciplines. In no way do I pretend to be an expert on those rich and diverse concepts and theories employed to construct the proposed paradigm of development.

Postscript

History changes through evolution or revolution. Human life flows with the tide of history most of the time with little control over the current, and the mission of academia is to describe, explain, and predict the nature and impact of the historical tide. If the impact is disruptive and problems are found along the procession of the tide, the challenge of the intellectual is to resolve or prevent the problems. Karl Marx in the last Century saw the problem of exploitation of people without the means of production by others and offered an explanation of the course of historical change. Based on his paradigm (theory) of social change, in order to rectify the problems inherent in the capitalist system, Marx advocated an actionable recourse in the form of a proletariat revolution. Under Marxism and its variations, half of the world was swirled into economic socialism and political communism under the tutelage of the former Soviet Union for some five decades since the beginning of the Cold War era. In that part of the world, there was little room for alternative theoretical expositions, making that era a dark age for social and behavioral sciences. In the meantime, the other half of the world became dominated by the ideals of liberal democracy under the leadership of the United States and its Western allies. Unlike the Soviet bloc, the Western bloc produced a myriad of theories of social change and development, but mostly they were designed to justify the Western experience; thus, they are characterized as being "Western-biased." These biased conceptual and theoretical explorations are largely inaccurate and inadequate, and unable to **explain** the course of social change and development. As a result, the actual problems in real history have been unattended to and often neglected; yet worse, the leading Western scholars refuse to acknowledge their shortcomings with scientific or logical self-assessment. Instead, some of them, notably Francis Fukuyama (*End of History*) and Samuel Huntington (*The Third Wave*) observe that Western democratization is not only historical reality but also inevitable. Scholarship in the 21st Century is entirely unprepared to deal with the many real problems; ready or not, life-threatening problems have intensified and proliferated.

301

This book made has made an effort to: first, assess the inadequate state of Western scholarship for the study of development; second, formulate a theory of development that is claimed here to have great explanatory power for the process of development as it actually happened; third, offer a theoretical architecture for a desirable course of development; and finally, propose an alternative conception and theory of development – along a sample of specific actions for changing the course of social engineering toward the possibility of an ideal community for human race.

These ideas are the outcome of my life-long soul searching through both personal experience and intellectual journey over an extended period of time that includes my childhood in China in the middle of the Chinese Civil War that gave birth to Mao's China (1949), the agonies of separated families across the great divide of the Korean peninsula and the Korean War itself, coming to the United States to further my education in 1965, and teaching at the University of Georgia for more than 40 years. While in the United Stated, I witnessed the evolution of the diplomatic and political impasse between Washington and Pyongyang, which prompted me to visit North Korea on numerous occasions for the purpose of acquiring in-depth knowledge about the cause of the diplomatic stalemate. These personal experiences made me not only more knowledgeable but wiser. Many ideas that I used in this book are the outcome of my rich and painful experience, but I also benefited tremendously by my education in the United States both as a student and an educator.

It is my wish and hope that the ideas contained in this book will invoke serious discussions and soul searching across a wide range of readership. In the end, I hope that we will be able to see the sustenance of human history without succumbing to the forces working to extinguish humanity.

Bibliography

Allen, George C. *A Short Economic History of Modern Japan,* 1867-1937. London: Routledge, 1946.

Almond, G. and J. Coleman, eds. *The Politics of the Developing Areas.* Princeton, NJ: Princeton University Press, 1960.

Almond, G, and G. B. Powell *Comparative Politics:* A *Developmental Approach.* Boston: Little Brown, 1966.

Almond, G., and S. Verba. *The Civic Culture.* Princeton, NJ: Princeton University Press, 1963.

Almond, Gabriel A, and G. Powell. "Determinancy- Choice, Stability-Change: Some Thoughts on a Contemporary Polemic in Political Theory," *Government and Opposition,* Vol. 5, No.1 (Winter 1969-70): 22-40.

Almond, Gabriel A. "The Development of Political Development." *A Discipline Divided: Schools and Sects in Political Science.* Sage Publications, 1990.

Almond, Gabriel A. "Capitalism and Democracy." *PS: Political Science and Politics* 3 (1996): 467-474.

Appadurai, Arjun. "Disjuncture and Difference in the Global Cultural Economy." *Public Culture* 2, no.3 (1990): 1-24.

Apter, David E. *The Politics of Modernization.* Chicago: University of Chicago Press, 1966.

Apter, David E. *Some Conceptual Approaches to the Study of Modernization.* Englewood Cliffs, NJ: Prentice-Hall, 1968.

Apter, David E. "Norms, Structure, and Behavior and the Study of Political Development," In Nancy Mammond, eds., *Social Science and the New Societies.* East Lansing, MI: Social Science Research Bureau, Michigan State University, 1973.

Banks, Arthur S. *Cross Polity Time Series Data.* Cambridge, MA: The MIT Press, 1971.

Aron, R. Progress and Disillusion: The Dialectics of Modern Society. New York, Praeger, 1978.

Banks, Arthur S. and Robert B. Textor. *A Cross-Polity Survey.* Cambridge, MA: The MIT Press, 1963.

Barber, Benjamin R. *Jihad vs. McWorld.* New York: Ballantine, 1996.

Barnet, Richard J. *The Economy of Death.* New York: Atheneum, 1969.

Barnet, Richard J., and Ronald E. Muller. *Global Reach: The Power of- the Multinational Corporations.* New York: Simon and Schuster, 1974.

Baudrillard, Jean. "The Precession of Simulacra." *Simulacra and Simulation.* Ann Arbor: University of Michigan Press, 1981.

Bauer, P. T. and B. S. Yamey, "Against the New Economic Order," *Commentary* 63, no. 4 (1977): 25-31.

Beck, Ulrich. *What is Globalization?* Cambridge: Polity Press, 2000.

Bell, Daniel. *The Coming of Post-Industrial Society.* New York: Basic Books, 1973.

Bell, Daniel. *End of Ideology.* New York: Collier Books, 1969.

Berger, Bennett M. "The Sociology of Leisure," in Erwin O. Smigel, eds. *Work and Leisure.* New Haven, CT: College and University Press, 1963.

Berger, Peter L, and Samuel P. Huntington. *Many Globalizations: Cultural Diversity in the Contemporary World.* Oxford University Press, 2002.

Bertsch, Gary K, and Thomas W. Ganschow, eds. *Comparative Communism.* San Francisco: W.H. Freeman and Company, 1976.

Beynon, John, and David Dunkerley, eds. *Globalization: The Reader.* London: Athlone, 2000.

Bill, James A, and Robert L. Hardgrave. *Comparative Politics: The Quest for Theory.* Columbus, OH: Charles E. Merrill, 1973.

Binder, Leonard. *Crisis and Sequences in Political* Development. Princeton: Princeton University Press, 1971.

Blaney, Harry G, III. Global Challenges. New York: New Viewpoints, 1979.

Blau, Peter M, and Otis D. Duncan. *The American Occupational Structure.* New York: John Wiley and Sons, Inc, 1976.

Boorstin, Daniel J. *The Republic of Technology.* New York: Harper and Row, 1978.

Bosworth, David. "The Spirit of Capitalism, 2000." *The Public Interest* 138 (2000): 3-28.

Brandt, Willy. *North-South: A Program for Survival.* Cambridge, MA: MIT Press, 1980.

Breeze, Gerald. *Urbanization in Newly Developing Countries.* Englewood Cliffs, NJ: Prentice Hall, 1966.

Brickman, Philip, and Donald T. Campbell. "Hedonistic Relativism and Planning of the Good Society," in M. H. Appley, ed., *Adaptation-Level Theory.* New York: Academic Press, 1971.

Brodbeck, May. "Methodological Individualism: Definition and Reduction." *Philosophy of Science* 25, no.1. (1958): 1-22.

Brown, Lester R. and Christopher Flavin. "A New Economy for a New Century." *State of the World* (1999): 3-21.

Buchanan, James M. and Gordon Tullock. *The Calculus of Consent.* Michigan: University of Michigan Press, 1967.

Campbell, Angus. *The American Voter.* New York: Wiley, 1960.

Caporaso, James A. "Dependency Theory: Continuities and Discontinuities in Development Studies." *International Organization* 39 (1980): 605-628.

Carothers, Thomas. "The End of the Transition Paradigm." *Journal of Democracy* 13, no.1 (2002): 5-21.

Charlesworth, J, eds. *Contemporary Political Analysis.* New York: The Free Press, 1967.

Charlesworth, James C, eds. *Leisure in America: Blessing or Cure?.* 1964.

Chilcote, Ronald H. *Theories of Development and Underdevelopment.* Boulder, CO: Westview Press, 1984.

Chilton, Stephan. *Defining Political Development*, Boulder & London: Lynne Rienner, 1988.

Chilton, Stephan. *Grounding Political Development*, Boulder & London: Lynne Rienner, 1991.

Converse, Philip E. "The Nature of Belief Systems in Mass Public," in David E. Apter, eds. *Ideology and Discontent.* New York: The Free Press, 1967.

Collier, David, and Steven Levitsky. "Democracy with Adjectives: Conceptual Innovation in Comparative Research." *World Politics* 49 (1997): 430-451.

Cooling , Benjamin F., ed. *War, Business, and American Society.* New York: Kennikat Press, 1977.

Dahl, Robert. *Democracy in America.* Chicago: Rand McNally, 1973.

Dahl, Robert, and Charles Lindblom. *Politics, Economics and Welfare.* New York: Harper and Row, 1958

Dahl, A. Robert. "Development and Democratic Culture." In Larry Diamond, Marc F. Plattner, Yun-han Chu, and Hung-mao Tien, eds., *Consolidating Third Wave Democracies: Themes and Perspective.* Baltimore and London: The John Hopkins University Press, 1997.

Dahl, A. Robert. *Dilemmas of Pluralist Democracy.* New Haven: Yale University Press, 1982.

Dahrendorf, Ralf. *Class and Class Conflict in Industrial Society.* Stanford, CA: Stanford University Press, 1959.

Dallmayer, Fred R., ed. *From Contract to Community.* New York: Marcel Dekker, Inc., 1978.

Davies, James C. "A Formal Interpretation of the Theory of Relative Deprivation," *Sociometry* 22 no.4 (1959): 280-296.

Davies, James C. *Human Nature and Politics.* New York: John Wiley and Sons, Inc., 1963.

Davies, James C. "Toward a Theory of Revolution" in James C. Davies, eds. *When Men Revolt and Why.* New York: The Free Press, 1971.

Deutsch, Karl W. "Social Mobilization and Political Development." *American Political Science Review* 55 (1961): 493-514.

Deutsch, K.W. *Political Community and the North Atlantic Area: International Organization in the Light of Historical Experience*. Princeton, NJ: Princeton University Press, 1957.

Diamant, Alfred. ''The Nature of Political Development" in Jason L. Finkle and Richard W. Gable, eds. *Political Development and Social Change*. New York: John Wiley, 1966.

Diamond, Larry. 1997. "Introduction: In Search of Consolidation." In Larry Diamond, Marc F. Plattner, Yun-han Chu, and Hung-mao Tien, eds. *Consolidating Third Wave Democracies: Regional Challenge*. Baltimore and London: The John Hopkins University Press.

Diamond, Larry. "Is the Third Wave Over?" *Journal of Democracy* 7, no. 3(1996): 20-37.

Diamond, Larry. 1994. "Introduction: Political Culture and Democracy." In Larry Diamond, ed. *Political Culture and Democracy in Developing Countries*. Boulder and London: Lynne Rienner Publishers, Inc.

Diamond, Larry. 1994. "Causes and Effects." In Larry Diamond, ed. *Political Culture and Democracy in Developing Countries*. Boulder and London: Lynne Rienner Publishers, Inc.

Diamond, Larry. 1989. "Introduction: Persistence, Erosion, Breakdown." In Larry Diamond, Juan J. Linz, and Seymour Martin Lipset, eds. *Democracy in Democratic Countries: Asia*. Boulder and London: Lynne Rienner Publishers, Inc, 1989.

Domhoff, William. *The Higher Circles*. New York: Random House, 1970.

Dorsey, John T., Jr. "The Bureaucracy and Political Development in Viet Nam," in Joseph LaPalombara, eds. *Bureaucracy and Political Development*. Princeton, NJ: Princeton University Press, 1963.

Downs, Anthony. *An Economic Theory of Democracy*. New York: Harper and Row, 1957.

Dube, S. C. *Modernization and Development: The Search for Alternative Paradigms*. London: Zed Books, 1988.

Durkheim, Emile. *The Division of Labor in Society*. New York: Macmillan Co., 1933.

Durkheim, Emile. *The Rules of Sociological Method*. New York: Free Press, 1938.

Easton, David. A *Framework for Political Analysis*. Englewood, NJ: Prentice-Hall, 1965.

Easton, David. *The Political System; An Inquiry into the State of Political Science*. NY: Knopf, 1953.

Eckstein, Harry. "The Idea of Political Development: From Dignity to Efficiency." *World Politics* 34 (1982): 451-486.

Edwards, Alba. A *Social and Economic Grouping of the Gainfully Employed Workers in the United States*. Washington, D.C.: Bureau of Census, 1938.

Eisenstadt, S. N. "Theories of Social and Political Evolution and Development," in *The Social Science: Problems and Orientations*. The Hague: Mouton, 1968.

Eisenstadt, S. N. 1963. "Problems of Emerging Bureaucracies in Developing Areas In New States," in Bert F. Hoselitz and Wilbert E. Moor eds., *Industrialization and Society*. Paris: UNESCO.

Eisenstadt, S. N. "Breakdowns of Modernization," *Economic Development and Cultural Change* 12 no.4 (1964): 345-367.

Enloe, Cynthia H., The Politics of Pollution in a Comparative Perspective. New York: David McKay Co., Inc., 1975.

Erikson, Erik. *Childhood and Society*. New York: W. W. Norton and Co., Inc., 1950.

Estall, R. C., and R. Ogilive Buchanan. *Industrial Activity and Economic Geography*. London: Hutchinson University Library, 1961.

Easton, David. *The Political System*. New York: Alfred A. Knopf, Inc., 1953.

Frank, Andre Gunder. *Capitalism and Underdevelopment in Latin America:* historical studies of Chile and Brazil. New York: Monthly Review Press, 1967.

Friedman, Milton. *Essays in Positive Economics*. Chicago: University of Chicago Press, 1953.

Falk, R. A. *A Study of Future Worlds*. New York: The Free Press, 1975.

Finkle, J. A., and R. W. Gable, eds. *Political Development and Social Change*. New York: John Wiley and Sons, Inc., 1966.

Finkle, Jason L. and Richard W. Gable, eds., *Political Development and Social Change*. New York: Wiley and Sons, 1966.

Flanigan, William, and Edwin Fogelman. "Functional Analysis" in James C. Charlesworth, eds. *Contemporary Political Analysis*. New York: Free Press, 1967.

Fukuyama, Francis. *The Great Disruption*. New York: Free press, 1999.

Fukuyama, Frances. *The End of History and the Last Man*. New York: Avon, 1992.

Fukuyama, Frances. "The End of History?" *National Interest* 16 (1989): 3-18.

Galtung, Johan, and Richard C. Vincent. *Global Glasnost: Toward a New World Information and Communication Order?* Cresskill, NJ: Hampton Press, 1992.

Gappert, Gary. *Post Affluent America: The Social Economy of the Future*. New York: New Viewpoints, 1979.

Gerth, H. H., and C. Wright Mills. *From Max Weber: Essays in Sociology*. London: Oxford University Press, 1946.

Giddens, Anthony. *The Consequences of Modernity*. Cambridge: Polity Press, 1990.

Gillespie, J. V., and B. A. Nesvold, eds. *Macro Quantitative Analysis*. Beverly Hills, CA: Sage Publications, 1971.

Goldsworthy, David. "Thinking Politically About Development." *Development and Change* 19 (1988): 504-530.

Golembiewski, Robert T., William A. Welsh, and William J. Crotty. A *Methodological Primer for Political Scientists*. Chicago: Rand McNally, 1969.

Goslin, D. *A.,* ed. *Handbook of Socialization Theory and Research*. Chicago: Rand McNally, 1969.

Goulet, Denis. "Development for What?" *Comparative Political Studies* 1, no. 2 (1968): 295-312.

Goulet, Denis. *The Cruel Choice: A New Concept* in *the Theory of Development*. New York: Atheneum, 1971.

Groth, Alexander J. "Structural Functional Analysis and Political Development: Three Problems," *Western Political Quarterly* 23 no. 3 (1970): 485-499

Gurr, Ted. "A Causal Model of Civil Strife: A Comparative Analysis Using New Indices." *The American Political Science Review* 62 (1968): 1104-1124.

Gurr, Ted. *Why Men Rebel*. Princeton, NJ: Princeton University Press, 1970.

Hagopian, Frances. "Political Development, Revisited." *Comparative Political Studies* 33 no. 6 (2000): 880-911.

Hansen, Birthe, and Bertel Heurlin. *The New World Order: Contrasting Theories*. New York: St. Martin's Press, 2000.

Hardt, Michael, and Antonio Negri. *Empire*. Cambridge, MA: Harvard University Press, 2000.

Harris, Dale. "Problems in Formulating a Scientific Concept of Development." in *The Concept of Development : An Issue in the Study of Human Behavior*. Minneapolis: University of Minnesota Press, 1967.

Hauser, Philip. "The Analysis of 'Over-Urbanization'." *Economic Development and Cultural Change* 12 (1964): 113-22.

Harvey, David. T*he Condition of Postmodernity*. Cambridge, MA: Blackwell, 1990.

Harvey, Robert. *Global Disorder*. New York: Carroll & Graf, 2003.

Heilbroner, Robert. *An Inquiry into the Human Prospect*. New York: Norton, 1974.

Held, David. *Global Transformations : Politics, Economics and Culture*. Stanford, CA: Stanford University Press, 1999.

Hempel, Carl G. and Paul Oppenheim. "Studies in the Logic of Explanation," *Philosophy of Science* 15 no.2 (1948): 135-175.

Hempel, Carl G. "The Logic of Functional Analysis" in May Brodbeck, eds. *Readings in the Philosophy of the Social Sciences.* New York: Macmillan, 1968.

Hertzler, J. O. *Social Institutions.* Lincoln: University of Nebraska Press, 1946.

Hirschman, Albert O. "The Changing Tolerance for Income Inequality in the Course of Economic Development," *Quarterly Journal of Economics* 87 no.4 (1973): 544-566.

Ho Ping-ti. *The Ladder of Success in Imperial China.* New York: Columbia Press, 1962.

Holsti, K. J. "Underdevelopment and the 'Gap' Theory of International Conflict." *American Political Science Review* 69 no. 3 (1975): 827-839.

Holt, Robert T., and John E. Turner. *The Political Basis of Economic Development.* Princeton, NJ: D. Van Nostrand Co., Inc., 1966.

Holt, Robert T., and John M. Richardson. "Competing Paradigms in Comparative Politics." in Holt and Turner, eds. *The Methodology of Comparative Research.* New York: The MacMillan Co., 1968.

Holton, Robert. "Understanding Globalization: History and Representation in the Emergence of the World as a Single Place." in *Globalization and the Nation-State.* New York, N.Y.: St. Martin's Press. 1998.

Horowitz, L. Donald. "Democracy in Divided Societies." in Larry Diamond and Marc F. Plattner, eds. *Nationalism, Ethnic*

Conflict, and Democracy. Baltimore and London: The John Hopkins University Press, 1994.

Hoselitz, B.F., and W.E. Moor, eds. *Industrialization and Society*. Paris: UNESCD and Mouton, 1963.

Huntington, Samuel P. "Political Development and Political Decay." *World Politics* 17 (1965): 386-430.

Huntington, Samuel P. "The Change to Change." *Comparative Politics* 3 no. 3 (1971): 283-322.

Huntington, Samuel P. *Changing patterns of military politics*. New York: Free Press of Glencoe, 1962.

Huntington, Samuel P. "Democracy For the Long Haul." *Journal of Democracy* 7, no. 2(1996): 3-13.

Huntington, Samuel P. *The Third Wave: Democratization in the late Twentieth Century*. Oklahoma: University of Oklahoma Press, 1991.

Huntington, Samuel P. "Will More Countries Become Democratic?" *Political Science Quarterly* 99 no.2 (1984): 193-218.

Huntington, Samuel P. "The Clash of the Civilizations?" *Foreign Affairs* 72 no. 3 (1993): 22-49.

Isaak, Alan C. *Scope and Method of Political Science*. Homewood, IL: The Dorsey Press, 1969.

Jaguaribe, Helio. *Political Development.* New York: Harper and Row, 1973.

Jameson, Frederic. "The Cultural Logic of Late Capitalism." in *Postmodernism, or The Cultural Logic of Late Capitalism.* Durham: Duke University Press, 1991.

Johnson, Dale L. "Dependency and the International System," in James D. Cockcroft eds., *Dependence and Underdevelopment.* New York: Anchor Books, 1972.

Johnson, John J. eds., *The Role of the Military in Underdeveloped Countries.* Princeton, NJ: Princeton University Press, 1962.

Kalb, Don. eds., *The Ends of Globalization: Bringing Society Back In.* Lanham, MD: Rowman & Littlefield Publishers, Inc., 2000.

Kaplan, Abraham. *The Conduct of Inquiry.* San Francisco: The Chandler Publishing Company, 1964.

Karatnycky, Adrian. "The Decline of Illiberal Democracy." *Journal of Democracy* 10 no.1 (1999): 112-125.

Kautsky, John H. *Political Change* in *Underdeveloped Countries.* New York: Wiley, 1962.

Kautsky, John H. *Communism and Politics of Development.* New York: John Wiley and Sons, 1968.

Kennedy, Gavin. *The Economics of Defense.* Great Britain: Western Printing Service, 1975.

Kennedy, Paul and Dirk Messner, and Franz Nuscheler. eds., *Global Trends and Global Governance*. London: Pluto Press, 2002.

Kline, Wanda. *Latin American Politics and Development*. Cambridge: MIT Press, 1979.

Kohlberg, Lawrence and June L. Tapp. "Developing Senses of Law and Legal Justice." *Journal of Social Issues* 27 no.2 (1971): 66-91.

Kohlberg, Lawrence. "State and Sequence: The Cognitive Developmental Approach to Socialization," in D. Goslin, ed., *Handbook of Socialization Theory and Research*. Chicago: Rand McNally, 1969.

Kuhn, Thomas S. *The Structure of Scientific Revolutions*. Chicago, IL: University of Chicago Press, 1962.

Kupchan, Charles A. *The End of the American Era*. New York: Alfred A. Knopf, 2002.

Lane, Robert E. "Political Belief Systems," in Jeanne D. Knutson ed., *Handbook of Political Psychology*. San Francisco: Jossey-Bass, 1973.

Lane, Ruth. "Structural-Functionalism Reconsidered: A Proposed Research Model." *Comparative Politics* 26 no.4(1994): 461-477.

LaPalombara, Joseph ed., *Bureaucracy and Political Development*.Princeton, N.J.: Princeton University Press, 1967.

Lasswell, Harold. *Politics: Who Gets What, When, How.* New York: Meridian Books, 1958.

Lawson, Stephanie. "Conceptual Issues in the Comparative Study of Regime Change and Democratization." *Comparative Politics* 23 (1993): 183-205.

Lens, Sidney. *The Military-Industrial Complex.* Pilgrim Press, 1970.

Lenski, Gehard E. *Power and Privilege.* New York: McGraw-Hill Book Co., 1966.

Lerner, Daniel. *The Passing of Traditional Society.* New York: The Free Press, 1958.

Levy, Marion J. Jr. "Patterns (Structures) of Modernization and Political Development," *The American Academy of Political and Social Science* 358 (1965): 30-40.

Li, Dun J. *The Ageless Chinese.* New York: Charles Scribner's Sons, 1971.

Lindblom, Charles E. *The Intelligence of Democracy.* New York: The Free Press, 1965.

Linz, J. Juan. "Transition to Democracy." *The Washington Quarterly* 13 (1990): 143-164.

Linz, J. Juan, and Alfred Stephan. "Toward Consolidated Democracies." *Journal of Democracy* 7 no.2(1996): 14-33.

Lunden, Walter A. *The Suicide Cycle.* Montezuma, Iowa: The Sutherland Printing Co., 1977.

Manent, Pierre. "Democracy without Nations?" *Journal of Democracy* 8 no.2(1997): 92-102.

Mannheim. Karl. *Ideology and Utopia.* New York: Harcourt, Brace and World Inc., 1939.

Martindale, Don. *American Society.* New York: D. Van Nostrand Company, 1960.

Martindale, Don. *Social Life and Cultural Change.* New York: D. Van Nostrand Company, 1962.

Martindale, Don. *Community, Character; and Civilization.* New York: The Free Press, 1963.

Masannat, George S. ed., *The Dynamics of Modernization and Social Change.* Pacific Palisades, California: Goodyear Publishing Company, 1973.

Maslow, Abraham H. *Motivation and Personality.* New York: Harper and Row Publishers, Inc., 1954.

Mayer, Lawrence C. *Comparative Political Inquiry:* A *Methodological Survey.* Homewood, IL: Dorsey Press, 1972.

McClelland , David C. *The Achieving Society.* Princeton, NJ: Van Nostrand, 1961.

McPhee, John. *The Curve of Binding Energy.* New York: Ballantine, 1974.

Meadows, Donella H., Jorgen Randers, and Dennis Meadows L. *The Limits to Growth.* New York: Signet Books, 1974.

Mendlowitz, S. H. *On the Creation of a Just World Order.* New York: The Free Press, 1975.

Merelman, Richard. "The Development of Policy Thinking in Adolescence," *American Political Science Review* 65 no.4 (1971): 1033-47.

Milbrath, Lester W. *Political Participation.* Chicago: Rand McNally and Co., 1965.

Mische, Gerald. *Toward a Human World Order.* New York: Paulist Press, 1977.

Mitchels, Robert. *Political Parties:* A *Sociological Study of the Oligarchical Tendencies of Modern Democracies.* Trans. by Eden and Cedar Paul. Glencoe, IL: The Free Press, 1949.

Mitchell, William C. *Public Choice in America.* Chicago: Markham Publishing Co., 1971.

Morris, Morris David. *Measuring the Condition of the World's Poor: The Physical Quality of Life Index.* New York: Pergamon Press, 1979.

Muthu, Sankar. *Enlightenment Against Empire.* Princeton University Press, 2003.

Nagel, E. *The Structure of Science*. New York: Harcourt, Brace and World Inc., 1961.

Nesvold, B. and J. Gillespie, eds. *Marco Quantitative Analysis*. Beverly Hills, CA: Sage Publications, 1970.

Neibuhr, Reinhold. *Moral Man and Immoral Society*. New York: Charles Scribner's Sons, 1932.

N.O.R.C. "Jobs and Occupations: A Popular Evaluation," *Opinion News,1947*.

Nodia, Ghia. "Nationalism and Democracy." in Larry Diamond and Marc F. Plattner, eds. *Nationalism, Ethnic Conflict, and Democracy*. Baltimore and London: The John Hopkins University Press, 1994.

Nye, Joseph S. and John D. Donahue, eds., *Governance In a Globalizing World*. Cambridge, MA: Visions of Governance for the 21st Century, 2000.

O'Donnell, Guillermo A. "Illusions about Consolidation." *Journal of Democracy* 7 no.2 (1996): 34-51.

O'Donnell, Guillermo A. "Delegative Democracy." *Journal of Democracy* 5 no.1 (1996): 55-69.

Ohmae, Ken'ichi. *Borderless World: Power and Strategy in the Interlinked Economy*. London: Fontana, 1990.

O'Neill, Bard. 'Towards a Typology of Political Terrorism: The Palestinian Resistance Movement." *Journal of International Affairs* 32 no.1(1978): 17-26.

Organski, A. F. K. *The Stages of Political Development.* New York: Alfred Knopf, 1965.

Owen, John D. *The Price of Leisure.* The Netherlands: Rotterdam University Press, 1969.

Parenti, Michael. *Democracy for the Few.* New York: St. Martins, 1977.

Park, Han S. "Socio-Economic Development and Democratic Performance: An Empirical Study." *International Review of Modern Sociology* 6 no.2 (1976): 349-361.

Park, Han S. *Human Needs and Political Development: A Dissent to Utopian Solutions.* Cambridge, MA: Schenkman Books, 1984.

Park, Han S. "Development and Global Consequences." in *Human Needs and Political Development: A Dissent to Utopian Solutions.* Cambridge, MA: Schenkman Books, 1984.

Park, Han S. *North Korea: The Politics of Unconventional Wisdom.* Boulder, CO: Lynne Rienner Publishers, 2002

Park, Han S. *North Korea Demystifies.* Amherst, NY: Cambria Press, 2012

Parker, Richard. *The Myth of the Middle Class.* New York: Harper and Row, 1972.

Parsons, Talcott. *Essays* in *Sociological Theory: Pure and Applied.* Glencoe: The Free Press, 1949.

Parsons, Talcott. *The Social System.* New York: The Free Press, 1951.

Parsons, Talcott. *The Structure of Social Action.* New York: The Free Press, 1937.

Pennock, J. Roland. "Political Development, Political Systems and Political Goods." *World Politics* 18 no.3 (1966): 415-434.

Peterson, John M. and Ralph Gray. *Economic Development of the United States.* Homewood, IL: Richard D. Irwin Inc., 1969.

Piaget, Jean. *The Origins of Intelligence in Children.* New York: W. W. Norton and Co. Inc., 1952.

Piaget, Jean. Psychology of Intelligence. New Jersey: Littlefield, Adams, 1963.

Pieterse, Jan P. Nederveen. *Empire & Emancipation: Power and Liberation on a World Scale.* New York: Praeger, 1989.

Plamenatz, John. *Man and Society.* New York: McGraw-Hill Book Co., 1963.

Przeworski, Adam and Henry Teune. *The Logic of Comparative Social Inquiry.* New York: Wiley-Interscience, 1970.

Przeworski, Adam, Michael Alvarez, Jose Antonio Cheibub, and Fernand Limongi. 1996. "What Makes Democracies Endure?" in Larry Diamond, Marc F.Plattner, Yun-han Chu, and Hung-mao Tien, eds. *Consolidating Third Wave Democracies: Regional Challenge.* Baltimore and London: The John Hopkins University Press, 1996.

Purcell, Victor. *The Boxer Uprising.* Cambridge: The University Press, 1963.

Pursell, Carol W. *The Military-Industrial Complex.* New York: Harper and Row, 1972.

Putnam, D. Robert. "Bowling Alone: America's Declining Social Capital." *Journal of Democracy* 6(1995): 65-78.

Pye, Lucien. *Politics, Personality, and Nation Building.* New Haven, Conn.: Yale University Press, 1962.

Pye, Lucien. *Aspects of Political Development.* Boston: Little Brown, 1966.

Pye, Lucien. "The Concept of Political Development." *The Annals of the American Academy of Political and Social Science 358 (1965): 1-13.*

Renshon, Stanley A. *Psychological Needs and Political Behavior: A Theory of Personality and Political Efficacy.* Riverside, N.J.:Macmillan Publishing Co., 1974.

Rieff, David. "A Global Culture?" *World Policy Journal* 10 no.4 (1993): 73-81.

Rike, William H. *The Theory of Political Coalition.* New Haven: Yale University Press, 1962.

Riggs, Fred W. "Agraria and Industria-Toward a Typology of Comparative Administration" in William Siffin ed., *Toward the Comparative Study of Public Administration.* Bloomington: Indiana University Press, 1957.

Riggs, Fred W. *Administration in Developing Countries: The Theory of the Prismatic Society.* Boston: Houghton Mifflin, 1964.

Riggs, Fred W. "The Dialectics of Developmental Conflict," *Comparative Political Studies* 1 no.2 (1968): 197-228.

Robertson, Ronald. *Globalization: Social Theory and Global Culture.* Sage Publication, 1992.

Rokeach , Milton. *The Open and Closed Mind.* New York: Basic Books, 1960.

Rosenau, James N. "The Complexities and Contradictions of Globalization." *Current History.* 96 no.613 (1997): 360-364

Rostow, Walt W. *The Process of Economic Growth.* Cambridge: Cambridge University Press, 1952.

Rostow, Walt W. *The Stages of Economic Growth: A Non-Communist manifesto.* Cambridge: Cambridge University Press, 1960.

Rousseau, J. *The Social Contract* trans. by G. D. Cole, E. P. Dutton and Company, 1762.

Russett, Bruce M. *World Handbook of Political and Social Indicators.* New Haven: Yale University Press, 1964.

Russett, Bruce M. *Trends in World Politics.* New York: The Macmillan Co., 1965.

Rustow, Dankwart A. "Transitions to Democracy: Toward a Dynamic Model." *Comparative Politics* 2 no.3 (1970): 337-363.

Rustow, Dankwart A., and R. E. Ward. *Political Modernization in Japan and Turkey*. Princeton: Princeton University Press, 1964.

Rustow, Dankwart A. and R. E. Ward. A *World of Nations: Problems of Political Modernization.* Washington: Brookings Institute, 1967.

Sadowski, M. Christine. "Autonomous Groups as Agents of Democratic Change in Communist and Post-Communist Eastern Europe" in Larry Diamond ed., *Political Culture and Democracy in Developing Countries*. Boulder and London: Lynne Rienner Publishers, Inc., 1994.

Sampson, Anthony. *The Sovereign State of ITT.* New York: Stein and Day, 1973.

Satori, Giovanni. "Politics, Ideology, and Belief Systems," *American Political Science Review* 63 no.2 (1969): 398-411.

Schedler, Andreas. "What is Democratic Consolidations?" *Journal of Democracy* 9 no.2 (1998): 91-107.

Schlesinger, Arthur Jr. "Has Democracy a Future?" *Foreign Affairs* 76 no.5 (1997): 2-12.

Schmitter, C. Philippe. "More Liberal, Preliberal, or Postliberal?" *Journal of Democracy* 6 no.1 (1995): 15-22.

Schmitter, C. Philippe. "Dangers and Dilemmas of Democracy." *Journal of Democracy* 5 no.2 (1994): 57-74.

Schmitter, C. Philippe. "The International Context of Contemporary Democratization." *Stanford Journal of International Affairs* 2 (1993): 1-34.

Schmitter, C. Philippe, and Terry Lynn Karl. "What Democracy Is...And Is Not." *Journal of Democracy* 2 (1996): 75-88.

Scholte, Jan Aart. *Globalization: A Critical Introduction.* Palgrave Macmillan, 2000.

Schumacher, E. F. *Small Is Beautiful: Economicsas if People Mattered*. New York: Harper and Row, 1973.

Sederberg, Peter C. "The Betrayed Ascent: The Crisis and Transubstantiation of the Modern World." *The Journal of Developing Areas* 13 no.2 (1979): 127-142.

Sigmund, Paul, ed., *The Ideologies of the Developing Nations.* New York: Praeger Publishers, 1967.

Smelser, Neil J. "Mechanisms of Change and Adjustment to Change" in Bert F. Hoselitz and Wilbert E. Moor eds., *Industrialization and Society.* The Hague: UNESCO and Mouton, 1963.

Snyder, Jack. *Myths of Empire.* Cornell University Press, 1991.

Sørensen, George. *Democracy and Democratization.* Boulder: Westview Press, 1993.

Sussman, Marvin B. and Ethel Shanas eds. *Family, Bureaucracy, and the Elderly.* Durham, NC: Duke University Press, 1977.

Sutton, Frank X. "Social Theory and Comparative Politics" in Harry Eckstein and David Apter eds. *Comparative Politics:* A *Reader.* New York: Free Press, 1963.

Teng Ssu-yu and John K. Fairbank. *China's Response to the West.* New York: Atheneum, 1954.

Teune, H. and Adam Przworski. *The Logic of Comparative Social Inquiry.* New York: Wiley Interscience, 1970.

Thurow, Lester C., *The Zero-Sum Society* (New York: Basic Books, 1980).

De Tocqueville, Alexis. *The Old Regime and the French Revolution.* Trans. by John Bonner. New York: Harper, 1856.

Treadgold, Donald. *Twentieth Century Russia.* Chicago: Rand-McNally and Company, 1964.

Veblen, Thornstein. *The Theory of the Leisure Class: An Economic Study of Institutions.* New York: Macmillan and Co., 1912.

Verba, Sidney and Norman H. Nie. *Participation in America.* New York: Harper and Row, 1972.

Verba, Sidney, Norman H. Nie, and Jae-on Kim. *The Modes of Democratic Participation.* Beverly Hills, California: Sage Publications, 1971.

Virilio, Paul. *Polar Inertia.* London: Sage Publications, 2000.

Vosburgh, William. *Social Class and Leisure Time.* Thesis. Yale University, 1960.

Wallerstein, Immanuel. *The Modern World System. Vol.1.* New York: Academic Press, 1974.

Ware, Alan. "Liberal Democracy: One Form or Many?" *Political Studies* 40 (1992): 130-145.

Warner, W. Lloyd, Marchia Meeker, and Kenneth Eells. *Social Class in America: A Manual Procedure for the Measurement of Social Status.* New York: Harper and Row, 1960.

Waters, Malcolm. *Globalization.* London and New York: Routledge, 1995.

Weber, Max. *The Methodology of the Social Sciences.* New York: The Free Press, 1949.

Weber, Max. *The Theory of Social and Economic Organization.* New York: The Free Press, 1947.

Weiner, Myron. "Political Integration and Political Development." *Annals of the American Academy of Political and Social Science* 358 (1965): 53-64.

Weis, Paul. "A Philosophical Definition of Leisure," in James C. Charlesworth, ed., *Leisure in America: Blessing or Curse?* Philadelphia: American Academy of Political and Social Science, 1964.

Willrich, Mason and Theodore B. Taylor. *Nuclear Theft: Risks and Safeguards.* Cambridge, MA: Ballinger Publishing Co., 1974.

Yanaga, Chitoshi. *Japanese People and Politics.* New York: John Wiley and Sons Inc., 1956

Young, Michael. *The Rise of Meritocracy.* New York: Penguin Books, 1958.

Zakaria, Fareed. "The Rise of Illiberal Democracy." *Foreign Affairs* 76 no.6 (1997): 22-43.

www.ingramcontent.com/pod-product-compliance
Lightning Source LLC
Chambersburg PA
CBHW060025030426
42334CB00019B/2185